Greenville's Grand Design

by **Tom Poland**
with an introduction by
Mayor Knox White

J Robert Towery — Publisher, Editor, & Art Director
James Tomlinson — Executive Publisher
Ardith Bradshaw — Editor
Nikki Sepsis — Profile Editor

Published by
a division of the Publishing Resources Group, Inc.
Jacques Verhaak, President & CFO
www.pubresgroup.com

URBAN Renaissance BOOKS

Photo by Paul Ringger

Greenville's
Grand Design

URBANRenaissanceBOOKS

Copies of this book may be ordered at:

www.pubresgroup.com/greenville.html

If you're an urban designer eager to scale the rarified heights where Jane Jacobs and Andrés Duany dwell, your fame will rest on mastery of fundamental design elements. Buildings. They form your city's walls. Within them you create a sense of place. Public Space. Consider this your city's living room. Give it energy and art. Streets—your conduits and people connections. Courageous decisions here lead to people-friendly patterns and widths. Transport. Give your city movement. Exalt in the pedestrian. Relegate the automobile. Landscape. Bring greenery and water to parched walls and streets. Give people spacious sidewalks with park-like ambience.

Question. Where is the city to which your fame will bond? Wherever your city waits, be hopeful that nature blessed it, for here you must integrate man and nature's elements with order, unity, balance, and proportion. The gods you serve are harmony, beauty, and people.

Your success hinges on other skills.

Mastering concepts such as density, diversity, and mix. Engaging nearby communities and developing savvy people and political skills. (Engage your city's senior residents.) Developing economic acumen can't hurt either. Hope for a pinch of good luck and fortuitous coincidences.

You intend to transform lives through urban design. How best to proceed? You can attend the Harvard Graduate School of Design and minor in psychology and economics. You can pour over the top ten books on urban design. You can analyze theoretical models, and you can shadow the country's top urban designers.

Or you could do yourself a big favor.

Visit a city where a renaissance blossomed by a river. Witness this city's rise from humble beginnings to resort status. It will teach you much about blending man and nature's elements. It's a story of transformation with deep roots that sprang from Earth's grand design.

Tom Poland

▲ The Old Cigar Warehouse and its vintage Coca Cola mural evoke a sense of the past. While the warehouse once housed cigars and cotton, it now serves as an event venue in the historic West End.

–Photo by Paul Ringger

Greenville's *Grand Design*

Library of Congress Control Number: 2015950824

Poland, Tom 1954 *Greenville's Grand Design* relates a story of courage, vision, and change. It details how a detoriating downtown, in a community whose principal industry had failed, was reinvented to become one of the most livable cities in North America. The themes are supported with lavish photography documenting the assets and attractions that make Greenville a place of grand design.

Published by
A Division of the Publishing Resources Group, Inc.
w w w . p u b r e s g r o u p . c o m
UrbanRenaissance**Books**
ISBN # 978-0-9847145-7-5   Printed in South Korea

Contents

Robert Clark, shot the front cover photo. The scene captures the spirit of the revitalized, reinvented Greenville. Lush, calm, and urbane. A trio of virtues that describe this city, this resort on the Reedy.

The back-cover photo was taken by Paul Ringger. This evening image suggests the excitement of being in Greenville's spectacular downtown. The city had forgotten that a river ran through it. No more. The Reedy River is now at the center of Greenville's colorful identity.

The Right Way

–Photo by Paul Ringger

GREENVILLE'S

—Inset Photo of Mayor White, above, by Robert Clark

—Mayor Knox White

We started with a big idea. Let's make Greenville the most beautiful and livable city in America.

As the pages of this pictorial of our city attests, we are well along on this journey.

You can sense it in the pride we all share in what has happened on Main Street. Visitors from across the country and planning experts say it, too. We've been included in those ubiquitous and ever-growing "Top 10" lists.

Greenville has set a new standard for how a city should grow by creating a vibrant urban center that is also green, inviting and a great place to walk.

How did it happen?

Greenville has always celebrated its natural beauty. A glimpse of the Blue Ridge Mountains provides an inspiring backdrop driving into downtown from the interstate. Paris Mountain and its state park are minutes from Main Street.

Grand Design

So it should come as no surprise that the first step in revitalizing our downtown was to plant trees, and that the next step was to reclaim a waterfall. The trees became the centerpiece of a redesigned Main Street and then, two decades later, we built one of America's finest public parks around the Reedy River waterfall, which gave birth to the city.

These two actions dramatically reshaped our downtown and set the stage for an extraordinary burst of private investment and creative endeavor. They also spoke to our values and to our unique history.

The once-abandoned Main Street has come alive with restaurants, cafes, retail shops, and homes. The streets draw people of all ages and backgrounds just to enjoy a stroll and a sense of sharing a special place.

These steps reflect a second attribute of Greenville — an ambition and drive to be a great city. Greenville has always had a plan and a willingness to stick to it. That alone separates us from most cities.

In 1907, city leaders brought in the best planners in America at the time and produced a road map for downtown. From this plan came Cleveland Park — a wonderful gift for all generations — and it brought about construction of the Main Street Bridge.

Even then, the Reedy River was seen as the city's greatest natural asset. By the middle of the 20th century, Greenville's leaders stepped up their commitment to planning by boldly declaring that our local economy must be diversified, opening the door to a post-textile economy that drives us today.

And they also recognized

–Photo by Stephanie Norwood

–Photo by Stephanie Norwood

Grand Design

struction Company (now Fluor), spoke directly to the aspirations of his city and called for bold, collaborative action in remarks during the 1964 groundbreaking for the then-tallest building in the state.

"The great cities of America

to answer the call for a greater Greenville today."

Daniel and his successor, Buck Mickel, carried through with plans to construct a landmark office tower on Main Street as a declaration of confidence in downtown's future.

that our downtown must change if it is to survive the retail shift to the giant shopping malls.

One of the foremost community leaders of this era, Charles Daniel, president of Daniel Con-

and those struggling for greatness have people who stand unafraid to commit themselves to the future," he said. "Greenville possesses such people in greater numbers than any city in eastern America. I urge them

In Remembrance
Buck Mickel

An extraordinary Leader
Whose Vision, Generosity
and Perseverance

Inspired the Transformation of Greenville
into a Vibrant and Beautiful
Community

2008

–Photo by Paul Ringger

This book illustrates how these words and actions have continued to resonate through the decades. It all comes down to a commitment to two principles: Good planning and great partnerships.

The tradition of partnership and collaboration are part of the culture of Greenville. It makes possible a generous philanthropic community. It nurtures a growing arts scene and is the driver be-

hind the Peace Center, the South Carolina Governor's School for the Arts and Humanities, Artisphere, local theater and other centers of creative talent.

It is why a city and a great garden club could work together for years to create an "oasis in the heart of the city," in the words of Harriett Wyche, then-president of the Carolina Foothills Garden Club.

Falls Park took an army of collaborators to tear down a state

highway bridge and put up a one-of-a-kind pedestrian bridge around a waterfall most residents had forgotten.

On the economic front, partnerships between the city and private investors support the hotels and office towers on Main Street and RiverPlace on the Reedy. Behind it all is a shared vision of what Greenville can be.

The planning tradition reflects a vision of a Main Street that is home to many corporate office

2 WEST WASHINGTON

towers yet maintains a human scale. It is a place for work and entrepreneurial activity and a venue for festivals, shows, shopping and fine dining.

Greenville's downtown is a serious place of employment, but it keeps no 9-to-5-office hours. Instead, it hums with activity nearly 24/7.

That's why the plan included residential units adjoining parking garages and a downtown baseball stadium surrounded by residential and retail so it never goes dark. Retail got a jumpstart with Mast General Store and then later the time was right for the return of national "destination" retailers to Main Street at the One Building. All of this drew shoppers to support new local retailers.

Add to this mix the magic of lights in the trees, eclectic public art, and welcoming public plazas on nearly every block and you have a pedestrian-friendly Main Street that every city in America longs to achieve.

Yet Greenville's downtown is reflective of its own unique personality.

Good planning. Great partnerships. Authenticity.

That's our "Grand Design" for making Greenville the most beautiful and livable city in America.

Knox White

–Photos on these two pages by Paul Ringger

Grand Design

From Trading Post to Renaissance

GREENVILLE'S

$\mathcal{S}$ ome 250 million years ago, two continental plates collided beneath North America shoving metamorphic and igneous rocks into hills of legend, the Blue Ridge Mountains. Gravity and weathering—rain, sleet, snow, ice, sun, and wind—went to work chiseling rocks, scouring declivities, gouging gorges, all of which forged a land destined to beckon explorers, lovers of waterfalls, and men of commerce. This folded land, cloaked in green, and running white with rapids and waterfalls, would become Upstate South Carolina.

Now, as then, Upstate waters churn, plummet, stairstep, flute, froth, and run white toward the sea. Water freefalls over ledges, a mesmerizing performance. Rivers coursing through rocks were the prototypal visitors bureau and chamber of commerce, for river magnetism has long pulled people from all points.

People drive great distances and make arduous hikes to witness the classic confrontation between rock and water. More fortunate souls, however, live in a city blessed with whitewater. They walk across "an ultra lightweight," 345-foot suspension bridge seemingly floating on air. Beneath them, a roar grows as river water pounds granite. Water shimmers down rock. Milky foam swirls like Atlantic surf over slabs of brown, ruddy rock. The unmovable object and the

irresistible force battle, and people–urban planners included–come to behold this spectacle from a bridge unlike any other.

That wasn't always the case, however, in Greenville, South Carolina. There was a time when people considered the falls an eyesore. The textile industry that drove Greenville's thriving economy had fouled the Reedy River and its falls. Moreover, a concrete bridge obscured the falls, not that anyone cared to see the river. Cracked, weed-infested

parking lots, vacant hotels, and a declining Main Street ruled the day.

THE RENAISSANCE CAME TOGETHER AT THE RIVER

Greenville's downtown resurgence emerged from a serious and balanced blend: mistakes, best practices, and examinations of "sister river cities" joined forces with public-private partnerships, thoughtful urban design, and an entrepreneurial spirit. The

city's energy and style is a far cry from the humble cityscapes of previous decades.

Today, Falls Park on the Reedy River in the historic West End is a great treasure. Before adversity arrived, Reedy River Falls attracted settlers, and today it's revered as the "cradle of Greenville." People consider the park an oasis within the city, and it is; but it wasn't always. They gather there to work, play, relax, and celebrate life. There was a time, though, when the citizens of Greenville wanted nothing to do with the river. The downtown went into deep decline. For a long time things looked bleak, but the falls would jumpstart Greenville's renaissance. Mayor Knox White said, "Falls Park is what started the inner-city visits, started *The Atlantic* magazine folks showing up. Falls Park was a game changer."

Things changed all right. Beautiful lighting, efficient parking garages, landscaped sidewalks, fascinating art galleries, coffee shops, sculptures, and other improvements broke the malaise that held Greenville. A

▲ The soothing sounds of whitewater draw people to a healthier falls that showcase the colors of Earth: greens, white, tan, and blue.

renaissance driven by partnerships, vision, and a collaborative culture turned Greenville into a resort by the Reedy, a diamond set amid mountains.

Today, it's a city blessed with European flair: green spaces, a graceful, walkable presence, and fabulous restaurants, which have gained national attention. So much love has been lavished on the city that bloggers and writers go to great lengths to come across as original "vocalists." Greenville native Chef John Malik, a self proclaimed, "writer trapped in a cook's body," wrote in the *Huffington Post* a blog titled *9 Reasons Not to Visit or Move to Greenville, South Carolina in 2015*. Said Malik, "In the past 24 months, we've been featured in *The Atlantic, The Pacific, Travel+Leisure, The Boston Globe, The New York Times, Outside Magazine, Inside, Money, Mo Money,* etc. Frankly, all this attention is starting to pile up into one enormous publicity jam. It's gotten to the point where our citizens can't take a walk down Main Street without running into a camera crew from the Happy Retirement Network. With that in mind,

I've decided to take a stand and point out nine reasons why you should not visit or move to my town."

Among his tongue-in-cheek reasons to shun Greenville are its restaurants, clean and delicious drinking water, and the Swamp Rabbit Trail. He even describes the city's newer architectures as subscribing to the UFO Theory of Architecture owing to their flying-saucer-like structures, saying Greenville is the Roswell of

the East Coast. Malik points out that the city's best restaurants aren't on Main Street though Main Street certainly has its share. We get the point. Those who live here or merely visit attest to the city's vibrant lifestyle, natural beauty, dynamic business culture, and storied past. Feature writers flock to Greenville—it's become a model for other cities; a destination for urban planners.

Greenville exhibited great patience in pulling itself out

▼ Falls Park, Greenville's jewel in waiting, is pictured here before the bridge obscuring its brilliance were torn down.

Grand Design

of decline. The city went from rags to riches, from nobody to celebrity. How did this transformation take place?

An Unraveling Textile Industry—Catalyst for Transformation

Key to Greenville's story of transformation is its recent history which Mayor Knox White describes in four words: "textiles and after textiles." It's the "after textiles"

where the story takes shape, and "after" takes root in the 1950s, an era that ushered in hard times. Crucial changes piled up and the overall effect diminished downtown Greenville. Cheap imported textiles hurt the textile industry, and textile jobs declined. Also, the mills began eliminating many jobs through automation, further aggravating a bad situation.

Another change—destined to become an American icon—was taking hold. A blossoming romance with the automobile was underway. By the mid-1950s a lot of American GIs were buying cars and the family vacation tradition established itself. A climate shift took place for the hospitality industry, and motels boomed at the expense of hotels. In time, Greenville's classic Poinsett Hotel would go into

foreclosure. Its decline symbolized the plagues downtown would suffer and longtime residents felt its loss acutely. The Greenville they had known was slipping away.

Yet another change involved the retail sector. Greenville got "malled." Malls promised an escape from bad weather, crime,

> "Around Reedy River Falls there was little or nothing to hold one's attention."
> **–David W. Cooley**

and parking woes: a siren song that seduced major retailers, nationwide, to relocate to the suburbs.

The city faced other problems as well. In 1958, David W. (Dave) Cooley served as the executive vice president of the Greenville Chamber of Commerce. He headed the chamber for six years and remembers

how the textile industry ran the show. "When I arrived in Greenville in 1958 to manage its Chamber of Commerce, the textile industry had the town by the throat and was choking it to death. Their owners had a common purpose—protect their industry, the rest of the community be damed. At the same time, downtown was in deep decline. Many stores had closed and others were barely holding on."

From Boarded Up to—

People moved out of the central city, and downtown Greenville withered in the 60s and 70s. Late in 1965 the Caine Company announced the construction of McAlister Square. It would be the largest mall in South Carolina, anchored by Ivey and Meyers-Arnold department stores. These two stores' departure from Main Street accelerated downtown's demise as the center of retail shopping.

Plagued with boarded-up buildings, downtown Greenville wasn't easy on the eyes. Vacant, they turned into detritus. When Main Street cash registers were clanging everything had been hunky-dory, but the people left and the register bells clanged no more. *"Down on Main Street,"* as Bob Seeger's song describes, disappointment had set in. A Hollywood location scout could have chosen the city as a setting for a depression-era movie. Vagrants sought refuge in the boarded-up Poinsett Hotel. Few people seemed to care about this once-proud area.

But this proved not to be the case.

Determined not to let this vital part of the city become a wasteland, city planners took action. In 1966 the Total Development Campaign encouraged retailers to modernize downtown by giving old buildings a veneer of aluminum siding. They razed the Ottaray Hotel, one of the more beautiful buildings in Greenville's history, and replaced it with a new motel. Down went the Woodside Building. Charles Daniel built the 25-story Daniel Building and Roger Peace built the new *Greenville News* Building close by the Reedy. These early efforts were regarded by many as mere window dressing;

of little avail as the city languished through the 1960s.

Downtown appeared incapable of rescuing itself. Enter a dynamic leader. Max Heller, elected mayor in 1971, developed a vision based on improving downtown's image through streetscape and traffic improvements.

Help for that vision came from a unique individual's fascination with a water feature far across the country. The late C. Thomas (Tommy) Wyche, a prominent local attorney, recalled a fetching fountain in Portland, Oregon.

Malls like McAllister Square lost their grip on retailers who returned to a revitalized downtown, spurred by the decision to downsize Main to two lanes and establish green spaces and a canopy of trees. It's hard to believe the bland intersection pictured on the opposite page is the vibrant McBee Avenue of today as it is seen below.
–Photo courtesy of the City of Greenville

–Photo by Paul Ringger

Giving people less road to drive seemed irrational in this era devoted to the primacy of the automobile. Retail, already struggling, fought the change but Heller forged ahead. Working with business leaders Wyche and Buck Mickel he fashioned a new streetscape with free, angled parking.

To keep the city from becoming a concrete canyon, they planted trees on both sides of Main Street and installed decorative light fixtures. Things began to improve. Main Street was gaining a bit of charisma.

Razing the slab of concrete known as Camperdown Bridge let in the sunshine and brought a new day to the Reedy River Falls. Mayor Max Heller had already seen the light when he set into motion changes that would bring a touch of European ambience to downtown. Today, Heller's statue stands as a tribute to his vision for the city.

–Photo courtesy of the City of Greenville

In the 1960s that fountain gave him an idea—build one for Greenville. "I liked the look of a fountain I'd seen pictured in Portland and invited its architect to come to Greenville and meet with city officials." That architect was Lawrence Halprin.

Halprin told Wyche, "You don't need a new fountain. You need to fix your downtown."

Fixing it became the mission.

Halprin suggested that much of Main Street go from four to two lanes, widen the sidewalks, and plant trees. Mayor Heller—focused on reviving Main Street and the downtown area—listened. Changing Main Street's persona became the initial strategy.

In this car-dominated era, city leaders did the unthinkable. They downsized Main Street's four lanes to two and added angled parking.

–Photo by Paul Ringger

They added parks and small plazas. Main Street was getting some personality. As the 1970s unfolded, downtown Greenville looked a whole lot better. Greenville had been transformed into a cityscape with character and charisma. It wasn't without challenges. Heller caught flack from downtown merchants fearful that reducing Main Street's four lanes to two would send what few customers remained to the malls. Heller stuck with his goal to give Main Street European ambience.

In time, the decision paid dividends. Main Street and its green spaces, flowers, and lights became an inviting place to walk; a place with a European, village-like presence.

Lee Leslie, the son of local advertising scion, Bill Leslie, recalls that downtown Greenville wasn't always a good place to live, work, or shop. Or even to walk around. He remembers Heller's influence, "Max Heller helped change that. I'd give an awful lot of credit to him for making downtown Greenville what it is today."

Lee Leslie continues about Heller that, "he got the city fathers (people such as Charlie Daniel, the Hipps, Timmons, and others) to agree to turn Main Street from four lanes—perfect for cruising—into a lush, tree-lined, two-lane street perfect for walking. The transformation began to attract development, including a Hyatt Regency."

Leslie believes Heller gave the city momentum. "Max Heller started something that continued: the Peace Center,

the Bergamo, Italy sister-city development in the middle of downtown, the festivals, and, significantly, the privately raised money for bridge removal revealing the Reedy River Falls, which led to Liberty Bridge and a new baseball park."

Under Heller's watchful eye, a plan took shape that incorporated vision, resourcefulness, and public-private partnerships. All required patience. Greenville's leaders, businessmen, and residents settled in for the long haul. City leaders and planners were determined to redevelop downtown according to a blueprint that featured persistence, strategic planning, and inspiring innovation.

It worked and a man with two excellent vantage points believes revitalization rescued the city from a dismal downturn.

From 1978 to 1982 Greg Jansen worked as a producer/director at Greenville's Channel 4 (WFBC/WYFF). Jansen's work in media has taken him to seven cities, which has given him a good frame of reference for assessing Greenville. "I have lived in Macon, Athens, Greenville, St. Louis, Raleigh, Charlotte, and Columbia in my 59 years. Twenty-four of them have been spent in the Greenville area. The overall quality of life in Greenville has been tremendous. As for downtown, I well remember when the Hyatt opened as the anchor on North Main and when a public-private partnership led to the Peace Center anchor shortly thereafter on South Main. By then, Max Heller's vision for downtown had really begun to take shape. Max Heller was a true visionary and just an all-around good guy.

"A huge advantage of working at Channel 4 during the

Grand Design

late 1970s and early 1980s was meeting the 'movers and shakers' of not just Main Street revitalization but the Upstate in general. Max was *the* leader.

"Prior to his vision," continues Jansen, "if the textile industry sniffled, the Upstate caught pneumonia. The vision and resulting revitalization was truly a culture-changing event."

For all we know Heller's leadership, accomplishments, and influence kept the Upstate from becoming an Allentown, Pennsylvania or Youngstown, Ohio or similar-sized Rust Belt city. Appropriately, a statue of Heller graces Main Street.

But, of course, there were many others who joined with Heller to affect these changes.

Dave Cooley recalls the era, "Time—that stands still for no one—worked its inexorable

way on Greenville. The great change in the textile industry, its automation and off-shoring, forced industry diversification, affecting the community's growth in very positive ways. Around Reedy River Falls there was little or nothing to hold one's attention. Today it is the centerpiece of Downtown Greenville and its massive development.

"There were a number of individuals who made a difference in the city's future. Charles E. Daniel, affectionately known as 'The Big Carpenter' was the leading Southern building contractor with headquarters in Greenville. He headed the list of forward-thinking Greenville citizens like Alester Furman Jr., a real estate mogul; Roger Peace, publisher of the town's newspaper; Bob Jolly, owner of then WFBC radio and television; Bill Timmons, an insurance company owner; The Hipps of Liberty Life

Insurance; Tommy Wyche, and environmentalist and lawyer; Buck Mickel, a nephew of Daniel; Kenneth Cass and Dave Traxler, mayors; A.D. Asbury, chairman of the planning commission; and, of course, others. They forged a consistent "can-do spirit" that still exists today. That spirit and its leadership history spell the difference between Greenville and other Upstate South Carolina cities."

In addition to Heller, Tommy Wyche, championed having the Hyatt Regency on Main. A public-private partnership landed the Hyatt Regency and slowly the rudderless ship *Greenville* had an oar in the water.

When the Hyatt Regency opened in 1982, the $34 million hotel signified a new era. The Greenville Commons/Hyatt Regency became the city's first luxury/convention hotel. The plan called for creating a vibrant setting for retail, offices, and living space as well as places for restaurants and entertainment venues. The community partnership that brought the Hyatt to the city, came up with $ 27.2 million. It used funds from a HUD grant, city reserve funds, money from Hyatt, and a grant from the U.S. Economic Development Administration. This unique venture paved the way for future partnerships like the one tasked with creating a performing arts center, which resulted in the creation of the Peace Center.

The 1980s ushered in nation-wide economic challenges: foreign imports, environmental regulations, and worldwide inflation—all of which put more nails in the coffin of the disappearing textile industry.

Yet, the 80s were transformative. In 1981, Crane and Associates' ten-year plan set goals for the next decade: the Greenville Central Area Partnership (GCAP) spurred much of that era's growth. One of GCAP's goals? Get people back to downtown. The 1982 Fall for Greenville Festival attracted approximately 20,000 people to Main Street on a Sunday afternoon. It wasn't without its hitches. Local church groups weren't keen on seeing Sunday licenses granted to allow the serving of alcohol.

Of course the great engine that drives urban revitalization is money. In 1986, the creation of a Tax Increment Finance (TIF) district offered an innovative way to let South Carolina cities use tax dollars normally spent on the city, county, and school districts for economic development. This funding mechanism was essential in 1984. It pumped millions upon millions into downtown and allowed Greenville to invest when other cities couldn't.

From 1983 to 1986, U.S. Shelter built what's known today as Liberty Square. Soon, new restaurants arrived. Other developments took place and downtown boomed in the mid-1980s. The workforce grew dramatically, nearly doubling office space, which rose to 2.1 million square feet.

The Liberty Square Towers went up just off I-385. Zoning laws were changed to allow mixed-use development. Keeping streets clean and adding law enforcement became a priority. Historic preservation resulted in the West End becoming a historic district.

Tommy Wyche worked with investors to start RiverPlace. *The Greenville News* first reported on RiverPlace in 1986 but more than twenty years would pass before the plan blossomed into reality. (Wyche, himself, worked on RiverPlace for 25 years before seeing it completed.)

But not all the dreams were realized. People consistently voted down a plan to pay for a new coliseum.

In 1988, the schoolchildren of Greenville got in on the urban revitalization act. It began when Dorothy Hipp Gunter pledged $3 million to the construction of a 400-seat theater as part of the Peace Center. Gunter bought a Steinway piano for the theater

Summer concerts, family events, and other festivities take place outdoors at the TD Stage. With a seating capacity of more than 1,400 and ample room for blankets and lawn chairs, food vendors find a receptive crowd down by the water. It's a great place for outdoor entertainment in the summer and adds a compelling facet to Falls Park.
–Photo courtesy of the Peace Center

Upscale and historic, this grand hotel sits on a site that has deep roots in the hospitality field. For one hundred years, the Mansion House Hotel stood where the Westin Poinsett is today. In 1924, the old hotel was demolished to make room for construction of the Poinsett Hotel. Besides maintaining the city's long tradition of housing a hotel on the very same plot, the opening of the Westin Poinsett Hotel helped the city develop downtown toward the Reedy and Falls Park.

but a second one was needed. People from many walks of life heard of the need for the matching pianos. The 88 Keys Campaign: 88 cents for 88 keys in 1988 came to life and thousands of school kids raided their piggy banks to help the cause. A spirit of engagement swept over the city. More good things were coming in the 1990s. A new Greenville was waiting down river.

BOOMING

The 1990s brought an up-surge. Momentum was build-ing, overcoming the inertia of the past. The city was inventing a charming new personality featuring the arts, restaurants, and the Reedy River. Major developments took place and the skyline took on character. The Peace family's start-up pledge of $10 million jump-started the cam-paign to build the Peace Center for the Performing Arts.

In the early 1990s, the city both tightened and lightened up. The Chamber of Com-merce took action to give downtown more contempo-rary governance. They helped draft and pass ordinances on noise, Sunday alcohol sales, ones making it okay for people to enjoy beer and wine in cups outdoors—all key to making the many new festivals work.

The 1990s would bring hope that the venerable Poinsett Hotel would regain its former glory, an accomplishment sure to please the city's older resi-dents. During the days of its demise, something about the Poinsett Hotel brought to mind the rusty, silt-covered ruins of the *Titanic*—all former glories gone. Razing the hotel—un-bearable words to Greenville seniors—had been a possibil-ity. From 1971 to December 1986, the hotel had suffered foreclosure and remained empty until November 1997 when Steve Dopp and Greg Lenox, owners and developers of Charleston's historic Fran-cis Marion Hotel, purchased it. Costly and serious renovations

–Photo by Paul Ringger

–Photo by Paul Ringger

One, a mixed-use complex, sits where the old Woolworth building was. Tenants include a restaurant, Haynesworth Sinkler Boyd, and high-end retailers such as Orvis, Brooks Brothers, and Anthropologie. Clemson University maintains offices there as does Hughes Development Corporation, the complex's developer

began. What was once considered one of the eleven most endangered sites in the Southeast, according to the South Carolina Chapter of the American Institute of Architects, had a reprieve.

Greenville's revitalization provided a path along which the restoration of the grand, old hotel could proceed. The opening of the Westin Poinsett helped the city develop downtown toward the Reedy and Falls Park. "Re-opening the Poinsett had a huge impact on Greenville's older residents," said Mayor White. "It broke a psychological barrier about developing downtown and brought us a lot of goodwill."

When the Bi-Lo Center opened in 1998 Greenville at long last had a coliseum. Sports and concert enthusiasts took joy in seeing the 16,000-seat facility rise from the earth. Scheer-Stern Development (ScheerGame) found a way to build it without tax money. The Bi-Lo Center is known today as the Bon Secours Wellness Arena.

The new energy fired up a desire not just to be downtown but to also live downtown. Housing—apartments and condominiums—went up. Greenville became *cool* to its residents. Greenville became *cool* to outsiders, too. There came a time when people in Columbia began talking

about driving up to Greenville for no reason other than to be there. They just wanted to enjoy the city's ambience and newfound identity. Greenville's dreams of rejuvenation were not just dreams anymore. The proof was all around. In 1995, the West End Market brought the city 35,000 square feet of retail and restaurant space and 10,000 square feet of office space. 1999 to 2000 saw the development of the Poinsett Plaza/Hotel, including 220,000 square feet of office space, four residential penthouses, the 204-room Westin Poinsett Hotel, and an 843-space parking garage, along with streetscape and park improvements to Main Street.

Grand Design

— Photo by Stephanie Norwood

— Photo by Stephanie Norwood

Falls Park offers something for everyone: dining, physical activity, and sheer relaxation. At its entrance you'll find the Passerelle Bistro. Properly enough, passerelle is French for footbridge. Nearby Liberty Bridge's sweeping arc—Miguel Rosales's aerial amphitheater—ferries a constant flow of people over the falls.

1995 proved to be a pivotal year. Looking back to the center of the decade's accomplishments, **December 11, 1995** merits bold type. When Mayor White took office that day, he, like Heller, had a vision to sell. Alex Crevar wrote about that vision in the *New York Times* titled *Opening the Gate to a Vibrant Main Street in Greenville, S.C.* In it he said, "Back in 1998, few could have imagined Greenville's transformation when Mayor Knox White began selling the idea of a park on Main Street incorporating the Reedy River's 40-foot waterfall. Falls Park became a spark for a pedestrian-friendly city center when it opened in 2004. Last year, the newly erected ONE building—located at 1 Main

—Photo by Paul Ringger

The falls are an eyesore no longer and its white noise is easy on the ears. It is a focal point like few others and even a weeknight near the falls seems like a Saturday night.

Street—provided yet another stamp of validation and a new home for high-end retailers to complement an already dense selection of restaurants, cafes and shops. 'Main Street was not an attractive destination,' the mayor said. 'Today, it's the most vibrant place in the region.'"

THE 2000's REVITALIZATION

Vibrant indeed, and the 2000s brought more of the same. A roll call of years reveals that while some cities sleep, Greenville doesn't.

In 2003, Mast General arrived. The "store that has everything" brought a lot to Main Street: creaky floors, memories of old country stores, and a cult-like following. It's always filled with shoppers.

In 2004, Falls Park and Liberty Bridge—the city's stars—brought Greenville a new identity and it's best brand according to Mayor White. Making use of nature's gifts is one of urban design's tenets and the river and falls held great appeal to Liberty Bridge's renowned designer, Boston architect Miguel Rosales. "I thought the site was unique and a

great opportunity to design a bridge that would respond to its natural features. The location of the waterfall was a very important consideration in the bridge design as we tried to relate to it by curving the bridge away from the falls creating an aerial amphitheater effect."

Rosales's designs take him all over the world and he gives Greenville high marks. "Downtown Greenville has one of the best main streets I have ever seen in the United States. The human scale, variety of uses, tree canopy, traffic-calming features, and sculptures all add to an excellent walking experience." He adds that small European cities often have similar features and qualities.

Rosales also has generous praise for city leaders. "Working with Mayor White, the City Council and stakeholders was one of the most rewarding experiences of my career. I am very grateful that they endorsed and supported my bridge design. I had never worked for the City of Greenville before the Liberty Bridge, so in a way they took a calculated risk with a new consultant and a challenging

bridge project." Rosales says Liberty Bridge and Falls Park "are unforgettable and very special. I am very pleased that the Greenville community embraced the Liberty Bridge. It's become the symbol of the regeneration of the river and falls."

In 2005, River-Place brought the city two residential condominiums, the 115-room Hampton Inn and Suites Hotel, an 87,000-square foot office building, a 285-space parking garage, and 5,000 square feet of art studio spaces.

In 2006, the West End Baseball Stadium/Field House gave the West End a Fenway Park-like mixed-use stadium and a 40-unit condominium.

In May 2009, the Greenville Health System Swamp Rabbit Trail officially opened with its inaugural 5K Race. More than 2,000 people took part.

In 2011, JMH Hotel's renovation of the Hyatt Regency added new virve to downtown Greenville. The multi-million dollar renovation incorporated a redesign

> "Downtown Greenville has one of the best main streets I have ever seen in the United States. The human scale, variety of uses, tree canopy, traffic-calming features, and sculptures all add to an excellent walking experience."
>
> **—Miguel Rosales**

Greenville's first anchor was Greenville Commons and its Hyatt Regency Hotel, office complex, and parking garage. Today, the Hyatt's Southern style and unique events such as "Yappy Hour," a Humane Society event that takes place the second Wednesday of each month, draw people to NOMA Square.

of the entire property, including all 328 guestrooms, additional meeting and event space, and launched a new soil-to-city restaurant, Roost.

DJ Rama, president of JMH Hotels, said his company wanted to help bring new energy to the downtown area. "Since our forefathers had such extraordinary vision in bringing the Hyatt to North Main as a catalyst for redevelopment of the declining downtown in the late 1970s, we wanted to make sure that we were good stewards of the hotel during our repositioning and renovation of the asset. We sought a lot of input on what was needed, as well as

researched successful models in other cities to create something special for Greenville. Our hope was that by creating a well-designed outdoor space for community events and a great restaurant, people would be drawn back to the north end of downtown. We created a new identity, calling it NOMA Square."

Draw people back it did. Said Rama, "It has been a pleasure to watch the community embrace the repositioned Hyatt and NOMA Square. The downtown community and our traveling guests seem to feel at home and take pride and ownership of the space. They love our free events, like yoga or 'yappy hour,' and make the festivals and concerts part of their regular

routine. Development in the North Main area is growing and retailers in the area are happy to see the increased foot traffic."

"Greenville," added Rama, "is a community with thoughtful leaders who have a strong sense of stewardship to protect what we have and build something great for the next generation with quality of life as the focal point."

In 2013, ONE, a sparkling, new, mixed-use hub brought office space, shopping, and dining to the Falls Park area.

CITY OF GREAT APPEAL

Had Richard Pearis and his trading post endured over the ages, he would have seen Greenville experience a

−Photos on these two pages by Paul Ringger

renaissance that would draw for people from around the world. A city with appeal to all. Mayor White says that the retirement community as well as young people come to the city for the ambience of downtown—the cycling community, the coffee shops, the apartments. "It's very healthy for a city to see that happen, and then there is certainly the tourist phenomenon."

Add retail, too. Greenville continues to build a reputation as the number-one downtown in the southeast. For business. For living. And for fun. ONE attracted national retailers Anthropologie and Brooks Brothers, and is home to the headquarters branch of CertusBank.

Today, Main Street booms. You'll find nearly every major bank in the Southeast downtown and a multitude of restaurants, coffee shops, lounges, and taverns. Now if you see a boarded-up building the explanation is obvious: it's undergoing renovation.

Interesting, too, are the multi-colored fronts of Main Street's buildings. No cement-like tones you'd see in concrete canyons. You get a Charleston Rainbow Row-effect

that plays well with the green canopies. Walk the street and see tans, reds, greens, burgundies, mustard, and hues both flashy and subtle. Picturesque sidewalk umbrellas sprout like parasols, their colors bubbling everywhere.

These days, downtown Greenville feels like a Saturday in a European resort. It's friendly and cosmopolitan. A happy city. No frowns. No one scurrying to escape a broiling sun. Walking in complete shade feels luxurious in a Southern city, and it makes people-watching here great sport. You'll see tour groups, businessmen, students, and casual strollers striking a pace that's anything but frenetic. It's relaxing... even the people on Segways spend more time standing than whirring along. And you have to recheck your eyes. No parking meters. Talk about saying good riddance to a blight. You'll not see parking meters sprouting like alien weeds from the sidewalks. You will see spacious sidewalks, benches and greenery thanks to streetscaping.

Walking Main Street will test your internal GPS and sense of geography. If you don't believe that, ramble Main Street on a Monday

morning. When you see the leafy green tunnel arching over Main, you'll think of the Lowcountry and picturesque avenues of green oaks. Look skyward. All you'll see are leaves. On the breeze, your ear will catch accents, dialects, and languages. Because Main Street is a melting pot of sorts. The bevy of international businesses in this city on the I-85 corridor proves staggering, and those from abroad flock to the city.

Seeing the myriad sidewalk cafés, may put you in mind of a stroll along Paris's Rue St. Germain with its legendary sidewalk bistros. And when you catch the delicious fragrances on the wind, you

Trees and umbrellas provide a Paris-like venue for dining. Sidewalk cafes abound and overflow with patrons. Aromas of fine foods create a rich sensory experience for passersby.

There's no shortage of fine restaurants along Main Street or anywhere in Greenville for that matter. Southern, American, and international cuisine—you'll find it here. A sumptuous repast near gleaming ice sculptures and outdoor dining are yours in the reinvented city by the Reedy River.

Il Porcellino, a wild boar of Florence, Italy fame, seems to stare down one of the Mice on Main. The idea for the mice came from Jimmy Ryan when he was a senior at Christ Church Episcopal School. Zan Wells sculpted the mice, which "hide" along Main Street. Statuary and art abound on Main Street, and downtown, where you'll see over twenty works of art.

will quickly focus. Let's have lunch.

You can go light. You can go sumptuous. You can choose French cuisine or enjoy refined seasonal American food featuring local and regional stocks. There's always pizza and old-school Southern deep-fried fare. Got a sweet tooth? Nine flavors of chocolate moose wait on North main. Just need a jolt of java? At the corner of Main and Coffee streets (where else?) you'll find an underground coffee shop known for its hot coffee and cool vibe. Up on NOMA Square (NOrth MAin), you'll find soil-to-city foods and great surroundings.

The list of great foods goes on. (Reader Alert: By the time you finish reviewing this roster you might gain a few pounds.) Jambalaya and raw oysters. Fresh salads and breads. Fabulous burgers. Fried green tomatoes and barbecued shrimp. Mediterranean-themed fare. Custom-blended ice cream. Moonshine, yes moonshine! Persian cuisine. Sizzling steaks. Grilled fish.

Or, there are places you can take cooking classes and learn to make many of these culinary delights at home.

STATUARY AND MORE

After lunch, checkout the statuary. Down along the south end of Main you can sit by the figure of Joel Poinsett. Tell him how much you love poinsettias. Don't expect a reply; he's a man of few words. From nearby fountains comes

the glassy crash of falling water—a sound older than mankind. Up along Main's northern end, the Roost restaurant combines fire and water—and firewater—in a delightful way. Alongside the outside dining area, its firebowl-in-a-fountain evokes images of an Olympic torch.

Down on the south end of Main Street, the sound of more falling water will draw you to Poinsett Plaza. You'll come across a most unusual statue: *Il Porcellino*, a wild boar of Florence, Italy fame. Originally sculpted and cast by Baroque master Pietro Tacca a bit before 1634. Now there are four things you

need to know about this wild hog: 1) it is a replica of the Florence statue; 2) water dribbles from its snout making it a fountain of sorts (or snorts); 3) it protects one of those canny Mice on Main; and 4) appropriately enough, as WYFF-TV 4 reporter Sean Muserallo drolly reported, "It doesn't hog up the sidewalk."

The Young Friends of Florence championed the placement of *Il Porcellino* on Main Street, further enriching this cultural landscape and strengthening artistic ties between Greenville and Florence.

Another example of the emblematic courage of the city is its investment in the West End. Beginning well before the boom times, the city's initiatives in this blighted area are among those which paid big dividends. The city converted a languishing industrial area adjacent to the West End Historic District into a thriving performing arts complex. Growth, excitement, and goodwill prove contagious, too. Development stabilized the stagnant neighborhood by transforming an abandoned cotton warehouse into the West End Market, a mixed-use project of shops, restaurants, and offices. Strong public-private partnerships gave the historical district a historic lift. That, in turn, encouraged adaptive reuse of several other historic buildings throughout downtown. Such farsightedness encouraged the necessary private investment and garnered recognition from municipalities across the United States.

No complacency here either as you see all too often in cities. In 2010, on its 20th anniversary, the Peace Center underwent an extensive $21.5 million makeover. Mayor Knox White said that prior to the makeover the Center was "pretty much sealed away from both Main Street and the river." A sweeping glass facade and front plaza enhanced the Center's drawing power. At night it gleams like a jewel. Adjacent to Falls Park, this performing arts center features the Peace Concert Hall, Dorothy Hipp Gunter Theater, and an amphitheater. The Peace Center takes its name from the Peace family

who donated $10 million towards its development. Today, entertainers from the world over perform where factories once stood building Confederate Army wagons, producing textiles, and serving as home base of Duke's Mayonnaise. Today the arts thrive here.

Things keep getting better in this ongoing renaissance. Greenville consistently makes top ten lists: best place to live, best downtown in America, etc. Developing the area adjacent to Falls Park brought dazzle and acclaim to the city. No wonder downtown Greenville and its beautiful falls attract 2.5 million visitors a year. All this, as you'd expect, continues to attract national attention.

A MEDIA DARLING

Greenville, long a destination for travelers, was considered a health-resort getaway in the early 1800s for South Carolinians in the lower part of the state. Today, the arts, cultural events, and outdoor recreation pull people to the city—and not just from the Lowcountry. They come from everywhere. Top businesses follow people who can't get enough of this Upstate jewel.

Any resort worth its salt offers great things to do—beautiful vistas, fabulous food, and entertainment. Well, Greenville's worth its salt and more. The media have taken notice. If you believe Greenville has grown into a media darling, you are correct. Let's review just a nano-fraction of the accolades media heap upon this dynamic city. *Atlanta Magazine*'s Amanda Heckert writes: "While driving through downtown Greenville, South Carolina, after a recent visit

Unlike the all-too-common concrete canyons of other cities, splashes of floral colorful flora set amid lush greenery draw people to Greenville. Hardscapes and winding paths direct leisurely strolls through one of America's best downtowns.

Grand Design

the eight years since I left the Upstate, this stretch has somehow evolved into one of the Southeast's most vibrant Main Streets. The Reedy—whose currents powered Greenville's early settlements and mills—buoyed the city again when Falls Park opened by its shoals in 2004. Here visitors can rent Reedy Rides bikes and hop on the Swamp Rabbit Tram Trail, a new thirteen-plus-mile greenway that runs to neighboring Greenville Zoo.

"Falls Park also forms a gateway to the revived historic West End, a once-derelict landscape of warehouses and rail yards. A free trolley rolls by, taking sightseers past na-

to my parents' house nearby, my husband—who has called New York and L.A. home—turned to me and said, "I wouldn't mind living here one day." I was stunned to realize that I agreed with him. In

tive "Shoeless Joe" Jackson's house museum and five-year-old Fluor Field—home to a Red Sox affiliate and a miniature Green Monster.

"When hunger calls, I face a dilemma unfathomable a few years ago: too many buzzed-about, chef-driven restaurants. Greenville's dining revival took off in the late nineties when

Carl Sobocinski opened nouveau southern Soby's in a renovated cotton exchange. Now Soby's has its own farm, and its owners have other hits like the Lazy Goat (with tapas such as bisteeya, a savory Moroccan pastry) and the Nose Dive gastropub. I finally settle on American Grocery Restaurant, known for sustainable seafood.

Another marvel: global eats. Popular downtown spots like chichi Persian Pomegranate on Main and Belgium-focused The Trappe Door, with its 150-plus beers, are a byproduct of Greenville's influx of international firms. Michelin and BMW top that list, and the latter's Performance Driving School draws fast-lane fans from across the nation."

CNN Money reports: Once known for textile manufacturing, Greenville has become an international powerhouse, hosting companies from all parts of the globe. The city, along with Spartanburg, Anderson, and other nearby towns known as "The Upstate," boasts more than 250 international firms, including BMW (Germany), Michelin (France), GlaxoSmithKline (United Kingdom) and Kyocera (Japan).

"That's the highest international investment per capita in the nation," said Nancy Whitworth, Greenville's Director of Economic Development.

Bicycling Magazine named Greenville as one of the Best Small Cities for Cycling. Home to the U.S. Pro national road and time-trial championships and American cycling legend George Hincapie, Greenville has worked

–Photos this page by Paul Ringger

tirelessly to update and develop its bike network. One of the most popular routes: the 17.5-mile Greenville Health System Swamp Rabbit Trail, which snakes along the Reedy River into the city's center. The trail has grown nearly 5 miles a year since opening in early 2009; new businesses that have recently opened along the path include a bike shop and a grocery store selling locally grown produce. Another local bike shop, Pedal Chic, claims to be the nation's first to cater specifically to female cyclists.

Men's Journal had this to say: "George Hincapie (one of the world's most recognized cyclists) has become something of an ambassador for Greenville, South Carolina, his home some 60 miles south of Asheville, North Carolina, for the past decade. A small city of 60,000, it sits in between the Sumter, Pisgah, and Chattahoochee National Forests. 'This is a town for you if you're an outdoors person,' he says. "There's mountain biking, world-class climbs on a road bike, and hiking." But beyond the attractions of the great outdoors, there's some pretty attractive indoor experiences as well. "There are tons of restaurants downtown, like Soby's, The Lazy Goat, and Rick Erwin's. And bars—"that's something I'm going to have to explore more in retirement." Hincapie also has a place for you to stay: He recently bought La Bastide Hotel, which he hopes will become a base camp for adventurous visitors to his chosen home. "We want people to come in from all over the world and do high-end cycling and triathlon camps and go running and just see why we love Greenville so much."

Southern Living, the quintessential Southern magazine, says "Greenville has the best little food festival in the South. Greetings from a sparkling Saturday in Greenville, South Carolina, where Euphoria, one of the most appealing food festivals in the South, is in full swing. We're talking bluegrass banjos, bacon-infused cocktails with industry legend Allan Benton, she-crab soup with Restaurant Eugene's Linton Hopkins, and a

–Photos by Tom Poland

Hiking trails, baseball, cycling, and more appeal to outdoor-minded Greenvillians. Baseball's legendary "Shoeless" Joe Jackson died in Greenville in 1951. Although a 1921 Chicago jury acquitted Jackson of fixing the 1919 World Series, Commissioner Kenesaw Mountain Landis banned Jackson and seven other players from baseball for life. Honored in bronze in downtown Greenville, you'll note the famed athlete is no longer "shoeless". Fluor Field at the West End draws fans of the Greenville Drive. The BMW Performance Center Driving School offers outdoor action for new BMW owners who put their car through road test rigors.

> " This is a town for you if you're an outdoors person..."
>
> **–George Hincapie**

–Photo by Paul Ringger

–Photo by Paul Ringger

34   G R E E N V I L L E ' S

guaranteed return home in tighter trousers (we know it's a tough job, but someone's got to try the moonshine cocktails and pork belly polenta at American Grocery Restaurant). It's all part of the fun.

Founded in 2006 by local hero (and platinum-selling singer/songwriter) Edwin McCain and restaurateur Carl Sobocinski (of Greenville's Table 301 restaurants), Euphoria is dedicated to showcasing the brightest star chefs in the South (including Joseph Lenn of Blackberry Farm, Edward Lee chef at 610 Magnolia) as well as the town's eclectic culinary and cultural scene.

Nestled in the foothills of the Blue Ridge Mountains, Greenville's revitalized downtown, confluence of international businesses (including Michelin and BMW) and world-class entertainment venues have made it an emerging dining and drinking destination. "Ten years ago we'd have to take visiting family and friends to Atlanta or Charleston to entertain them," Chris Stone, president of the Greenville CVB said over coffee, "but all that's changing. Now people actually want to come here to vacation, and they can't wait to get back to our restaurants."

Lonely Planet likes Greenville's location among many things. "With the Blue Ridge Mountains in its backyard, outdoor adventure is one of Greenville's main draws, and it starts right in town in Falls Park on the Reedy. The banks of the Reedy River were once lined with mills, textile factories, and warehouses. Today, inviting trails and gardens greet visitors, leading off to a revitalized Main Street, with local shops, craft-beer pubs, and a global array of restaurants.

Museums cluster in Heritage Green, just west of Main Street. Works by Andrew Wyeth and South Carolina artist Jasper Johns are highlights at the Greenville County Museum of Art, and families can head next door to The Children's Museum of the Upstate. Public art spills out on to Main Street with the small bronze statues of "Mice on Main," doubling as a scavenger hunt.

Greenville's B-Cycle (greenville.bcycle.com) bike-share program lets travelers wind their way through the city's extensive network of trails and roads. Grab a bike and follow an old railroad route along the still expanding GHS Swamp Rabbit Trail (greenvillerec.com), following the Reedy River. For day trips, six rugged state parks are easily reached from the Cherokee Foothills Scenic Highway 11. Hikers head for popular views atop Table Rock Mountain and Caesars Head State Park where birdwatchers gather from September to November for the annual Hawk Watch.

The accolades from media go on and on. Let's read two more, this one from *Better Homes and Gardens*. "This hill country city is alive with stylish indie twists on Southern charm." And this one from *Parade* magazine. "Year-round, the tree-lined Main Street is strung with twinkling lights that give it a 'fairy tale' feeling."

Okay, one more. Greenville is anchored by what *Forbes Magazine* calls one of America's Best Downtowns.

"Featuring a one-of-a-kind 'floating' suspension bridge and set against the scenic Blue Ridge Mountains, Greenville boasts a thriving arts scene, hundreds of restaurants, shops and boutiques, popular annual festivals, numerous historic sites and museums housing significant art collections. Excellent interstate service and a user-friendly international airport make access easy."

THE STORY CONTINUES

Just like Hans Christian Andersen's "The Ugly Duckling," the fairy tale continues for this resort that John Pearis would be proud of. Pearis knew a good thing when he saw it. Today, Greenville is recognized as having one of the country's top "in-town" waterfalls—watery stairsteps on the Reedy River aptly named Falls Park. Kayakers shoot rapids in the midst of an urban area boasting more than 300,000 people. You'll see bikers on the trail edging the river. Greenville's Falls Park and its "Big Brother" waterfall provide a relaxing setting for yoga classes' physical, mental, and spiritual discipline.

Few cities can boast of a whitewater park in its heart. Greenville can.

Greenville grew up on the banks of the Reedy, a river flowing out of the Smoky Mountains. Though the river went through some tough times due to pollution, you can now dine in outdoor venues overlooking a healthier stream—a hometown waterway rushing past city vistas and urban landscapes.

Mayor White sums up how the city's revitalization took place. "It's all about mixed

Yoga is another facet of outdoor life in Greenville. Falls Park's "Big Brother" waterfall provides a relaxing setting complete with white noise and splendid views.

use: the office, retail, and residential, the mix of those. Each one is an important ingredient. We got retail back into downtown and now we have Brooks Brothers and Anthropologie and all the big retailers, but we had to work hard to secure it. We created pockets of public spaces along the downtown area where people can gather. The spaces are carefully designed to do what they do. Then, there's the star of the show—the river and the waterfall—an asset we finally embraced as the centerpiece of the whole downtown."

It all works and it works beautifully. Sure, there were battles and a lot of ups-and-downs, but Greenville, "Yeah, *That* Greenville," persevered. From bust to boom, from boarded-up to booming, from trading post to resort, Greenville's transformative story keeps getting better. And it's nowhere near done.

–Photo by Paul Ringger

Greenville ... the metamorphosis of a Grand Design

Events and elements that figure in the city's rise, decline, and remarkable transformation.

1786 —Greenville County is created from Spartanburg District.

1831—"Pleasantburg" changes to "Greenville."

1850—Greenville's population is 1,305.

1853—The first train on the Greenville & Columbia Railroad arrives in the West End.

1860—Greenville's population is 2,757.

1869, February—The SC General Assembly establishes Greenville, the town, as a city.

1870—Greenville's population is 1,518.

1880— Greenville's population is 8,160.

1889—Carolina, Knoxville and Western Railway launched connecting Greenville County to Atlantic ports and Tennessee. Passengers call it the Swamp Rabbit, probably because of the bouncy ride.

1890— Greenville's population is 8,607.

1895 to 1910—Textile mills locate outside the central city; earlier mills along the Reedy River experience difficult financial conditions.

1900—Greenville's population is 11,860.

1900s, early—Cars and trolley cars make the downtown scene; Greenville's is becoming the Upstate's economic center.

1900s to 1930s—Some of the nation's largest textile mills go up on the city's western edge; Greenville's "textile crescent" attracts over 40,000 workers.

1874—A.M. Speights establishes a daily newspaper, The Greenville News. A weekly, The Mountaineer published in Greenville since 1829, later becomes a daily, The Greenville Piedmont. B.H. Peace and sons, owners of The Greenville News, purchase it in 1927.

1910—Greenville's population is 15,741.

1910—The trolley line extends to city outskirts, what would become the Overbrook Historic District.

1910 to 1930—Most of the buildings in the Pettigru Historic District go up.

1915—Nobel Laureate Charles Hard Townes, physicist and laser developer, is born in Greenville July 8.

1917—Greenville is known as the "Textile Center of the World."

1917—During World War I, the Army opens Camp Sevier where over 100,000 soldiers train; a building boom follows.

1920—Greenville's population is 23,172.

1928—James B. Davis founds the Dixie Hummingbirds from church choir members. In 1973 the group backs Paul Simon in the hit "Loves Me Like a Rock."

1930—Greenville's population is 29,154.

1940—Greenville's population is 34,734.

1941—Civil Rights leader Jesse Jackson is born in Greenville October 8.

1942—Donaldson Air Force Base is built. It brings thousands of airmen to Greenville after World War II.

1942—National companies purchase local textile mills and sell off their villages.

1945—Postwar Greenville grows rapidly with industrial development led by Charles Daniel.

1950—Greenville's population is 58,161.

1954—Greenville is the location where Frank Lloyd Wright builds one of his final homes.

1956—Eisenhower's Federal-Aid Highway Act will bring two interstates into the Greenville region.

1960—Greenville's population is 66,188.

1960s—Civil rights tensions lead to biracial committees that collaborate to ensure racial unrest won't harm growth

1967—Greenville Technical College opens, a major asset to South Carolina.

1970—Greenville's population is 61,208, a 7.5% drop.

1970—Austrian immigrant, Mayor Max Heller, implements European urban features. Landscape Architect Lawrence Halprin will design downtown streetscape renovations.

1977—All original members of Lynyrd Skynrd play their last concert in Greenville on October 19.

1980—Greenville's population is 58,242, a 4.8% drop.

1980s—The city lays the foundation for its downtown vision.

1990—Greenville's population is 58,282, a 0.1% increase.

1995—The Greenville News and The Mountaineer merge.

2000—Greenville's population is 56,002, a 3.9% drop.

2005—The first shovel of dirt May 8 signifies a new baseball stadium will sit where an old lumberyard existed.

2005—Artisphere celebrates the arts and Greenville's rich international and multi-cultural heritage.

2006—Greenville Drive plays and wins it first game in Fluor Field at the West End Field April 6.

2006—West End Field is the 2006 Ballpark of the Year as designated by Ballparks.com August 31.

2008—West End Field is officially renamed Fluor Field at the West End.

2009—Over 3,000 attend the opening of GHS Swamp Rabbit Trail and 1st Annual GHS Swamp Rabbit 5K.

2010—Greenville's population is 58,409, a 4.3% increase.

2010—Greenville and its surrounding population of 400,492 is SC's third largest and fastest growing urban area.

2011—The Center for Emerging Technologies opens, providing leading edge industry R&D.

2103—Greenville's estimated population is 61,397, a 5.1% increase.

2015—Artisphere has its best year yet.

Grand Design

How Greenville Brought the

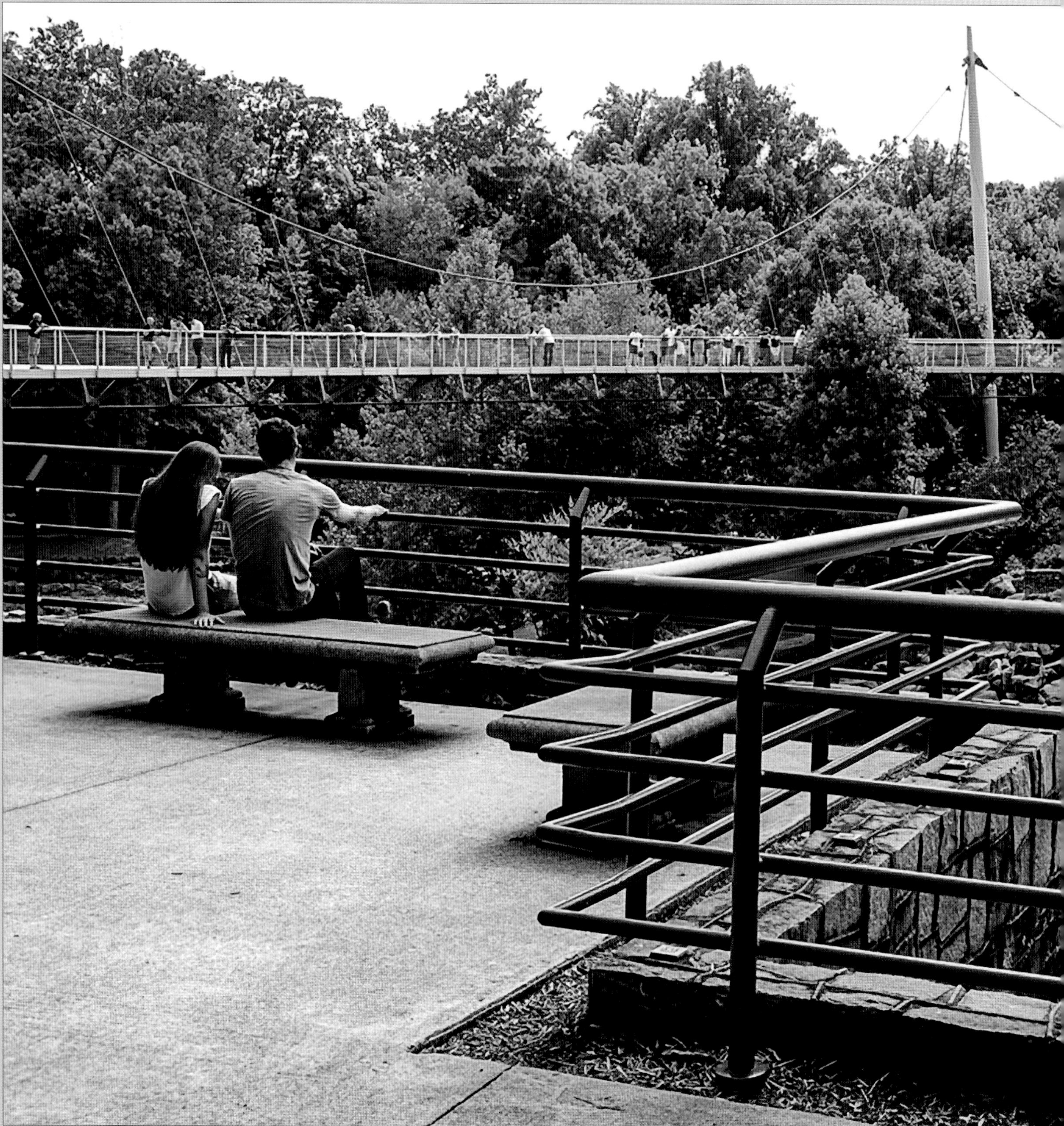

Reedy River Back

From Cesspool to Centerpiece

–Photo by Stephanie Norwood

The Reedy's headwaters rise north of Travelers Rest in the foothills of the Blue Ridge Mountains. From spring seeps it grows and is fed by creeks and streams until it empties into Lake Greenwood to the south-southeast of Greenville. In between and across the decades, the Reedy's journey tells a story. Unlike the river's straightforward flow, the story doubles back and stops and goes with periods of stagnation. The briefest of synopses might summarize it in ten words: From cesspool to centerpiece, from low point to high point. Or you could write that the Reedy went from gristmills to stagnant green water to greater times.

A river's demise at the hands of man is an old, sad story. Many a river has offered cities a tempting way to dispose of wastes in less-learned times. The Kanawah in Charleston, West Virginia comes to mind. Today, we know that what happens to a river affects other places. Trouble flows downstream.

Once valued for its waterpower, industries began to view the Reedy as a way to get rid of effluent in the late 1800s and early 1900s. Various factories came and went—a manufacturer of wagons and carriages, a lumber supplier, and the two Camperdown Mills that arrived in the late 1870s. As steam power, and later hydroelectric arrived, mills no longer needed the water to drive machinery. They needed it to wash things downstream. Textile mills discharged wastes without treatment or worry.

After the 1920s Greenville and its suburbs emptied sewage into the river. Add, too, what is termed non-point pollution today, urban runoff, and the river faced trouble for a long time. The river grew rank and nasty and by the 1970s it was shunned as if some evil miasma might rise off it and spread illness across the city. Odorous and overgrown, to see the river was to see downtown Greenville in retreat.

THE RAINBOW REEDY

When the Federal Clean Water Act of 1972 went onto the books, it signaled a turning point of sorts. Surely more stringent industrial discharge and wastewater treatment permits would bring better treatment to the Reedy. Nothing good, though, happened. People shied away from downtown. Some residents didn't even know a waterfall existed. Main Street retailers

The Camperdown Mills—the first modern textile mills to open within the City of Greenville and Greenville County—manufactured and exported cotton yarns throughout the United States. However, the Reedy River paid a price.
–Photo courtesy of Greenville County Historical Society

hightailed it for the suburbs, while the winds of change were blowing the textile mills out of business.

Some textile plants hung in there, however. Friends of the Reedy River posted on its website, "Many Greenville residents recall the days as recent as the early 1980s when the Reedy ran a different color every day depending on the dyeing operations of the textile plants." Folks referred

> The Greenville News ran a full front-page story: *Now They Call It The River of Death.*

to the river as the Rainbow Reedy but it was anything but pretty. The classic win-lose scenario was playing out. The textile mills that brought wealth and acclaim to Greenville were killing the river, but it wasn't just them. The river suffered at the hands of others, too. The construction of I-85 and Donaldson Air Force Base dropped huge loads of sediment into the river. Urban development's

housing projects did the river no favors. Water seeks its own level—poor stewardship is its own reward.

To make matters worse, a catastrophe was waiting downriver. June 26, 1996 a pipeline ruptured near Fork Shoals, filling the river with more than one million gallons of diesel fuel, one of the largest inland oil spills in U.S. history. *The Greenville News* ran a full front-page story: "Now They Call It The River of Death." The spill destroyed the entire food chain along a 23-mile stretch, ironically, one of the river's historically less-polluted stretches. Though the accident site was south of Greenville it reinforced the notion that the beleaguered Reedy could not catch a break.

Upstream, people had been fighting for the Reedy River, though, and despite this setback they did not give up. Back in 1967, a flicker of hope for the river had been kindled. The Carolina Foothills Garden Club bought land below the Reedy falls and reclaimed other lands along its banks as well. Furman University and the city pitched in to help. For the first time, steps toward re-creating a healthy, attractive river downtown had been taken. There was cause for optimism, even if it grew from darker clouds of change. If anything good came of the textile industry's demise it meant the river had a chance to course through the Upstate as a healthier waterway. Making that dream a reality would take time. A lot, and it would amount to a rollercoaster ride of ups and downs. By the 1980s, however, the Carolina Foothills Garden Club's efforts were reaping dividends. The river did run cleaner.

Widespread interest in rejuvenating the Reedy got two big lifts, the first when the Friends of the Reedy River formed in 1993, and the second from the establishment of Upstate Forever in 1998. With help from these groups and others, nature was given the opportunity to begin restoring balance to the river. Still, there remained something that separated the River from the identity of the city. Making the Reedy Greenville's "best brand", as Mayor White deemed it, required something transformative. It came in the vision of a beautiful park centered on the Reedy Falls. But first a lot of cement needed busting up.

The Camperdown Bridge lay across the falls like a huge ledge of granite. It provided one of four ways to cross the Reedy downtown. It served its purpose as intended but served, too, to obscure the falls. You couldn't see them for the bridge—a horizontal monolith that blocked views and access. Locals remember crossing that bridge regularly with the falls out of sight and out of mind.

As the river cleared, people began talking about taking down the Camperdown Bridge. Mayor White had a postcard made with a rendering of the newly conceived Liberty Bridge sans Camperdown on it. He carried it around showing it to whoever would listen to him. Seeing

the beauty, seeing the potential, people began to think differently about the old bridge. Cries went up for its removal. Others maintained that the bridge was needed. A divided public packed City Hall for public hearings.

When the people elected Knox White mayor in 1995, they elected a man who believed in the soaring potential of Reedy Falls and Liberty Bridge becoming the center-

piece of Greenville's future. The city mailed copies of White's old postcard widely. The desire for wholesale change gained momentum. In 1996, the Carolina Foothills Garden Club and the City of Greenville teamed up and embraced a Master Beautification and Development Plan for the 26-acre park. Women, dressed as if on their way to dinner,

kneeled and pulled up weeds. Anna Kate Hipp helped raise funds for a $3 million park endowment, including half a million dollars from Liberty Corporation, which led to the bridge's name.

FATE FINDS A FRIEND

In 1999, the Governor's School for the Arts went up and its view of the falls spurred more interest in rejuvenating the falls area. Early in 2001, the decision to tear down the Camperdown Bridge came to a vote. The City Council had undergone changes in recent elections; new members were favorable to tearing down the old bridge. Ballots were cast: the bridge would go.

There was just one problem. The South Carolina Department of Transportation, not the city, owned the bridge. Here's where coincidence joined Greenville's cause. In the article "Decade of growth follows Camperdown bridge removal,"

The earliest days of the Falls Park area's transition are frozen in time by the camera. Once you've been to the present-day Falls Park, it's impossible to look at this photo without your mind wandering to what's there today—a remarkable change fueled by vision, innovation, patience, and hard work.
–Photo courtesy of the City of Greenville

Greenville Online.com staff writer Lyn Riddle chronicled this remarkable act of providence.

(Anna Kate) Hipp remembers the highway department being a major obstacle because no one had ever asked for a roadbed to be torn down.

"They had no willingness to do this," she said.

That's where coincidence came in.

Mayor White was at an event at the Commerce Club when, standing over the hors d'oeuvres table, he told a friend he was soon to meet with the DOT head, Betty Mabry. The friend responded that Mabry was the sister-in-law of a Greenvillian and that she (Mabry) was the former head of the Columbia Garden Club.

After working the "connections" White had serendipidously discovered, Mabry came to Greenville. When she saw the falls, she said, "This is so amazing: Columbia just spent a lot of money to build a fake waterfall at Finlay Park, and Greenville has a spectacular one covered up by a state bridge."

She pledged her support.

White then called on state Senator Verne Smith to lead the effort in the General Assembly. Smith didn't tell White, but like so many people, he had never seen the falls. But after a single visit he was on board. Virginia Uldrick, then president of the Governor's School (which overlooks the falls), lent her support. White considers them unsung heroes.

Clemson University laid out the Reedy River Master Plan. The goal was to sustain, preserve, and use the Reedy's beauty and grandeur to their utmost potential. The Conestee Foundation fostered grassroots efforts. Architectural renderings built up enthusiasm for what was coming. When Falls Park opened in late 2004, Greenville entered a new era. The city's unique icons would generate unprecedented media attention, make the entire city proud, and become an economic blessing.

The idea to build a park on Main Street–making the Reedy River and its falls the centerpiece–took time to happen, but happen it did. What Knox White and the legion he summoned accomplished is the capstone of this narrative of *How Greenville Brought the*

–Photo by Paul Ringger

Reedy River Back. Indeed, a lot of things combined to bring the Reedy back, that fetid river and its waterfall that became the focal point of this city's renewal. A summarization is in order:

The textile industry went away due to economic change. A federal law underscored the importance of clean water. A garden club rose to a high calling. A coincidence took place. A bridge that served as a major artery was torn down. A sparkling 345-foot pedestrian bridge replaced it. A resolute man was elected mayor. A community became engaged. The City Council's make-up changed. Partnerships arose between the City of Greenville, Furman University, and Carolina Foothills Garden Club. Generous corporate and individual sponsors provided seed money. Women pulled weeds and a governor's school was erected on a river bluff. Add genuine vision (not the corporate-speak kind), an excited public, and the "Boston prophesy" and you have the elements in an equation that result in transformative change.

THE BOSTON PROPHECY

And what of that Boston prophecy? Boston architect Miguel Rosales, designed Liberty Bridge, which at night glimmers like a diamond bracelet. Mayor White keeps a small green book handy. That book documents how Greenville is implementing a vision dating back to the turn of the 20th century. The 1907, "Beautifying and Improving Greenville South Carolina," came from the Boston landscape architecture firm Kelsey & Guild and it presents a plan for Greenville that brings to mind today's vision of downtown.

[The falls are] "without doubt the most important single feature to be considered in the development and beautifying of the city," reads a passage from the chapter titled "Redeeming Reedy River."

The falls and the river stream "right in the heart of the city," they wrote, and are "an object of scenic beauty the likes of which few cities can boast."

Yet, they warned that the resource "is being rapidly destroyed and wasted and the proper use of one of the city's greatest assets perverted."

Well, Kelsey & Guild was right. Greenville's falls and river were a catalyst in transforming the downtown area. As in Hans Christian Andersen's "The Ugly Duckling", Greenville turned into a beautiful swan and it didn't take long for the accolades to arrive. Liberty Bridge received the Arthur G. Hayden Medal for outstanding achievement in bridge engineering at the International Bridge Conference a year after it was built.

When you remember how the people shunned their downtown river and then see the miraculous turnaround, it's fair to say the Reedy River is enjoying a long, overdue homecoming. Sure, it still has water quality problems just as most rivers do—but continued stewardship like that which led to Falls Park may yet fully redeem it.

At Falls Park it's difficult to tell residents, workers, and tourists apart. The mixed-use facilities along with the restaurants and falls' magnetism draw people to the area in good numbers, a complete turnabout from the days when people shunned the river.

–Photo by Paul Ringger

Grand Design

THE RIVER—GREENVILLE'S BEST BRAND

Marketing people study branding *ad infinitum*. They read books and articles, take classes, pour over websites and consult other experts. For Greenville, it's simple. The river. Mayor White doesn't beat around the bush. "Our best brand is the river."

It's a brand for which enhancement—for Knox White—is a given. "Continuing to go up the river, off Main Street, will be our focus in the years ahead." He pauses and adds, "It actually already is. We're getting a lot of unexpected development up the river from downtown and we're also working to create a new park along the river downtown that's pretty dramatic—a very large one."

Plans call for this spacious new park to sit along the Reedy and Swamp Rabbit Trail just past the Kroc Center and A.J. Whittenberg Elementary School. All the buzz says it could be Greenville's next cherished asset. It's on the West Greenville master plan as simply City Park, but the name Mayberry Park has taken hold in the community. It could cover 160 acres, making it larger than Cleveland and Falls parks combined.

Mayberry Park will add a huge swath of greenery to the city and could transform the West Side just as Falls Park revitalized the West End. Anticipated features include softball fields, playgrounds, an outdoor theater, soccer fields, tennis courts and a skate park. Estimated costs are put at $10 to $12-million.

> "It's all about mixed use—the offices, the retail spaces and residential areas... and great public spaces."
> **—Mayor Knox White**

Imagine another pedestrian bridge over the Reedy, abundant green space, a community garden and an amphitheater. The possibility of a farmers market has also been mentioned. The key to it all lies in funding and relocating the city's public works complex, a new location for which has already been acquired. The proposed park is already contributing to Greenville's economic boom, attracting a developer who plans to build a 215-unit West Side apartment complex with an architectural style reflective of the textile mill era.

GROWING THE BRAND

When your brand is vibrant, you keep it that way. Expect other parks to emerge along the Reedy. One such project, long in planning, is the Cancer Survivors' Park. A Greenville high school student's project involving improvements to the area around a cancer treatment facility took wing and developed into a park dedicated to those who beat cancer, those who continue to fight cancer, and to the memory of all those lost to the dreaded disease. The 6.8-acre park will be located along the Swamp Rabbit Trail and connect Falls Park to Cleveland Park. Cancer Survivors' Park will bring vitality and beauty to an area long plagued with graffiti and seedy surroundings. Among the plans for the park are a 2,000-square-foot education center, a labyrinth, a garden for children and manicured plazas. The park's projected opening is summer 2016.

Up river, the Greenville Textile Heritage Society is moving forward to develop a 6-acre park dedicated to the preservation and celebration of the region's rich textile history. Its concept includes a picnic area, walking paths, a playground, and a gazebo to host concerts and special events. The park's green space, Textile Heritage Park, may connect with the Swamp Rabbit Trail. The possible relocation of an original 1930s mill house to the park, where it would be restored as a textile museum, is also in the works.

The Greenville brand is the river and that brand is built on certain vital elements. Mayor White: "It's all about mixed use—the offices, the retail spaces and residential areas. Each one is an important ingredient and how we work to support each element is what has driven much of Greenville's revival."

While the concept of mixed-use seems clear on the surface, it is enigmatic in application—there's more than meets the eye. "The whole mystery of mixed use," said White, "is you have great public spaces. You have the 'walkable element'—a walkable downtown with personality, public art, the water, and the various things we employ all over downtown to make it an interesting place to be." (Children certainly find it interesting. Following tips, they search for the *Mice on Main* that play hide-and-seek.)

Great public spaces form that vital element. "We worked pretty hard to create these great pockets along the downtown area where people can gather. They're carefully designed to do what they do." Walk Main Street and it doesn't take long to see people sitting in lush landscaped retreats. An attractive iron fence cordons off a place to eat beneath umbrellas shaded by a green canopy. Here and there buffers of greenery separate the sidewalks from the street. The city has accomplished the goal of keeping downtown Greenville green. The sidewalks are best described as dappled ... sunlight filters through and the shadows form a soft, leafy lace upon the sidewalks where if you pay attention, you'll see bits of advice engraved into dark gray tiles:

"The best way to knock the chip off someone's shoulder is to pat him on the back." —Anonymous.

Humor, too:

"I've been on a constant diet for the last two decades. I've lost a total of 789 pounds. By all accounts, I should be hanging from a charm bracelet." —Erma Bombeck

Mayor White says another element is where "you hit the star of the show, which is the river and the waterfall and its story—and that story is having an asset you didn't know you had, discovering it and turning it into the centerpiece of the whole downtown."

City-Renewing Water

Mayor White's office occupies a corner of the City Hall building at 206 South Main. Looking at South Main from ten stories you see the changes that revitalized downtown. Angled parking.

A canopy-covered street (look closely and you see the trees are of different ages; staggered planting assures a continual canopy). Green spaces. Stylish lighting. Statuary and fountains. Even the Main Street asphalt is colorful. It has a fresh surface and a bold double yellow stripe divides it. As you proceed down South Main you cross two brick-red areas. One features vertical stripes, the other a herringbone pattern. And even from ten stories up it's what you don't see that adds so much. No parking meters.

All of this freshness—all this bold renewal and life— flow from the river. The Greenville brand is the river and the brand attracts people. People who like to build things. Therein lies a challenge Mayor White understands. "We need to make sure we grow the right way and

that means green space, bike and walking trails, and parks. It means being attentive to creating pedestrian zones and pedestrian commuting areas. It means having design standards and being sensitive to neighborhood concerns. Communities most successful in dealing with growth have focused on those kinds of things."

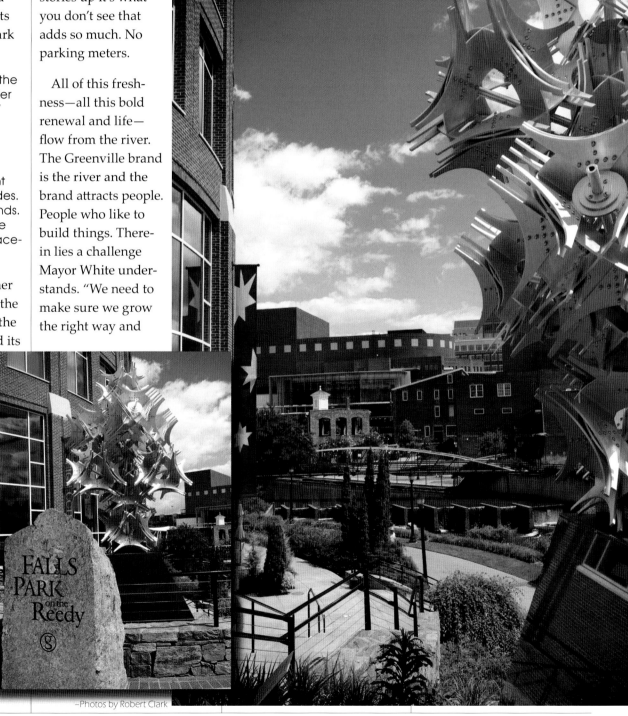

–Photos by Robert Clark

A Yearning to Know

History Complements Progress

Greenville's story makes people curious. "People who live in the Greenville area cannot get enough information, stories, whatever, about Greenville," said Mayor White. The mayor knew what *The Greenville News* discovered when it conducted a readership survey. "I knew from the speaking circuit that everybody wanted to ask 100 questions about this project and that project. There's a tremendous sense of pride in "ownership" people have taken of Greenville. If you ask anybody directions to something in downtown Greenville, you'll pick up on this sense of ownership. 'This is my city. Let me show you my part.' As a result of the newspaper's survey, the front page is very often a big story about downtown Greenville. They found out that readers who live in Simpsonville and Greer and far outside all want to know what's happening in downtown Greenville."

The people in Greenville's outlying areas aren't the only ones curious to know more. As we've seen from the media who cover Greenville, the yearning to know more is nationwide and much has been written about the city's rebirth and advances. The city's story also includes jewels from the past. They can't be forgotten. Historic homes, historic districts, structures, and sites on the National Register of Historic Places give Greenville and its surroundings a backstory and sense of place that balance and complement the city's forward movement.

Grand Design

The Gassaway Mansion

One mile from Main Street, the Gassaway Mansion is the Upstate's largest house and is on The National Register of Historic Places. A Christian non-profit owns the mansion, which now houses over 1,000 pieces of religious art. The Gassaway Mansion is also known as Issaqueena, in honor of a legendary Indian maiden.

Whitehall

One of Greenville's oldest residences, Whitehall

◄ Gassaway Mansion ►

Historic Homes

Kilgore Lewis House

Built around 1831, this home is thought to be one of the oldest surviving buildings in Greenville County. Josiah Kilgore built the home as a wedding gift for his daughter. Today the home and its 3.5 acres provide a setting for weddings and is a favorite stop during spring garden tours.

▼ Whitehalll

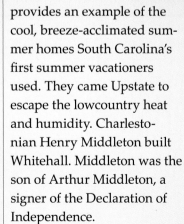

provides an example of the cool, breeze-acclimated summer homes South Carolina's first summer vacationers used. They came Upstate to escape the lowcountry heat and humidity. Charlestonian Henry Middleton built Whitehall. Middleton was the son of Arthur Middleton, a signer of the Declaration of Independence.

OLD DUNHAM BRIDGE

Built in 1929, this steel truss bridge spans the Saluda River. Picturesque and graceful, it brings to mind the scenes depicted in Fannie Flagg's *Fried Green Tomatoes*.

RICHLAND CEMETERY

Richland Cemetery played an important role in the development of a distinct, self-sustaining African American community in downtown Greenville. The cemetery is the final resting place for many of Greenville's most notable African American educators, health practitioners, and community leaders. The cemetery is a treasure trove of funerary art, landscape design, and cultural artifacts.

STRADLEY AND BARR DRY GOODS STORE

The Stradley and Barr Dry Goods Store represents an excellent, largely intact, example of late nineteenth century Romanesque Revival commercial architecture. It's significant for its role in the development and evolution of the South Main Street business district from the late-nineteenth through the mid-twentieth centuries. Built circa 1898, it housed the Stradley and Barr Dry Goods Store until 1919 when it became home to Efird's Department Store.

AMERICAN CIGAR FACTORY

This was one of Greenville's larger brick buildings when it was constructed around 1902. The American Improvement Company built it, one of five factories the American Cigar Company located in the South. Located in the heart of the central business district, it employed 150 girls and young women when it began production. It is one of the largest brick masonry buildings remaining in downtown and reflects Greenville's industrial growth at the turn of the century.

ROBERT QUILLEN LIBRARY

The Robert Quillen Office and Library is associated with American journalist and humorist Robert Quillen, a local literary figure nationally known for his humorous newspaper columns. Born in Syracuse, Kansas, Quillen moved to Fountain Inn in 1911 to start the *Fountain Inn Tribune*. He wrote paragraphs, editorials, one-liners, and cartoons for the *Baltimore Sun*, *Saturday Evening Post*, and *The American Magazine*.

—Photos by Paul Ringger

▲ American Cigar Factory. Known also as Stone Manufacturing Company, the American Cigar Factory, above, was built very early in the 1900s. It is one of the largest brick masonry buildings remaining downtown and reflects Greenville's industrial growth at the turn of the century. Listed in National Register July 1, 1982.

photo © Jack E. Boucher, Library of Congress Prints and Photographs Division/Wikimedia

◄ Frank Lloyd Wright's Broad Margin was designed in 1951 and completed in 1954. It is considered an excellent example of Wright's natural-style, referred to as Usonian.

Grand Design

PETTIGRU HISTORIC DISTRICT

Unique in the city for its evolution of styles from the Victorian era to 1930, this large neighborhood was nominated to the National Register of Historic Places in 1981. It's the city's largest historic district and features a wide variety of building styles, including the Queen Anne and local interpretations of the bungalow and Colonial Revival forms.

The Pettigru Street Historic District is significant for its wide range of architectural styles mirroring Greenville's growth from 1890 to 1930. These models include Victorian, Queen Anne, Colonial Revival, Craftsman, and Bungalow homes.

▶▲ This 1895 Queen Anne/Colonial Revival home stands at 104 Broadus Avenue.

▶ Pettigru Place Bed and Breakfast is just one of the many gracious homes in the Pettigru Historic District.

Grand Design

The Colonel Elias Earle District is significant for its range of early twentieth century architecture. The district originally was part of the estate of Colonel Elias Earle, a prominent early nineteenth century Greenville citizen. After 1900, the area was subdivided into lots and houses soon went up. The demand for textile products during World War I created a housing boom and the area developed into a major middle class neighborhood.

EARLE
STREET
HISTORIC
PRESERVATION
AREA

SOUTH CAROLINA
WHITEHALL
Built by Henry Middleton on land bought from Elias Earle in 1813, Whitehall served as his summer home until 1820 when it was sold to George W. Earle, whose descendants have occupied it ever since. Henry Middleton was son of Arthur Middleton. Signer of the Declaration of Independence. He served as Governor of South Carolina from 1810 to 1812.

ERECTED BY
KANETHLAND BUTLER CHAPTER, D.A.R.
1964

▶ Whitehall is among the numerous, well-preserved period homes found in the Earle Street Histoic Preservation Area. Photo on page 48.

Grand Design

UNIVERSAL JOINT

EAST PARK AVENUE HISTORIC DISTRICT

The East Park Avenue neighborhood received Historic-Architectural Overlay Zoning protection in 1989 and was listed on the National Register of Historic Places in October 2005. The city's oldest public park, McPherson, is situated on the southern boundary of the district and provides a buffer between the neighborhood and the downtown Central Business District.

—Photos on these two pages by Paul Ringger

With a service station look and auto part name, Universal Joint stands out in an area known for historic homes and bungalows. The Atlanta-based restaurant brings good food in casual surroundings to the growing East Park neighborhood just a few blocks from downtown. People walk and bike to it for filling up that doesn't involve fossil fuels.

G R E E N V I L L E ' S

HAMPTON-PINCKNEY HISTORIC DISTRICT

In 1815 Vardry Mc-Bee spent $27,550 for 11,028 acres of land in what is now the center of Greenville. McBee had great aspirations for the little frontier village of Greenville. A philanthropist, he donated land for the Greenville Male and Female Academies and for the city's first four churches. Hampton-Pinckney became Greenville's first trolley-car neighborhood.

HERITAGE HISTORIC DISTRICT

The City Council designated this neighborhood in the West Park area as a local preservation overlay in December 2001. About 126 structures stand in the neighborhood with the most prominent architectural style being the bungalow. Construction in the district peeked during the 1920s.

OVERBROOK HISTORIC DISTRICT

Overbrook began with the expansion of the Greenville trolley line. It was one of the first suburbs of Greenville, and attracted many people with its easy access by trolley. The popularity of the "Toonerville Trolley," as it was called, continued despite the switch to bus transportation around 1928.

—Photos on this page by Paul Ringger

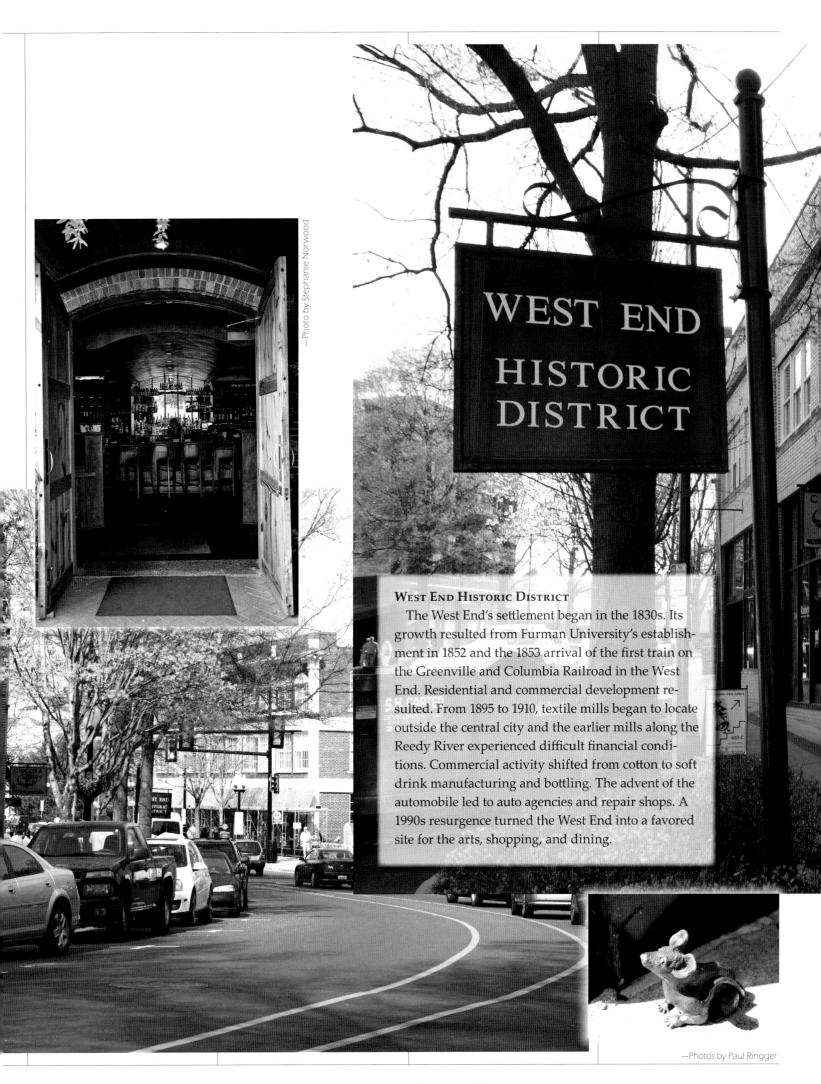

—Photo by Stephanie Norwood

WEST END HISTORIC DISTRICT

WEST END HISTORIC DISTRICT

The West End's settlement began in the 1830s. Its growth resulted from Furman University's establishment in 1852 and the 1853 arrival of the first train on the Greenville and Columbia Railroad in the West End. Residential and commercial development resulted. From 1895 to 1910, textile mills began to locate outside the central city and the earlier mills along the Reedy River experienced difficult financial conditions. Commercial activity shifted from cotton to soft drink manufacturing and bottling. The advent of the automobile led to auto agencies and repair shops. A 1990s resurgence turned the West End into a favored site for the arts, shopping, and dining.

—Photos by Paul Ringger

City of Commerce

Fortune 500 to I-85; the Numbers Add Up

The numbers tell a profitable story. More than forty *Fortune 500* companies, more than 240 international companies, and over 20 headquarters' operations call Greenville home. Greenville Technical College's emergence foreshadowed Greenville's ascension to a center of commerce. This tech school, or vocational school as it was initially known, was South Carolina's first technical college. It's widely acknowledged that the technical college system that spread from Greenville early in the 1960s altered South Carolina's destiny. Before Greenville Tech came along, the state was losing people to industry up north. Farming and textile manufacturing were in dire straits.

South Carolinians today build BMWs, develop pharmaceuticals, and rethink how to build airplanes. All that progress started in Greenville where state leaders envisioned a systematic way to train people. The following anecdote concerning how and where Greenville Technical College began—on a landfill—underscores the importance of that school to all of South Carolina.

The old axiom that one man's trash is another man's treasure holds merit. Ernest Fritz Hollings went to Dayton, Ohio to a training camp for United Way campaigners. While there, he saw a building where late-night classes in drafting, welding, and punch

The Zentrum
BMW Visitors Center

Open Monday – Friday
9:30am – 5:30pm

—Photo by Robert Clark

Grand Design

drills were underway as late as eleven pm. It made a huge impression on Hollings. A mantra of sorts grew within him. "The rich are getting richer and the poor are getting poorer. We don't have anything like that in South Carolina."

Inaugurated January 20, 1959, Governor Hollings fo-

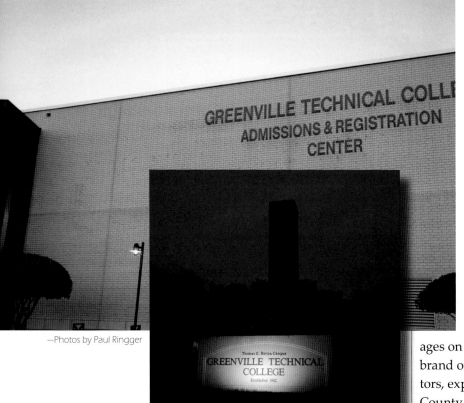

—Photos by Paul Ringger

GREENVILLE TECHNICAL COLLE
ADMISSIONS & REGISTRATION CENTER

Thomas E. Barton Campus
GREENVILLE TECHNICAL COLLEGE
Established 1962

cused on creating the technical education system. Training, he knew, would mobilize a great resource, and industry would follow. Greenville had the chance to get the state's first vocational training school. In the early 1960s, though money was tight, state senator Morrow Bradley pushed Greenville TEC forward. Bradley who was all-powerful said, "Build it. I'll find the money." Bradley had a team designing the building before the money was available. Sapp Funderburk, Greenville native and

businessman, got the site—a garbage dump. The vocational school, South Carolina's first, went up.

When the day for Greenville TEC's groundbreaking arrived, a cold wind swirled around Governor Fritz Hollings, state leaders, and Sapp Funderburk. Hollings quietly advised the men holding shovels, "Don't dig too deep. You'll hit garbage." They struck gold instead. In 2009, half a century later, Charleston landed Boeing thanks to that cold day in Greenville.

The "Boom-Belt"—A Good Place To Be

As for Greenville and Greenville County, the beat goes on. Companies like Cott Beverages, U.S. subsidiary to Cott Corporation, one of the world's largest producers of beverages on behalf of retailers, brand owners and distributors, expanded its Greenville County operations with a $10 million warehouse and distribution center. The facility's location on the I-85 corridor provides quick and easy access to East Coast customers. Atlanta is 145 miles from Greenville and Charlotte is 102. That's good positioning along an interstate that gave rise to the term, "Boom Belt" for the region.

Boom is right. "The big picture here is that the region is strong economically," said Mayor Knox White. "It has a robust, diverse economy. That's the big picture behind the international business. A

lot of that came to us via I-85. For Greenville, being on the I-85 corridor between Charlotte and Atlanta is a good place to be."

A Strong, Diverse Economy

The list of the businesses operating in Greenville is a long one. From advertising and media to arts, culture and entertainment; to automotive, aviation and marine, it covers about any aspect of life you can think of. Communications. Business and professional services. Finance and insurance. Government and education. Healthcare. Home and garden. Public utilities. Real Estate. Manufacturing—lots of technical manufacturing. And of course, restaurants, shopping, and specialty retail.

Greenville's our Home

When BMW said, "Lassen Sie uns unsere Hauptsitz in Greenville verlagern (Let's call Greenville our home), it started a flood of international businesses to the I-85 corridor near Greenville and Spartanburg. The region is progressive, business-friendly,

> "Lassen Sie uns unsere Hauptsitz in Greenville verlagern."
> —translation, "Let's call Greenville our home."

and alluring. In its own words, BMW has this to say about Greenville and the Upstate. "With fine dining and entertainment in the heart of its cities and breathtaking natural beauty in the nearby foothills and mountains,

—Photo by Robert Clark

Upstate South Carolina may seem like a hidden treasure at first glance—but the world is quickly discovering all that this sophisticated region has to offer.

The past few decades have seen the arrival of several international companies, including BMW Manufacturing, and the resulting growth has transformed the region into an economic engine for the state and the Southeast at large.

Thousands of talented professionals have come to call Upstate South Carolina home in recent years, thanks in part to the affordable cost of living, flourishing cultural scene and family-friendly communities around the region."

Upstate South Carolina Alliance, formed in 2000, is a public-private regional economic development organization designed to market the dynamic 10-county Upstate

region to the world. "Come discover what BMW, Michelin, Fuji, and more than 1,400 other manufacturing companies already know. Upstate South Carolina is what a competitive advantage looks like."

BMW realized that Upstate South Carolina offered advantages. "Project Pretoria" sounds exciting and it is. That was BMW's code name for its search for a plant site to for its 3-series models. Over three years, the automaker scoured 250 locations in 10 countries. By spring 1992 only two places remained in the hunt and both weree in the United States: Nebraska and South Carolina.

Nebraska gets mighty cold. South Carolina offers year-round golf. After a change in the proposed site, South Carolina closed the deal. In June 1992, BMW announced it would bring 2,000 jobs and a $66.5 million annual payroll

to South Carolina. South Carolina would screen and train job applicants and then train BMW's entire workforce through the state's technical schools. Financial incentives including a $1-a-year lease on the 1,000 acres proved enticing, as did the region's comparatively affordable labor, low taxes, and few unions.

A PRO-BUSINESS STANCE

Business advocacy and the establishment of tax credits and transportation and infrastructure funding are part of Greenville's pro-business climate. The Greenville Chamber's legislative agenda reflects input from its more than 2,300 members. Repairing an

Cars and tires contributed a chunk of history to the Upstate thanks to Greenville. In 1988 Michelin opened its new headquarters in the city where it consolidated operations and manufacturing. Michelin set the stage for making South Carolina the country's number one tire manufacturer.

—Photo by Robert Clark

aging infrastructure, educating the workforce, promoting entrepreneurship, and ensuring that a streamlined, efficient government contributes to a free-market economy are priorities.

The Chamber's Manufacturer's Roundtable encourages and supports competitive, world-class manufacturing across the Upstate. Its forum for plant managers in various industry sectors helps them address issues that affect their ability to compete successfully.

THE I-85 CORRIDOR—BETWEEN ATLANTA & CHARLOTTE

South Carolina's section of I-85 runs 106 miles. The I-85 route, which includes 10 exits in Anderson County, follows the Atlanta-to-Charlotte railroad line built 82 years earlier. From the start, I-85 brought an economic boom to the

Upstate South Carolina. Built at a cost of $267 million, the South Carolina section of I-85 transformed the Upstate economically. In 1973, Michelin broke ground on a commercial manufacturing plant, a 1.4-million square foot facility just three miles from I-85's Exit 19.

All this bodes well for Greenville. Thanks to I-85, Greenville is a premiere location for corporate headquarters. Hubbell Lighting opened its new headquarters in Greenville, and Michelin Tire Corporation built its largest manufacturing plant and North American headquarters close by. These successes are the stuff of development legend. Contact lenses, tires, cars, lighting, advanced materials such as optics, biotech products—that and more are manufactured in Greenville County. How about call centers, data centers, and logistics' warehousing and distribution facilities? Consider it the centerpiece of the region's manufacturing

capabilities. One statement sums up Greenville's corporate charisma: The South Carolina Department of Commerce says Greenville is home to more corporate headquarters than any other region in South Carolina.

Add to this a deep pool of skilled and talented workers and excellent technical college training, and Greenville continues to attract key players in aerospace and other advanced industries.

Being located along the booming I-85 corridor brings a strong corporate presence to Greenville and its environs.

> Thanks to I-85, Greenville is a premiere location for corporate headquarters.

A corporate-like edifice near Falls Park further demonstrates that this area is on the map as a desirable location for business headquarters.

European Influence, Upstate Roots

—Photo by Paul Ringger

G R E E N V I L L E ' S

*W*illkommen to Main Street. A great street to walk; a great place to be. Residents and visitors alike find its spacious walkways and plazas, its sidewalk dining evoke comparisons to European cities. There's nothing lethargic about Main Street. It brims with energy and cosmopolitan élan. Thanks to international businesses and the people they bring to the Upstate, a certain European ambience is now native here.

"It's like a street you'd find in Paris or Naples," a recent visitor commented.

"We hear statements like that often," says Mayor White. "We have a lot of foreign investment. We hear it from Europeans who visit as well as those who live here: the French, Germans; a lot of people comment on the European feel of downtown. People pick up on that."

White relates a story about a former head of the German consulate in Atlanta. "There's someone new in the job now, but the former one used to come here frequently and that's what he said. He'd bring his wife here on weekends, and say, 'I feel like I'm back in Europe.' He lived in Munich, so that's quite a compliment."

Greenville and the region are becoming more and more international. You can literally hear it. "You can't walk along the streets of downtown Greenville without hearing German and French and other languages," said White. "It's very internationalized."

Grand Design

Today, over 150 international firms from twenty-seven countries operate in Greenville County. Mayor White adds that people who fly into the Greenville-Spartanburg Airport are frequently on flights with people from all over the world.

Companies such as Ahold, Bosch Rexroth, Eurokera, Kyocera Mita, Magna, Michelin, Mitsubishi, Nutra, Saint Gobain, and Samsung Networks America operate in Greenville. The list of coun-

> "You can't walk downtown without hearing German, French, and other languages."
> **–Mayor Knox White**

tries with businesses located in the Upstate include Australia, Belgium, Canada, Hong Kong, Iceland, Israel, South Africa, Switzerland, Taiwan, and the United Kingdom.

One result of the international influence is a cosmopolitan atmosphere. Comments on the city's European flair fill blogs, social media, and conversations.

Coffeehouses, international festivals, and a lifestyle evocative of the Old World give Greenville charm; a charisma enhanced by a business presence with roots throughout the hemispheres.

—Photos on this page by Robert Clark

INTERNATIONAL COMMERCE

During the 70s when Michelin's U.S. business was expanding dramatically, it opened two plants in South Carolina. A few years thereafter, in 1988, Michelin moved its U.S. headquarters to Greenville concentrating operations and manufacturing in the same area. Michelin had been in New York since 1950, but made the decision to move its executives to South Carolina.

A EUROPEAN FLAVOR

"European atmosphere, excellent schnitzel and beer. Just off Main. Don't miss it." "A taste of Holland in the States. Come for the Old World décor, stay for the food and beverages."

You'll find, appropriately enough, a bistro at the base of Liberty Bridge: *Passerelle*, French for "footbridge". Soak up some French atmosphere here and enjoy a great view of Falls Park.

Around the city, it's easy to find Italian, Mediterranean, Persian, and Mexican cuisine as well. If your southern palate craves fried chicken and barbecue, no worries. Y'all will find them readily available. And if you want to improve your second language, check out the International Center of the Upstate. In Greenville, of course.

Greenville claims international associations serving Chinese, German, Italian-American, Indian, and Japanese vistors and residents.

Greenville's chapter of Sister Cities International partners with three sister cities: Bergamo, Italy; Kortrijk, Belgium; and Tianjim, China.

Greenville is home to the South Carolina Hispanic Chamber of Commerce as well as the Hispanic Alliance, an organization serving the that community.

Greenville has one of the United State's largest concentrations of Scots-Irish descent. Gallabbrae, the community's Scottish games, stages athletic competitions such as the caber toss. Brawny, kilt-wearing men toss the caber—a roughly trimmed tree trunk—in a competition of accuracy not distance, developed from the need to lay logs across narrow chasms in order to cross them. The games are popular, and the Standing Council of Scottish Chiefs ranks Greenville's contests among the world's top. In 2010 His Royal Highness Prince Edward attended the Greenville games, the first member of the British Royal Family to attend a competition outside Scotland.

—Photo Paul Ringger

America's Most Livable City

—Photo by Paul Ringger

G R E E N V I L L E ' S

Greenville's Ineffable Something

For well over forty years Greenville's city leaders have been heavily involved in renewing the city's downtown area. Their efforts certainly haven't been in vain. Today, Greenville consistently ranks high as one of the country's more livable cities. But, just what is this ineffable quality that makes a city livable?

Five fundamental aspects apply to great, livable cities: robust and complete neighborhoods, accessibility and mobility, a diverse and resilient local economy, lively public spaces, and affordability. What else contributes to great livability? Climate, location, vibrancy, nature, open spaces, outdoor living, walkability, and jobs. Greenville does well across the board.

Greenville's climate is mild. A little snow in winter, perhaps, but otherwise quite pleasant.

Greenville's location in this mountainous province is a plus. Greenville grew up on the banks of the Reedy, and though the river went through some tough times, it is now a much healthier environment. And Greenville is located on the bustling I-85 corridor—good for business.

The cost of living, 6.80% lower than the U.S. average, is quite affordable and the abundance of businesses and jobs contribute to livability.

cycling, hiking and, no doubt, rock climbing. Nearby lakes offer boating, fishing, and skiing opportunities.

Though small compared to major cities, it resides in the midst of one of the larger U.S. metropolitan statistical areas and is located midway between two of the country's most robust metropolises. Greenville offers a wonderful consortium of attractions: great museums and cultural opportunities, a thriving restaurant scene, festivals, and rich and diverse music. These amenities complement residential options, from million-dollar riverfront condos to affordable housing. A highly-ranked consolidated public school system includes both city and county students, and there's Furman University, Greenville Technical College, Bob Jones University, and Clemson University. Moreover, another ten colleges and schools in the area round out higher learning opportunities.

An Upstate snowstorm leaves in its wake a crystal-like sparkle on the trees.

The Furman Bell Tower is a statuesque nod to the beauty of the University campus.

—Photos on these two pages by Robert Clark

Green spaces, the Swamp Rabbit Trail, and parks offer open spaces. Falls Park and the Reedy River provide opportunities to enjoy nature. As for outdoor living, check out the many outdoor restaurant venues. Falls Park and its "Big Brother" waterfall provide a relaxing setting for the physical, mental, and spiritual discipline of yoga. There's

GREENVILLE'S

Livability.com listed Greenville as one of the Top 10 Best Downtowns in 2015, coming in at number four behind Indianapolis, Minneapolis, and Pittsburgh. Downtown played a part in getting Greenville on *Livability's* two previous Top 100 Best Places to Live lists.

What else makes Greenville livable? Downtown's luxury condos, apartments, and lofts attract new residents and businesses. Falls Park brings a touch of a mountainous, whitewater region to the city. The park includes gardens, and Liberty Bridge provides overlooks of the Reedy River and waterfalls. Two red and blue open-air trolleys make continuous loops from West End to the Colonel Elias Earle Historic District, and offer a vintage look and feel. They even have cowcatchers on the front and wooden bench seats inside. They're fare-free and operate year-round.

Balance is the key to making Greenville a highly desirable

place to live. As *Livability.com* puts it, "Balance between the old and the new. Between growth and quality of life. Between economic vibrancy and day-to-day livability." These qualities fuel the city's high scores in these indexes.

As one of *Livability.com*'s **Best Places to Live**, this energetic city has much working

Any trip through the area during peak foliage season, whether by car, bike, or on foot will create a breath taking memory.

Grand Design

in its favor, from an enviable location in the booming Charlotte-Atlanta corridor and a welcoming cultural mix of ur-

ban sophistication and traditional Southern charm, to its talented young workforce and diversified economy.

"It's all about getting the balance right," says Knox White, a Greenville native who has served as mayor since 1995 and overseen the city's emergence as one of the nation's most saluted places to live. "You want a robust local economy that creates jobs and

opportunities, but at the same time, you need to balance growth with a strong quality of life—you want to have a

place people love, lots of activities, lots of green space, a lot of attention paid to walkability."

GREENVILLE WALKS THE WALK

Greenville holds onto its small-town charm yet overflows with entertainment options, from galleries and restaurants to museums and sports events. The Peace Center, one of many venues for concerts and performances,

provides patrons first-class accommodations. There's the oft-mentioned Fluor Field to delight baseball fans. Families love The Children's Museum of the Upstate, an 80,000-square-foot educational playland touted as "a place of possibility where children and adults alike can explore, discover, imagine, pretend, and be anything." Other attributes that bring Greenville accolades for its livability include walkability

(an important factor), cycling, restaurants, museums, sports, and arts and music.

How do you sustain all this success? Mayor White says Greenville's challenge is to be authentic, "to keep what gives us our unique personality." Bringing even more green space to the city ranks as high a priority as further commerical or residential development.

—Photos on this page by Paul Ringger

Greenville ... a Few Facts and Figures

A city that's a top performer consistently earns praise and lands on top-ten lists. A strong economy and flourishing business climate bring multi-cultural strength, fiscal resources, and energy to a vibrant lifestyle.

Accolades & Acknowledgments

2014 Best Cities for Job Growth
Newgeography.Com (2014)

Top 10 Competitive States
Site Selection (2013)

No. 4 Best States for Business
Development Counsellors International (2014)

No. 6 Cities With the Greatest Capacity For Innovation
Forbes (2014)

American Cities of the Future (Micro Cities Category)
No. 2 Overall

No. 3 Foreign Direct Investment Strategy
fDi Magazine (2013/14)

10 Fastest Growing U.S. Cities
CNN Money (2012)

No. 13 Best Cities for Young Professionals
Forbes (2011)

No. 3 America's Strongest Job Market
Bloomberg Business Week (2013)

No. 9 Among States for Small Business Friendliness
Thumbtack.Com/Kauffman Foundation (2013)

Most Export-Intensive Metro Area
Brookings (2012)

Greenville Is the Knowledge Economy's Next Big Thing
Fast Company (2012)

South Carolina Ranked

No. 8 Best Business Climate

No. 3 Nuclear Power Generation Leader

No. 7 Automotive Manufacturing Strength

No. 10 Auto Parts Supplier Leaders

No. 7 Lowest Cost Of Labor
Business Facilities (2013)

No. 5 Export Intensity

No. 6 Top States For Exports

No. 8 Export Intensity Growth

No. 8 Stem Job Growth
Us Chamber Of Commerce (2014)

Greenville by The Numbers

Distance to Asheville	63 miles
Distance to Atlanta	145 miles
Distance to Augusta	115 miles
Distance to Charleston	210 miles
Distance to Charlotte	100 miles
Distance to Columbia	103 miles
Distance to Savannah	256 miles
Distance to Spartanburg	29 miles
U.S. Cost of Living average	6.8% lower
Population of Greenville County	475,000
Population of Greenville	61,414
Median Age	35.5 years
Median Home Value	$187,612
Average Annual Temperature	61° Fahrenheit
Average Rainfall	42 inches
Average Annual Snowfall	5 inches
Average Number of Sunny Days	220
Hotel Rooms in Greenville County	8,511
Downtown Hotel Rooms	860 +
Greenville event days per year	300 +
Distance to Nearest State Park	7 miles
Airlines serving Airport	77
Miles from GSP Airport to downtown	13
Number of Golf Courses within 20 Miles	31
Elevation	1,080 feet
Greenville County Square Miles	785.12
City of Greenville Square Miles	25.38

Beauty in the Hills

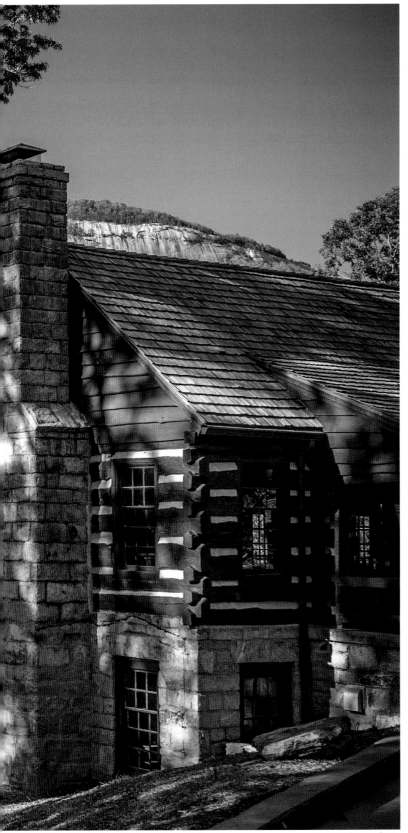

—Photo by Robert Clark

*A*ny city worth its salt shares a special connection with its outlying areas, whose residents love a jaunt to the city just as city dwellers delight in daytrips to area attractions. Number Brooke Stillwell among those who visited Greenville often from her home nearby. An expat of the area now living in Columbia, she grew up in Pickens County, in Six Mile (where Legend says Indian maiden, Issaqueena, named the community for her ninety-six mile horseback ride to warn her lover, English trader Francis Allen, of a Cherokee attack). Stillwell misses her home. Misses Greenville.

Six Mile is just 24 miles from Greenville as the crow flies, 28 by car or horseback.

Stillwell remembers "that *other* Greenville"; the comparison to today is a tale of redemption. "When I was growing up, the Reedy River was not something you'd want to get near. It smelled bad. Still, when I was young it didn't make sense to me that I couldn't go play in a river—especially one that was downtown with those huge rocks to climb around on. Now the Reedy is one of the city's greatest assets. Also, the Poinsett Hotel was derelict. Today—it's a restored gem."

Stillwell recalls that things began to improve in the late 1980s. "There was a smattering of good, new restaurants and some trendy little bohemian stores.

I'd go down there to a weaving class and then run around town with friends. The first time I ever heard the Indigo Girls was in one of those hippy stores on Main Street. Of course later the Peace Center was built and anchored everything—that was really the smartest thing the planners did, putting it in the middle of town in a place kind to pedestrians in every way. The Peace Center became a magnet for businesses around it. It made it possible for so many other good things to happen.

"We went to Greenville to the Warehouse Theater where my folks had season tickets and we'd go there to shop and sometimes for Chinese dinner. Greenville had Cleveland Park and the zoo was nice. And when the art museum opened my mom would take my elementary class on field trips to see the Andrew Wyeth exhibits and other things."

Greenville is perfectly positioned for indoor and outdoor adventure. Stillwell along with many others declare their love for the city and its surroundings. Together they give the region charisma and identity. Consider the jewels you'll find Upstate where the hills overflow with beauty.

Jones Gap State Park, Marietta

Discover the peace and tranquility of a deep mountain cove. Trails and 11,000 acres of pristine mountain woodlands connect the park with Caesars Head in the Mountain Bridge Wilderness Area. Trails let hikers travel between the two parks, as well as connect to a portion of the Foothills Trail. South Carolina's first designated scenic river, the Middle Saluda River, runs through Jones Gap and offers excellent trout fishing. Find here, too, a living lab for the park's hands-on ecology learning center.

photo courtesy of Wikimedia

—Photo by Robert Clark

> "It is a river that demands the utmost respect."
> **–National Wild and Scenic Rivers System**

Chattooga River, South Carolina Border

Born in springs and rivulets on the south side of Whiteside Mountain, near Cashiers, North Carolina, the Chattooga flows some 50 miles south-southwest forming the border between Georgia and Oconee County, South Carolina. As it runs it drops 3,000 feet to 950 feet. Geological processes 250 million years old carved out the Chattooga. It's the only mountain river in a four-state area devoid of significant development. Perhaps most recognized for its depiction in the film *Deliverance*, two distinct whitewater rafting sections exist on the Chattooga. "It is a river that demands the utmost respect," declares the National Wild and Scenic River System website.

Campbell's Covered Bridge, Gowensville

Campbell's Covered Bridge sits near the small town of Gowensville. It's South Carolina's last remaining covered bridge and it crosses Beaverdam Creek. Greenville County owns the bridge and closed it to traffic in the early 1980s. Built in 1909, the bridge was restored in 1964 and 1990. It was added to the National Register of Historic Places on July 1, 2009.

Doodle Trail, Easley

The Doodle Rail Trail connects Easley and Pickens. The paved trail follows the former Doodle Line railroad for a little over seven miles and includes two wooden bridges.

STUMPHOUSE TUNNEL, WALHALLA

Follow SC Highway 28 out of Walhalla and you'll discover a tunnel where men performed backbreaking labor pursuing a railroad dream. In the 1850s, Irish workers chipped and drilled through though solid granite, hoping to link Charleston to the Midwest. After six years, the Civil War and a lack of money brought the backbreaking work to a halt. The tunnel had been excavated to a length of 1,617 feet of the planned 5,863 total feet. Some 100 years later, Clemson University used the tunnel to age blue cheese but relocated the operation to air-conditioned cheese ripening rooms where they were able to duplicate the conditions indoors, chiefly the 85 percent humidity and constant 56 degrees Fahrenheit. The tunnel measures 17 feet wide by 25 feet high.

◄ Whitewater Falls sits off secondary road S-39-171 where two falls form the highest series of falls in the eastern United States. They plunge just over 800 feet before their waters ultimately flow into Lake Jocassee. The North Carolina-South Carolina state line actually passes between the upper and lower falls.

▼ The unfinished Stumphouse Tunnel stands s just one remider of how the Civil War left its imprint on the Upstate.

The railway began passenger and freight service in 1898. The "Doodle" ran backwards like a doodlebug between Pickens and Easley due to its inability to turn around.

WHITEWATER FALLS, WALHALLA

Ease up Highway 130 near the North Carolina line to glimpse Whitewater Falls' twin cataracts, the South Carolina-North Carolina boundary running between them. It's the eastern United State's highest vertical falls. The falls plunge 411 feet. South Carolina's Lower Whitewater Falls drops another 400 feet. In all, the 811-feet fall provides a stunning view.

—Photo by Tom Poland

Grand Design

The Middle Saluda was the first river South Carolina's 1978 Scenic Rivers Program protected. Roughly five miles of the Middle Saluda and its major tributary, Coldspring Branch, enjoy a 600-foot wide scenic corridor from U.S. Highway 276 to one mile upstream of the defunct Cleveland Fish Hatchery. The river,

running through northern Greenville County within Jones Gap State Park, drops nearly 1,000 feet in four miles. Its clear, cold water supports self-sustaining trout populations.

POINSETT BRIDGE, LANDRUM

When you first see the arch of Poinsett Bridge (circa 1820), it's easy to imagine it's the entrance to an underground fortress. Named for Joel R. Poinsett, it is South Carolina's oldest intact bridge. Elegant in design, the 14-feet high

The gristmill on Hagood Creek near Pickens operated from 1845 until the mid-1960s and is South Carolina's only wooden waterwheel. The Middle Saluda River looks like a quaint setting for a fairy tale. Adding to the elegance, Poinsett Bridge's 14-foot high Gothic stone arch provides access for the Little Gap Creek to flow through near County Road 42. The bridge is listed on the National Register of Historic Places.

—Photos on these two pages by Robert Clark

HAGOOD MILL, PICKENS

A fine example of nineteenth century technology, this gristmill operated from 1845 until the mid 1960s. The mill is located on Hagood Creek, a tributary of Twelve Mile River. The wooden waterwheel, which produces 22 horsepower, is 20-feet in diameter by 4-feet wide and is the only wooden waterwheel in South Carolina. The wheel and its mechanical components were rebuilt in the mid-1970s using as many original parts as possible. Restoration continued in the mid-1980s and mid-1990s.

Grand Design

Gothic stone arch lets Little Gap Creek flow through unimpeded. The bridge was part of the original State Road that ran from Charleston, through Columbia and on into North Carolina.

▲ Areas surrounding Falls Park include lush landscaping and pristine places to dine, all set against a serene backdrop of falling water's white noise.

—Photo by Stephanie Norwood

FALLS PARK AND "BIG BROTHER" FALLS, GREENVILLE

The sound of falling water provides a relaxing setting. Just out-of-sight Liberty Bridge, a unique curved suspension footbridge, overlooks the Reedy River and its surprising falls.

LIBERTY BRIDGE, GREENVILLE

This curved suspension footbridge overhangs Reedy River and its rare urban falls. A single suspension cable supports the bridge. From afar, it seems to float. Below the bridge is where Greenville's first European settler, Richard Pearis, set his trading post in 1768.

PEACE CENTER FOR THE PERFORMING ARTS, GREENVILLE

Adjacent to Falls Park, this arts center features the Peace Concert Hall, Dorothy Hipp Gunter Theater, and an amphitheater beside the Reedy River. Named after the Peace family who donated $10 million towards its development, entertainers from the world over perform where three factories once stood: one built Confederate Army wagons, one produced textiles in the 1880s, and the other served as Duke's Mayonnaise home. Now the arts thrive here.

GREENVILLE COUNTY MUSEUM OF ART, GREENVILLE

Art historians regard Andrew Wyeth (1917 - 2009) as one of the most important American artists of the 20th century. To see the Greenville County Museum of Art's Andrew Wyeth collection is to see the full scope of the artist's extraordinary career, including significant decade-by-decade examples, from the 1930s to the 21st century. It's a collection Wyeth himself described as "the very best collection of my watercolors in any public museum in this country."

REEDY RIVER FALLS, GREENVILLE

The refined environment built by the city is an oasis to which the white noise of the Reedy's rushing water presents a soothing backdrop. Residents and tourists enjoy this Chattooga-like setting without having to drive into the rugged northwest corner of the state.

FURMAN UNIVERSITY, GREENVILLE

The university's Bell Tower, built in 1955, is a Greenville County landmark. Historically a Baptist College, the Reverend Richard Furman founded Furman in Edgefield County in 1826. The university relocated to Greenville in 1851.

BOB JONES UNIVERSITY, GREENVILLE

The Old Master Painting Collection at the Bob Jones University Museum & Gallery provides a rare viewer experience outside European cities: masterworks by recognized artists and their students—all aesthetically exhibited with period furniture, sculpture, and tapestries to lend a period ambiance to the galleries and give patrons a panoramic view of ages past. M&G's baroque paintings represent one of the most important collections in America.

BROAD MARGIN, FRANK LLOYD WRIGHT HOME

Designed in 1951 and completed in 1954, the house serves up a fine example of Wright's natural or "Usonian" homes. One of fewer than 20 of Wright's buildings in the Southeast and one of only two in South Carolina, the house illustrates Wright's dictum: "Shelter should be the essential look of any dwelling." Broad Margin comes from Thoreau's *Walden* in which he states, "I love a broad margin to my life."

AMPHITHEATER RUINS OF CLEVELAND PARK

Located near the corner of Cleveland Park Drive and Lake Crest Street, steep concrete stadium seats are all that remain of a local amphitheater.

Mill provided a setting where people gathered.

WOODSIDE COTTON MILL VILLAGE

The Woodside Cotton Mill Village Historic District pos-

SYMMES CHAPEL, GREENVILLE COUNTY

Known also as Pretty Place, Symmes Chapel overlooks Greenville County's Jones Gap State Park. The majestic view of the mountains

—Photo by Robert Clark

▲ When autumn arrives, the mountains don their coats of many colors and Greenville and Greenville County host hordes of foliage pilgrims hoping to witness the season's pageantry in its most magnificent color palette.

Moss and vines reclaim the remaining seats. You'll find this hidden gem by on the Swamp Rabbit Trail toward Hincapie Path in the opposite direction of the Greenville Zoo.

GILREATH'S MILL & WATER WHEEL

Gilreath's Mill is one of the few remaining mills in South Carolina that speaks to the vital tradition of rural industry. The mill was an integral part of the area's social and economic setting. Gilreath's

sesses industrial and architectural significance. It provides a good example of an early twentieth century urban South Carolina textile mill village. The village is largely intact over eighty years later despite modernizations a succession of mill and homeowners made to individual buildings.

and valley makes the chapel a popular site for weddings and a powerful draw for photographers.

LAKE JOCASSEE, SALEM

This deep-water reservoir possesses crystal-clear mountain water and is ideal for boating, fishing, and skiing. Its 75 miles of shoreline is near pristine. Trout live here in the cold clear water. Although most manmade structures were demolished

—Photo by Robert Clark

▲ Furman University, designated a *Tree Campus USA* by the Arbor Day Foundation, is assured many colorful autumns for decades to come. The University plants trees on its campus and practices sound forestry management to ensure the maintaining of their green investment.

prior to the lake's creation, divers discovered the remains of an intact lodge that now sits below 300 feet of water. A hilltop graveyard with headstones remains as well some 130 feet beneath the water. The cemetery provided a scene in the 1972 thriller, *Deliverance*.

CAESARS HEAD, CLEVELAND

Here you can stand atop the Blue Ridge Escarpment, 3,266 feet above sea level. The panoramic view includes Paris Mountain. In autumn people come to watch hawks wheeling and spiraling—"kettling"—as they migrate to Central and South America to overwinter. The view from Caesars Head reveals how the collision of continents during the early Paleozoic folded and crumpled the land, thrusting up mountains.

ISSAQUEENA FALLS, WALHALLA

Unlike many waterfalls, it's easy to walk to Issaqueena Falls. The route to a great overlook is only about 200-300 feet down a wide, gentle, graveled path. Legend holds that the falls is named for an Indian maiden, Issaqueena, who warned the white settlers of an Indian attack. Chased by Indians she appeared to jump over the falls. By hiding behind the falls she tricked her pursuers and survived.

TABLE ROCK STATE PARK, PICKENS

The towering monolith, which inspired the park's name, is South Carolina's most-photographed mountain. It serves as a backdrop for the 3,000-acre park and its facilities. To the Cherokee, the monadnock seemed to be a logical place for the Great Spirit, Yowa, to dine. The Cherokee referred to this mountainous region as "Sah-ka-na-ga," the Great Blue Hills of God.

PICKENS COUNTY MUSEUM, PICKENS

Housed in a 1903 jail and expanded in 2006, this museum houses artifacts representing Pickens County's heritage—from prehistory to current events. Three art galleries refresh every eight to ten weeks and feature the talents of local artists. The landscape is native gardens. The museum itself provides a wonderful example of turn-of-the-century architecture, featuring hand-rolled brick, and is quite distinctive with its crenellated turret and copper-colored tin roof.

Swamp Rabbit Trail, Greenville

Hiking the Greenville Health System Swamp Rabbit Trail is wildly popular, so popular it generates nearly $7 million in tourism-based revenues for Greenville County each year. This ever-growing (for now 20-mile) multi-use greenway system runs along the Reedy River connecting schools, parks, and local businesses. Its popularity with cyclists has, in Mayor White's words, created a "constellation" of bike shops and related suppliers." It wasn't always this way, however, for the trail named in part after a large cottontail rabbit.

The Greenville Health System Swamp Rabbit Trail's roots go back to a rail line launched in 1889. The dream was to connect Greenville County with the Atlantic and Tennessee. The line went though dizzying ownership and name changes. With a history of hauling timber and passengers and various industrial uses, the line experienced ups and downs and we're not talking hilly terrain. Openings and closings took place.

In 1998, the downtown Greenville-to-Travelers Rest section went on the market. Upstate Forever, a Greenville-based non-profit group, launched a public acquisition campaign with a vision to convert the line to a trail. A year later, Greenville County Economic Development Corporation, a county agency, acquired the rail line. In 2007, the Greenville County Recreation District agreed to become the line's full-time operator. Recognizing the trail's positive health benefits, the Greenville Health System partnered with Greenville Recreation and the "Greenville Health System Swamp Rabbit Trail" came to be. The trail is officially known as the Greenville Health System Swamp Rabbit Trail due to a $1 million contribution the local healthcare provider made to help develop and publicize the trail.

Ranging from 8 to 12 feet wide, a paved surface invites bicycles, skaters and walkers. A rubberized surface cushions the many runners' feet and knees. Trail amenities include lighting, picnic areas, benches, water fountains, restrooms, signage and bicycle racks. Each year the trail extends north and south, and over half a million people use the trail. One site popular along the trail is Medusa Tree, known also as the Root Tree on the trail in downtown Greenville. Here you can see what a beech's underground root system looks like. Sure enough it brings to mind Medusa, one of the Gorgon sisters; anyone who looked into her eyes turned to stone at once. You won't have that problem however along the Swamp Rabbit Trail. It has turned Travelers Rest, as you're about to see, into a flourishing village.

Traveler's Rest

Many compare the rolling hills along the Swamp Rabbit Trail to the peaks and vales of France and Italy. Something makes the air here a bit more energized, and cyclists love it. Cycling is huge up here, thanks in large part to legendary George Hincapie who now lives in Greenville.

Thanks to the many cyclists who pedal here, Traveler's Rest has assumed a bit of European ambience. The town that once received Conestoga wagons now welcomes cycles and their riders. This town in particular has benefited from Greenville's transformation. When Swamp Rabbit Trail hikers and bikers hopped into town it meant a shot in the arm as business goes. Cafes opened and so did the Swamp Rabbit Brewery. An old general store went though its own transformation and in time became an outfitter catering to bike enthusiasts.

Travelers Rest went from a place on the way to somewhere to a destination itself. It, too, has a remarkable story: an old railway bed turned greenway brought green to the town in a big way. The city of Greenville and Furman University, which owns the most land along the trail, pitched in and made the trail and amenities a reality. The word is out that people are even buying homes in Travelers Rest thanks to the Swamp Rabbit Trail's allure. Now and then folks refer to Travelers Rest as "T.R." That could easily mean "the rage."

▼ Time spent in Traveler's Rest is surely time well-spent. The town reaps trickle-down benefits of Greenville's transformation. It has long been a stopping point for drivers going to and from places like Asheville and the Blue Ridge Mountains. From ice cream to white lightening, from kayaking the Green River to cycling the Swamp Rabbit Trail, Traveler's Rest offers a myriad of treats and treks.

—Photo by Robert Clark

A Roadmap for Other Cities

DOWNTOWN
IS EVERYBODY'S
NEIGHBORHOOD.

—Photo by Paul Ringger

*G*reenville went from empty storefronts, abandoned warehouses, and a Main Street with four space-consuming lanes to a thriving city; from an aging mill town to a city with boutiques, art galleries, restaurants, entertainment venues, a heralded trail, baseball, and exciting nightlife. As we've seen, all this progress took innovation, partnerships, teamwork, and patience. Consensus-building was key. The city's approach to revitalizing downtown gave rise to a tagline: "Downtown is Everybody's Neighborhood," and that's exactly what it became.

A caveat is in order for municipal leaders and urban planners who read this story of revival: no magic pill exists for instant urban rebirth. No single approach to revitalizing a city exists, every community is unique. But, much can be learned from how Greenville went about things. Here are some of the landmarks along the road to the restoration of Greenville.

STEP BACK & EVALUATE

Greenville assessed its problems. Downtown was begging to be reinvented as extraordinary and appealing. Something dramatic was in order. The city invested in properties, developed anchors, and used private-sector development to occupy areas between anchors.

Grand Design

and cultural resources. It worked with the private sector to create partnerships that reinvigorated downtown businesses.

Greenville realized the public-sector needed to take the initiative if private investments were to occur.

DEVELOP A SOLID PLAN

The city began by looking at its main avenue. Lawrence Halprin and Associates, landscape architects, developed a plan that downsized Greenville's Main Street from four lanes to two. That made it possible to plant trees, Main Street's calling card

FOSTER PUBLIC-PRIVATE RELATIONSHIPS

With a commitment to abide by its master plan, Greenville formed alliances leading to public-private investments that created anchor projects. The goal was to attract visitors to the downtown core. Examples of public-private investments include the Peace Center for the Performing Arts, The Greenville Commons/Hyatt Regency Hotel, and West End Market.

DEVELOP ANCHORS

Anchor projects inspired redevelopment downtown.

The first anchor was Greenville Commons and its Hyatt Regency Hotel, office complex, and parking garage. The city bought the land, built a convention center and a parking garage. The anchor set a precedent. The city and public and private sectors collaborated to revitalize Greenville although this approach did not work with the next major anchor. The historic West End of downtown held no appeal to private sector investors. Though risky, the city

Mixed-use buildings, landscaped streets and creating a city with convenient opportunities for foot-traffic were key goals in Greenville's grand design.

—Photos on these two pages by Paul Ringger.

The city displayed courage, too. In the late 1970s when trends dictated that malls were the next big thing, Greenville bucked the trend. It chose instead to give Main Street an exemplary blend of vehicular and pedestrian design.

The city focused on anchor developments, and natural

of the future. Spacious sidewalks fostered outdoor dining. Plazas and public spaces gave people breathing space. Making Falls Park a showplace led to Liberty Bridge. Falls Park put Greenville on the map. The attractions worked. The people came. And were able to park for free.

developed the West End Market, creating a 45,000-square foot park-like setting offering office, retail, restaurants, artisans, and a farmers market.

Financing came from tax increment financing, a HUD Section 108 loan, grants, city general fund dollars, and other sources. The risk paid off and led to an arts and entertainment district of restaurants, theaters, and the Governor's School for the Arts.

Pursue Mixed-Use Developments

Fluor Field at the West End illustrates the strategic worth

of a mixed-use development and public-private partnership, funding came mainly from tax increment financing, sale proceeds from the West End Market, hospitality and other funds. Team owners used future stadium revenue to build the stadium.

Greenville renovated the donated Alliance Cotton Warehouse into the West End Market in 1994, which housed restaurants and shops. This project, along with Fluor Field at the West

End, turned the area into a thriving commercial district that tourists find attractive.

Bringing back the Reedy and creating Falls Park encouraged growth along the riverfront. When the timing was optimal for revitalization, environmentally sensitive development proceeded. The city constructed underground parking and private development went up over it. Walkways and plazas give people

The revitalized city offers residents and visitors memorable ways to enjoy life in the great outdoors—from the "great American pastime" to a unique array of special events near the banks of the Reedy.

Grand Design

access to the park, and Falls Park connects downtown and the West End District.

Once an eyesore and environmental blight, Falls Park offers residents and visitors greenways, amphitheaters, and botanical gardens. The private sector welcomed this development and invested in urban residences, theaters, galleries, and restaurants, all of which worked wonders for the city's tax base and did much to create a vibrant, diverse urban setting.

SMALL THINGS ARE VITAL

Festivals, music, and dining prove alluring. Greenville encourages downtown events that offer something for all. These events motivate people to come downtown. ARTISPHERE, for instance: an annual signature event, it celebrates the arts and the area's rich international and multi-cultural flair. Held each

People gravitate to water and Greenville is a water-rich city. Restaurants offering views of the falls seduce patrons seeking creative dining experiences in a mesmerizing environment.

year in May, Artisphere is an event that entertains, educates, inspires and enriches its diverse audience bringing the community together through the arts.

The narrow sidewalks that discouraged pedestrian traffic are long gone. Spacious ones now provide dining spaces where people can take in events beneath the green canopy for which Greenville is famed.

Signage clearly directs people to venues. Public art plays a vital role in this urban renaissance—embellishing the city; giving it pizzazz. Quotes etched in the sidewalk, lights in the trees, art, and sculptures give the landscape personality. Add all these factors together and going to one of America's Top 10 best downtowns feels special.

THE ROADMAP SIMPLIFIED

Make anchors accessible. They set the tone for development and standards.

Please tourists. Additional revenue comes from tourists, strengthening the city's economics. Mixed-use developments appeal not just to tourists but workers and residents as well. It's the proverbial win-win scenario for the city.

Innovate and take thoughtful risks. The public sector

Greenville is not just any old downtown city. Modern sculptures and a pleasing mix of historic and contemporary architecture give the city much of its eclectic personality.

—Photos on these two pages by Stephanie Norwood

Grand Design

—Photo by Stephanie Norwood

Lush landscaping is a major mile marker on Greenville's roadmap for other cities. Contours, hardscapes, the colors of Earth and tons of trees—that's how a city transcends from monotone to memorable.

became entrepreneurial, cognizant of the same risks involved in private development. Invigorating the West End proved to be a smart move.

Give private development incentives and other good things. In addition to money, other ways to provide value exist. Facilitate development. Cut through red tape. Expedite licensing and approval of building plans. Provide tax credits for redevelopment projects.

Make living downtown attractive. People who live downtown support retail, restaurants, and cultural venues. When people live downtown, they bring spirit to the city.

The Final Word

Greenville set standards and was sensitive to people's need by developing guidelines for historic neighborhoods. Preserving a sense of place is pivotal to a city's identity. Greenville invested in public spaces, parking facilities, and an infrastructure that attracted excellent private development. While public-private partnerships paved the way, the city developed previously undesirable areas to attract private developers. Today, the quality of life in Greenville is well known. In fact, it has become a magnet for the intellectual capital that is driving the city's economic boom.

Greenville's revitalization didn't take place overnight. It took 40 years. The city is

keeping the spirit of revitalization alive and well. Known once upon a time as the textile capital of the world, the city continues to reinvent itself proving that a business district can flourish from horizontal investments in public infrastructure, that vision can turn a city into a happenning urban setting.

Cities in need of rebirth should take heart in Greenville's accomplishments. Greenville shows us that where there's a will, there's not just one way. There are many. A good roadmap will lead you to them.

Grand Design

Twenty-Four Hours in Greenville

—Photo by Paul Ringger

G R E E N V I L L E ' S

reenville abounds with wonderful ways to spend a day. It does not bore. You won't have to work hard to fill a day, a night, and the wee hours with great things to do. If you're a decathlon type, you can DIY for 24 straight hours of outdoor recreation, music, art, entertainment of all sorts, culinary pleasures, physical fitness, museums, festivals, downtown mice adventures, shopping, and more. Or you can live vicariously through what others can do with 24 straight hours in Greenville. But what fun is that? Do it yourself.

Where to start? The Greenville Health System Swamp Rabbit Trail.

When to start? Sunrise.

Dawn. Droplets of dew reflect a million images of the yellow-pink horizon. The early light gives cyclists, joggers, and walkers a glow as they join you on this 20-mile multi-use trail. You'll glow, too, as you start the day off with some aerobic exercise. After some healthy jogging, great views, and green spaces, you head back downtown. Coffee sounds good.

8:00 A.M.—Having cooled down, you're glad you jogged the former Swamp Rabbit rail line as you sit down to a stack of chocolate-chip pancakes and a caffè latte at Coffee Underground on, where else, 1 East Coffee Street.

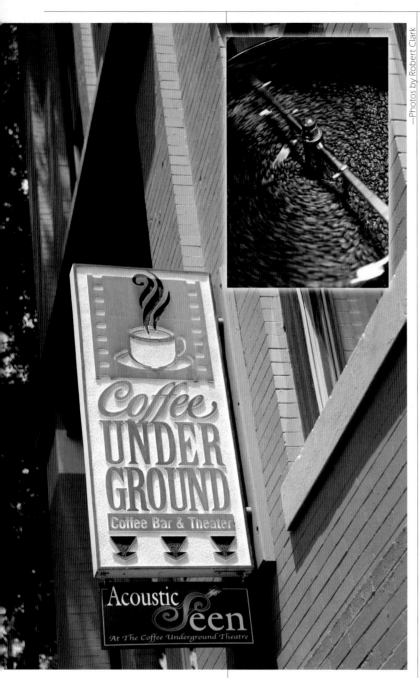

—Photos by Robert Clark

▲ Much like those heart-tugging coffee ads on TV, you really can wake up and smell the coffee brewing in downtown Greenville. Coffee shops appeal to trendy millennials as well as boomers and seniors who need a kick-start for their day. Coffee Underground delivers a Seattle-like vibe to the city and its gallery offers hanging space for local artists.

9:20 A.M.—A jolt or two of caffeine spikes your curiosity. Right now, you think, is a good time to find the bronze Mice on Main everyone talks about. If you're good, you'll find nine mice sculptures inspired by Margaret Wise Brown's children's poem, "Goodnight Moon." The mice hide on both sides of Main Street, from the Hyatt to the Westin Poinsett Hotel. You set out looking for Uncle Miles, Mr. Mickey, Mrs. Minnie, Mifflin, Mitch, Melissa, Milkey, Miss Minnie, and Mickey Jr. (Hint: get the Mice on Main book to expedite your search.)

11:30—Well, you didn't find all the mice. You'll finish that another day. Now it's time to return to your room, which commands a great view, at the venerable Westin Poinsett and get ready for a baseball game. Having read about the Poinsett's rich history, you realize that the earth beneath this grand hotel has supported great hotels from 1824 to today. After checking emails, it's shower time.

2:05 P.M.—At Fluor Field at the West End, you get a case of déjà vu. It looks so familiar. Then it hits you. It looks like Boston's Fenway Park. And it should. It's modeled after the home turf of the Boston Red Sox. The stadium even has its own "Green Monster," a 30-foot high wall in left field, equipped with a manual scoreboard. The dimensions around the outfield wall match Fenway Park's. It even has a "Pesky's Pole" in right field, the foul pole notorious at Fenway for the cheapest homeruns in major league baseball. You have a classic all-American afternoon ... hot dogs and Cokes, singing "Sweet Caroline," and best of all, the Greenville Drive defeat the Savannah Sand Gnats,

3 to 1 thanks to a ninth-inning home run.

5:10 P.M.—You wanted to see the Andrew Wyeth watercolors at the Greenville County Museum of Art but the museum closes at 6 p.m. Instead, having a love for photography, you make the 18-mile drive up Highway 276 to Cleveland, South Carolina to Symmes Chapel, known also as "Pretty Place." You want

—Photos above by Paul Ringger

to stand atop Stone Mountain and try out a new camera at this place renowned for its view of mountain ridges and valleys. You can see why over 100 weddings take place here a year.

7:00 P.M.—Back at the Westin Poinsett, you barely have time to change and make it to the Peace Center for "An Evening with Chris Botti" at 8 o'clock. Walking down Main toward the river, you note how the Reedy reflects the fading light. The river flaunts rainbow colors but this time they come from the streaks of yellow orange, and purple shading the western sky. White, silky threads of water lie across rock faces.

Couples walk hand-in-hand along the banks of the comeback river. What a beautiful evening, you think. At the Peace Center, the music flows smoothly from master trumpeter Botti. He's worked with Sting, Tony Bennett, Lady Gaga, Paul Simon, and others. Your ears tell you why. When the show ends, you walk along the Reedy River. You can see why performers refer to the Peace Center as a jewel. It, like the nearby Liberty Bridge, glitters.

10:10 P.M.—Where did the day go? And where did the time to get lunch go? Famished, you hear that Rick Erwin's West End Grille is open from 5 P.M. until ... sounds like your kind of place. The bar is dazzling; a perfect place to unwind. And it's filled with people enjoying life. The wine

Each season fans flock to Fluor Field to watch the city's Class A affiliate, the Greenville Drive, play more than 70 home games. "The Drive" got its name from the influence of nearby BMW US Manufacturing, Michelin and other contributors to Greenville's rich automotive history.

Grand Design

—Photo by Robert Clark

—Photo by Stephanie Norwood

The historic West End, just across the Reedy, developed into a beautiful district of shops, services, restaurants and bars. It brings art and entertainment offerings to the city. At night, a spectacle of lights fills its trees; pastel floodlights color its buildings and shop windows glitter like a Manhattan Christmas.

► Standing 3,266 feet above sea level, the panoramic view here includes Paris Mountain. In autumn you can see hawks wheeling and spiraling through Greenville County as they migrate to Central and South America to winter in warmer climates.

list is one of the most comprehensive you've seen. And the menu? Blackened scallops and sides of grilled asparagus and roasted mushrooms will do nicely.

2:00 A.M.—Back on Main near Piazzo Bergamo, it's fun to sit and people-watch. Lots of young people fill the street. After-hours bars prove popular, and the Piazzo Bergamo has been described as a miniature Times Square. The nightlife here is exciting.

3:30 A.M.—You find a late-night coffee shop and have another caffè latte. So far, your energy is holding up. It's amazing how many people come in for coffee. There's no danger of Greenville being branded "a sleepy little Southern town." You decide it's time to fulfill your dream of seeing sunrise from a special place where your parents honeymooned, Raven Cliff Falls and Caesars Head, a landmark atop the Blue Ridge Escarpment. Time to strike this off your bucket list.

4:25 A.M.—The drive to Caesars Head takes about an hour. Standing atop Caesars Head, you're 3,215 feet above sea level.

At 5:25, you can see the land begin to lighten. Dawn arrives and your view includes Paris Mountain near Greenville. Some believe this rock

outcropping resembles the Roman Emperor, Caesar, thus its name. Getting to nearby Raven Cliffs Falls involves a short drive but a bit of a hike. It's worth it though. Raven Cliff Falls, near Caesars Head, plummets some 420 feet. Feeling brave, you cross its swinging, suspension footbridge Indiana Jones-style.

You've done it. You've had a whirlwind 24 hours in Greenville and there's so much left do. First, it's time to head back to the Westin Poinsett for some well-deserved sleep. As Scarlett O'Hara might say, "After all, tomorrow is another day to enjoy Greenville."

Grand Design

GREENVILLE'S

—Photo by Robert Clark

Grand Design

G R E E N V I L L E ' S

—Photo by Robert Clark

Grand Design

GREENVILLE'S

—Photos by Robert Clark

A fog-shrouded mountain cove...the Middle Saluda River rendered into satiny threads...the music of fall color... a field of sunflowers or a tour of the Swamp Rabbit Trail—Greenville and its surroundings feed all the senses.

Grand Design

Grand Design

—Photos on these two pages by Paul Ringger

—Photos on these two pages by Paul Ringger

This place reflects its moods... it may be from a rainy day, or a sunny day; it could be because of busy streets or even empty streets. The memories of war, of a dirty river and an old bridge; fading murals and pastel brick all contribute to what makes Greenville days—and life here—unique.

G R E E N V I L L E ' S

—Photo by Paul Ringger

Grand Design

—Photos on these two pages by Paul Ringger

Glass, steel, rock, water, movement, and light—Greenville is a city designed for being outside; a city of lights and color where architecture, art, and activity are best appreciated from an outdoor point of view.

G R E E N V I L L E ' S

—Photos on these two pages by Paul Ringger

GREENVILLE'S

Grand Design

Grand Design

ABOUT 1765

NEAR REEDY RIVER FALLS STOOD THE HOME, TRADING STATION, AND GRIST MILL OF COL. RICHARD PEARIS, FIRST WHITE SETTLER OF THIS SECTION. HE WAS A NOTED INDIAN TRADER AND PROMINENT TORY OF THE REVOLUTION.

THIS MARKER PLACED BY CAMPS OF GREEN-VILLE COUNTY, WOODMEN OF THE WORLD, 1966.

—Photo by Paul Ringger

G R E E N V I L L E ' S

Grand Design

Grand Design

125

Grand Design

—Photo by Paul Ringger

127

GREENVILLE'S

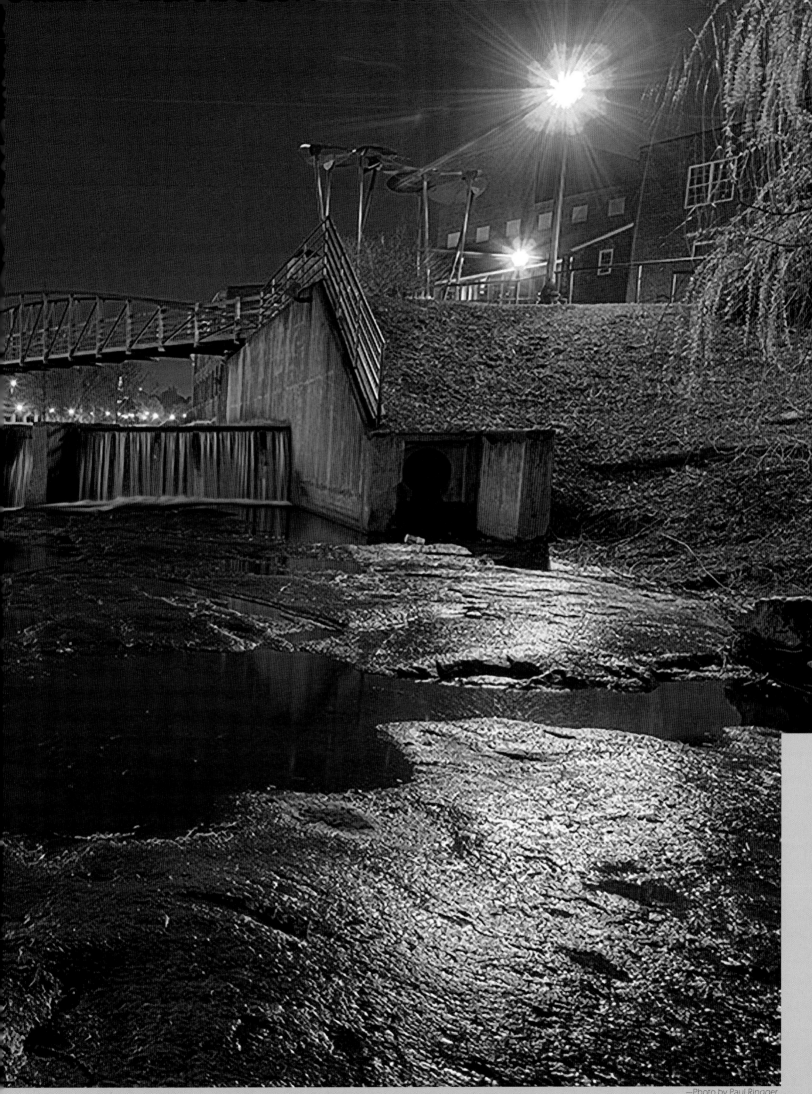

Grand Design

To say that the construction of Liberty Bridge and the timely clean-up of the Reedy River were catalysts for downtown Greenville's resurgence would be beyond an understatement.

The fact that the bridge is pedestrian created a curiosity that could only be fed by seeing the river and the falls someway other than simply driving-by or driving across. The bridge endears the falls to the public and the accessibility to the banks of the river lends a more hands-on feel to the entire area. It is a place where people want to be... allowing their children to explore the giant rocks and mossy boulders that line the river while they relax and take in sights many Greenville residents never dreamed they would see in their lifetimes.

—Photo by Robert Clark

GREENVILLE'S

—Photo by Paul Ringger

The contemporary design of Liberty Bridge is evident from any angle at any hour of the day or night. Angular steel masts and cables that almost seem to disappear stand out against a serene sunrise sky and glisten when the lights come up at dusk. Any way you look at it, form and function are fused and are obvious from every point of view.

—Photo by Robert Clark

Grand Design

131

Miguel Rosales is president and principal designer of Rosales + Partners, the firm that designed Liberty Bridge. According to the firm's website, "Greenville's downtown is split by a wooded valley park containing the falls of the Reedy River. Liberty Bridge replaced a demolished six-lane highway bridge. The new bridge has a curved clear span over the river that arcs away from the falls providing an aerial platform from which to view the cascading water. The bridge gently slopes into the ravine and is supported by twin inclined towers and a single suspension cable, allowing unobstructed views. The bridge appears to float over the landscape. The twin towers and suspension cable, visible from vantage points around the city, draw visitors to the public park, falls, and Reedy River."

—Photo by Robert Clark

Schlaich Bergermann and Partner worked on the bridge's conceptual design and construction. According to its website, "The curved pedestrian bridge over the Reedy River is supported by a single suspension cable at the outer edge of the bridge. Two inclined and tapered tubular steel masts, each 200 feet apart and stabilized with single sloped back stays, support the main cable. A circumferential steel truss below the outer edge of the concrete deck provides the necessary stiffness. The torsion in the deck created by the one-sided support is balanced by a series of pre-stressed ring cables below the deck."

Length: 380 feet   Width: 12 feet
Awards: Footbridge Awards 2005; Arthur G. Heyden Medal 2005; OCEA Award of Merit 2006, and Waterfront Center Excellence 2008 Annual Honor Award

GREENVILLE'S

River Lodge
Cleveland Park

Grand Design

GREENVILLE'S

No matter how much someone loves to walk—or run—for most there comes a time where they simply want to sit and rest a spell.

Options for this in Falls Park are abundant. Whether you treasure that old familiar feel of the slats of a porch swing against your backsides or cherish the touch that a soft cushion of warm green grass provides, you are in luck here.

A restful place to catch up on the local goings-on or just watch the river roll by, the swings and benches along the river banks provide a tranquil and peaceful setting for any such activity.

And if you prefer natural seating to man-made ones, lush greenery and colorful blossoms surround amphitheater-like areas suitable for play, people-watching or catching a few rays during the right season.

The truth be told, Falls Park, much like the city itself, truly has something for everyone.

GREENVILLE'S

Grand Design

—Photo by Paul Ringger

CAUTION
GARDEN STEPS
UNEVEN

$\mathcal{M}$aking striking public art available to all of its citizens may be one of the most notable contributions that sets Greenville apart from comparable cities.

The fluid angelic sculptures on this page, Meditation and Reminiscence, were created by Vietnamese native Tuan Nguyen. Tuan was sentenced to a concentration camp in 1985 for attempting to escape his native home to come to America. He made sculptures while imprisoned by mixing water and dirt from the floor of his cell. His incredible talent caught the eye of the warden who eventually helped him flee to the Philippines.

The bronze boar on the facing page is Il Porcellino—a full-sized replica of one from Florence, Italy. Legend has it that if you rub his nose you will one day return to the romantic Tuscan city.

Finally, the towering metallic spires located in Poinsett Plaza are Philip Whiteley's interpretation of mountains and water, two of the most notable elements that surround Greenville.

Such sensory experiences are "free for the taking" in Greenville; a city that assigns high value to the contributions of art to the heartbeat of the Upstate.

—Photos on these two pages by Paul Ringger

Grand Design

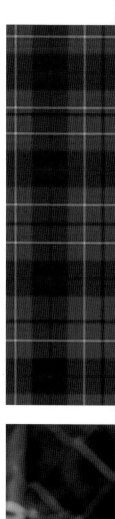
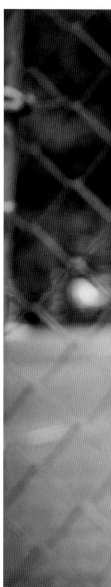

GREENVILLE'S

The Gallabrae Scottish games reflect that Greenville has one of the country's highest concentrations of Scot-Irish descendants. Bagpipes, athletic competitions, and Highland dancing are all part of the games that the Standing Council of Scottish chiefs rank among the world's best. Octo 2, stands at McBee Avenue and Falls Street. Kinetic artist Anthony Howe created the mesmerizing wind-driven sculpture that requires only a bit of oil now and then.

—Photos on these two pages by Robert Clark

Grand Design

GREENVILLE'S

The one-time textile center of the world reinvented itself into a city where a polluted river and a dying industry gave way to a vibrant city filled with greenways and high-end shopping venues.

—Photos on these two pages by Robert Clark

Entrepreneur and philanthropist Vardy McBee, referred to as the "father of Greenville" donated land for the first four churches built in the city and for the first male and female academies. And though he helped bring in the first railroad, today Segways scoot people along in a greener fashion. Now a clean Reedy River provides and abundance of atmosphere for outside activity in the leafy, artistically graced city.

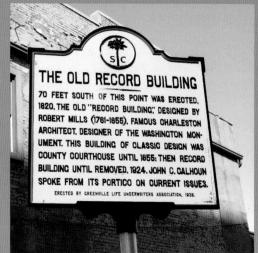

THE OLD RECORD BUILDING

70 FEET SOUTH OF THIS POINT WAS ERECTED, 1820, THE OLD "RECORD BUILDING," DESIGNED BY ROBERT MILLS (1781-1855), FAMOUS CHARLESTON ARCHITECT, DESIGNER OF THE WASHINGTON MONUMENT. THIS BUILDING OF CLASSIC DESIGN WAS COUNTY COURTHOUSE UNTIL 1855; THEN RECORD BUILDING UNTIL REMOVED, 1924. JOHN C. CALHOUN SPOKE FROM ITS PORTICO ON CURRENT ISSUES.

ERECTED BY GREENVILLE LIFE UNDERWRITERS ASSOCIATION, 1936.

—Photo by Paul Ringger

Past and present distinguish this river city. Robert Mills designed The Old Record Building that served as the county courthouse until 1855.

McBEE

Photo by Tom Poland

Photo by Tom Poland

—Photo by Paul Ringger

Grand Design

ARTISPHERE
ARTS. CULTURE. LIFE.

—Photos on these two pages by Paul Ringger

ARTISPHERE—THE BEST ARTS FAIR

Every year in May, downtown Greenville springs to life with a three-day event that celebrates the arts of every genre—Artisphere.

Tens of thousands of visitors and locals spill into the city streets to soak up the sights and sounds made possible by the many participants who bring their varied talents to the heart of the city.

G R E E N V I L L E ' S

Since its inception in 2005, this festival has built momentum with 2015 being the most successful to date. It has earned increasing recognition including a national honor taking third place in USA Today's 10 Best Readers' Choice contest.

Artisphere has something for everyone, regardless of age or artistic preference. Children are charmed by street art created on the Swamp Rabbit Trail next to the river.

artists of national and international caliber.

In addition to the visual exhibits, live performance art, demonstrations, and even culinary arts are showcased in grand fashion when the Upstate opens its arms during this much-anticipated event. Local tourism is boosted and the quality of life in Greenville and the surrounding area is enhanced by exposure to arts with such broad public appeal.

walk away with a new-found sense of appreciation for what they have seen and what their senses have experienced.

In Greenville, Artisphere truly gives an entire new meaning to "the merry month of May".

—Photos on these two pages by Paul Ringger

And people of all ages develop a greater appreciation of the arts by simply wandering through this explosion of color and creativity. It encourages local support for arts as it hosts award-winning visual

Greenville thrives as a diverse international and multicultural city and Artisphere generously supports every aspect of that. With its emphasis on education, entertainment and enjoyment, festival-goers

Grand Design

—Photo by Paul Ringger

—Photos on these two pages by Paul Ringger

GREENVILLE'S

Printmaking, an ancient Chinese art, is making an impression in Greenville. Printmakers practice and demonstrate their unique skills in woodcuts and other talents related to their very special craft.

GREENVILLE'S

—Photo by Paul Ringger

Grand Design

—Photos by Paul Ringger

GREENVILLE'S

—Photo by Robert Clark

The word "vibrant" is a workhorse when it applies to Greenville—full of energy and enthusiasm as in a vibrant cosmopolitan city. It can also mean (as color goes) bright and striking. Yet another definition is strong or resonating. All meanings apply when you refer to Greenville, which has experienced a renaissance during Mayor Knox White's administration.

Grand Design

—Photo by Robert Clark

—Photo by Paul Ringger

—Photo by Paul Ringger

—Photo by Paul Ringger

Traveler's Rest has seen a burst of bicycle shops thanks to the Swamp Rabbit Tail linking it to downtown Greenville, just as the city has seen retailers and restaurants arrive on the scene. The region's look and feel today is certainly one of energy and change.

—Photo by Paul Ringger

Grand Design

Elected mayor in 1971, Max Heller brought a vision that enhanced downtown's image through streetscape and traffic improvements. Sculptures and fountains have been added and the mid-1960s' aluminum veneer has been replaced, restoring the traditional façade of Main Street. Now, people are eager to visit and explore the city.

—Photos on these two pages by Paul Ringger

GREENVILLE'S

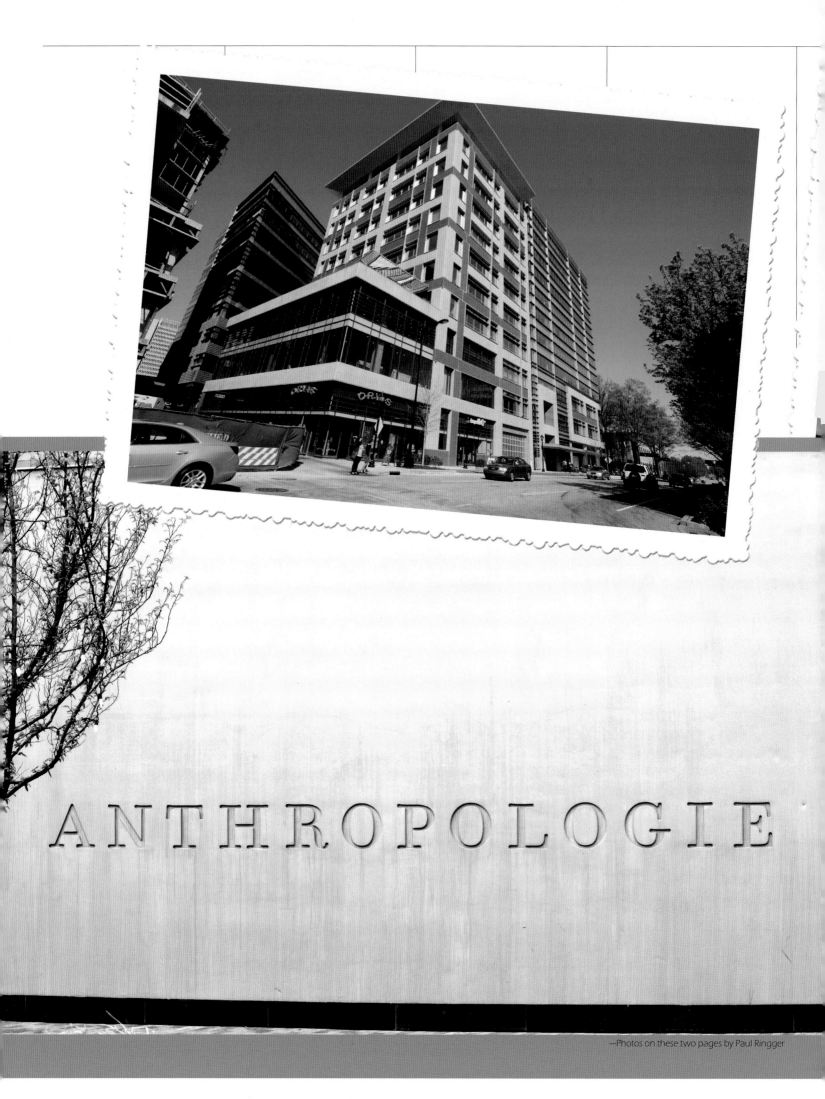

ANTHROPOLOGIE

—Photos on these two pages by Paul Ringger

New retailers like Orvis, new construction, and art give the city a higher tone. The renaissance continues on a good note, jazzing up the city by the Reedy.

GREENVILLE'S

Grand Design

The grand clock standing in front of the Greenville Chamber of Commerce building bears the name and founding date of Liberty Insurance—behind it stands the Westin Poinsett.

The Chamber Building, also known as the North Greenville College Building, was built in 1925 and is an example of the Chicago School style of architecture. It was added to the National Register of Historic Places in 1982.

CHARLES K. CHREITZBERG
GRAND MASTER

A∴L∴ 5925
A∴D∴ 1925

A GATE OF FRIENDLINESS
UPON THE HIGHWAY OF TRADE
JOHN A. RUSSELL   CHR. BLDG. COMM
BEACHAM & LEGRAND   J.E. SIRR
ARCHITECTS   ENGIN
                  THE MINTER HOMES CO.
                       BUILDERS

Grand Design

Greenville is dotted with a variety of architectural styles reflecting design trends through the decades.

Grand Design

G R E E N V I L L E ' S

—Photos on these two pages by Paul Ringger

Grand Design

—Photos on these two pages by Robert Clark

—Photos on these two pages byRobert Clark

International celebrations, the arts, and great cuisine contribute to Greenville's multicultural quality of life. Above, traditional weaver, Mary Alice, weaves split oak strands into what will no doubt become an heirloom basket, bringing function and beauty to generations of users.

Grand Design

GREENVILLE'S

Afterword

As the renaissance continues to blossom, Greenville bears beautiful urban fruit. The media continue to heap praise on the city by the Reedy, and the city's future looks brighter than ever. Success, however, brings new challenges. Community togetherness, innovation, and leadership can do much to maintain its beauty and livability. And if they do, all roads will continue to lead to Greenville, that city of grand design, that resort by the Reedy.

Greenville's *Grand Design*

Profiles in Excellence

Biographies of the organizations whose generous support of this work made it possible.

◄ A bronze likeness of former Mayor Max Heller
stands as a tribute to Greenville's revitalization.

Though listed alphabetically here, biographies of
organizations appear in the book in the order in
which they were established in Greenville.

Furman University

Engaging the Challenges of an Ever-Changing World

Furman University and Greenville share a history that dates to 1851 when the university staked its position along the Reedy River on land now occupied by the South Carolina Governor's School for the Arts. Today, Furman is a flourishing nationally renowned private liberal arts university that is widely lauded for the engagement of its students, top notch faculty and beautiful campus.

Some of the university's most notable alumni have been Greenville natives: former South Carolina Governor and U.S. Secretary of Education Richard Riley, Nobel Prize winner Charles Townes, physicist and color television pioneer Thomas Goldsmith and Federal Judge Clement Haynsworth among them.

EDUCATING FOR LEADERSHIP

Furman enrolls more than 2,700 undergraduate residential students representing 46 states and 53 foreign countries. Approximately one-fifth of these students are from South Carolina. The university also offers a range of enrichment, adult degree and professional certification programs that provide educational opportunities for people of all ages. Ninety-six percent of Furman's faculty have attained the highest degree in their respective field.

At the center of the university's rigorous academic program is a commitment to challenge students to think critically, to evaluate and create, and to view challenges and opportunities from multiple perspectives. This is achieved by an intentional and deliberate process of engagement inside and outside of the classroom that leads to meaningful engagement with the broader community.

Pointing to the success of the university in achieving its mission are some remarkable statistics:

• Furman has a job and graduate school placement rate of approximately 96 percent after graduation
• The university was recently ranked 81st among 1,500 U.S. schools in the percentage of graduates continuing their studies to earn doctorate degrees in the first decade of the new millennium.
• Furman's four-year graduation rate is greater than 80 percent, the highest in South Carolina.
• Six out of 10 graduates are working in some business-related field, including marketing, accounting, finance and public relations.

Those numbers, along with the exceptional learning environment, led U.S. News & World Report to rank the school as the top private university in South Carolina.

A CENTER FOR LEARNING

Outside the classroom, Furman has a vibrant student life program that includes 150 student organizations and focused on a variety of interests including academics, religion, the arts and politics. The university fields 18 NCAA Division I athletic teams and 23 intramural and club teams.

The University is led by President Elizabeth Davis. She was inaugurated as the school's 12th President in March, 2015 and is uniting the university behind a shared vision that calls for Furman to become more deeply embedded in the Greenville community.

While Furman's primary mission is dedicated to undergraduate education, the university is truly an educational center that serves people from pre-school age to retirement. Furman spon-

▼ Furman President Elizabeth Davis talks with Lindsay Eddy, a member of the Furman Class of 2016.

sors a Child Development Center; degree programs for working adults and graduate students; professional development for business and corporate leadership; a sought-after state Diversity Leadership workshop through the Richard Riley Institute for Government, Politics and Public Leadership that boasts nearly 2,000 graduates; and one the nation's largest Osher Lifelong Learning Institute programs.

A PROUD HISTORY

The university was founded in 1826 and is the oldest private university in South Carolina. Its namesake, Richard Furman, was a clergyman considered the most important Baptist leader before the Civil War. He served as pastor of the First Baptist Church in Charleston, and became the first president of the Triennial Con-

vention, the first national body of Baptists in America.

The South Carolina Baptist Convention established Furman's original campus in Edgefield, South Carolina, but over the next three decades, the campus changed locations three times before moving to Greenville in 1851. Originally founded as a men's academy and theological institute, the theological school broke away from Furman in 1858 to become the Southern Baptist Seminary.

In 1924, Furman was named one of four collegiate beneficiaries of the Duke Endowment whose grants sustained the university through the years of the Great Depression. Those endowments also helped the university coordinate with Greenville Woman's College in the 1930s, and bolstered the university's effort to pursue

a new campus location. Furman broke ground on its current location north of its home city in 1953. The school would also become independent in 1992, breaking ties with the South Carolina Baptist Convention. In 2000, Furman became the primary beneficiary of the estate of Greenville native John D. Hollingsworth.

Furman's leafy, beautifully landscaped campus has been ranked as one of the most beautiful in the world. A signature of the 750-acre site is a Florentine bell tower that chimes on the hour and watches over a spring-fed lake. The campus also features an Asian Garden, the Place of Peace (a Buddhist temple that was relocated from Japan), a replica of Henry David Thoreau's cabin, an 18-hole golf course and 13 miles of paved and wooded trails.

▼ Furman fields 18 men's and women's varsity sports.

Serving the Upstate Since 1874

▲ The Greenville News daily publications, as well as community weekly papers like the Tribune-Times, are printed and distributed from the production facility on Wade Hampton Blvd.

▼ Daily newsroom meetings allow journalists to monitor real-time stats and community discussion, review the current day's news and plan for upcoming features.

South Carolina and much of the South were still working through the painful years of Reconstruction in 1874 when the first copy of what is now known as The Greenville News rolled off the presses. A.M. Speights established the News as a small four-page, four-column daily journal to serve the almost 5,000 residents of Greenville. In those days, Speights' paper carried

more advertising than news. The annual subscription cost was $8 and records indicate that the paper's daily circulation during its first year in existence was fewer than 300 copies.

During the next quarter-century, as Greenville became known as "the textile center of the South," the News saw several different owners until B.H. Peace purchased controlling interest of the paper in 1919. A native of Spartanburg, South Carolina, Peace brought his talent for printing and business in general to the operation and eventually purchased the News. Peace's leadership, assisted by his sons,

ushered in a period of stability and prosperity that led to the paper being recognized as a leader in the Greenville area.

Peace and his sons also bought The Greenville Piedmont, the city's afternoon newspaper, in 1927. Upon the death of his father in 1934, Roger C. Peace became president and publisher of the Greenville News-Piedmont Company. His was the guiding hand as the newspaper company grew and expanded.

In 1954, the News-Piedmont purchased the daily newspapers in Asheville, North Carolina, an acquisition which included

Asheville Citizen-Times-owned radio station WWNC. Southeast Broadcasting Company, the Asheville Citizen-Times Publishing Company, and The Greenville News-Piedmont Company merged in 1968 to form Multimedia, Inc.

The Gannett Company, Inc. purchased Multimedia in 1995 ushering in yet another era of growth and opportunities for increased service to the people of the Upstate.

Today, The Greenville News is the Upstate's largest media organization, providing news, information and in-depth re-

porting to more than 265,000 adults across the region each week. The News has grown to a multi-platform media provider, offering The Greenville News print and electronic edition seven days a week and the 24/7 GreenvilleOnline.com site. For readers on the go, GreenvilleOnline is available via mobile and tablet platforms.

The Greenville News also serves the surrounding communities with weekly publications Pickens County News, Tribune-Times and Greater Greer News, as well as with monthly magazines Upstate Parent and TALK Greenville.

The business-to-business team, The Greenville News Media Group, provides local and regional businesses with marketing solutions utilizing The Greenville News publications and website, as well as a full suite of digital marketing options, including web site design, email marketing, video production, social media marketing, and SEO and SEM.

A LEGACY OF SERVICE

More than 300 Greenville News employees call the Upstate home. The Greenville News is deeply rooted in not only informing the community, but making it a better place to live, work and play.

A long-time fixture on Main Street in downtown Greenville, The Greenville News building stands in the middle of a vibrant business and entertainment district. While the current iconic building is no longer conducive for a next generation media company like The News, the company has plans to remain downtown and occupy a new, state-of-the-art facility.

"The Greenville News has been an integral part of the fabric of the community for more than 140 years. We strive every day to serve the greater good of Greenville and the Upstate. Our commitment to the community and the role we play in championing change in Greenville is one we take seriously," stated Dave Neill, President & Publisher, The Greenville News.

▼ The current Greenville News building anchors the south end of Main Street and has been home to newspaper operations since 1968.

Haynsworth Sinkler Boyd, PA

Providing Solutions to Complex Legal Problems

It comes as little surprise that businesses and companies with a national and international reach, including CSX Transportation, DuPont, GlaxoSmithKline, Marriott Corporation, Sonoco, and a host of others, have looked to the law firm of Haynsworth Sinkler Boyd, P.A. for legal representation they trust and depend on. The 115 lawyers of the firm are proud to represent a diverse clientele,

▲ Harry J. Haynsworth – HJH and William A. Williams open a law practice in 1887.

►▲ Miss Jim Perry – first woman to be admitted to practice law in South Carolina.

▼ Haynsworth & Park.er law offices (1888).

including a wide array of public and private, for-profit and non-profit entities, ranging from Fortune 500 companies to small and emerging businesses.

While the law firm as it exists today dates to 2001 when the Haynsworth firm merged with the Sinkler and Boyd firms, the history actually dates back to 1887 when Harry J. Haynsworth opened his law office in Greenville. Over the years, through growth and mergers with other leading legal firms in the area, Haynsworth Sinkler Boyd lawyers built a long, proud tradition of public service and involvement in civic, educational, professional and legal activities.

Many attorneys in the firm are actively involved in a variety of roles, including several who run cities and work to keep the pro-business climate in the Southeast. Among them are:

• The mayor of Greenville and the corporate counsel for the City of Charleston

• The former chair of the South Carolina Chamber of Commerce board
• A Greenville shareholder is president of the National Association of Bond Lawyers
• A Columbia shareholder was nominated by President George W. Bush for a seat on the U.S. Fourth Circuit Court of Appeals
• Current General Counsel for the Greater Greenville Chamber of Commerce
• Four Liberty Fellow Scholars

COMBINING PEOPLE AND TECHNOLOGY TO PROVIDE SOLUTIONS

Haynsworth Sinkler Boyd attorneys realize that people and the unique challenges they face in their personal and professional lives are the heart and soul of their business. They also understand the changing landscape of technology and transforming information to provide fast, dynamic and thorough legal service to their clients. The firm's technology decisions and applications are driven by client needs and expectations for cost effective service. The firm's technology investment is utilized to supplement its most valuable asset, the Haynsworth Sinkler Boyd attorneys, to ensure they remain client focused and driven to successful results.

Haynsworth Sinkler Boyd attorneys, practicing in offices in Greenville, Charleston,

Columbia, Florence, and Myrtle Beach, South Carolina deliver legal services in business and litigation practice areas ranging from administrative and regulatory law, utilities regulation, and tax and estate planning to medical malpractice, intellectual property, restructuring and insolvency, and others.

The law firm's managing partner Boyd B. (Nick) Nicholson, Jr. said, "Our firm has deep roots in Greenville, and we are proud to have served and to continue to serve this community through client service, public service and volunteer service. Haynsworth Sinkler Boyd has collaborated on public projects such as the Swamp Rabbit Trail, Bon Secours Wellness Arena, and ONE City Plaza. In addition to the local companies, both small and large, that we have represented over the years, we are proud to have assisted many foreign companies in establishing a presence in Greenville. Our firm's main purpose is to help our clients achieve their goals."

—Photo by Paul Ringger

Grand Design

Leadership and Service to the Upstate

When the Greenville Chamber received Four-Star Accreditation from the U.S. Chamber in March of 2015, the organization achieved a milestone reached by only 200 of the 7,000 chambers of commerce nationwide. That accreditation attests to the vision and groundbreaking work of the Chamber's founders and their legacy that the present leaders have embraced and advanced.

▼ The Honorable Merl Code has dynamically emceed the Chamber Annual Meeting for more than a decade.

▶▲ The Greenville Chamber's Accelerate initiative takes on high-level economic development strategies designed to increase community prosperity. Accelerate Co-Chair Toby Stansell presents strategies to Investors.

For more than a century, the Greenville Chamber has been the hub of the city's vision for the future. Founded in 1889, the Chamber is the epicenter of building Greenville's economy and has been for its entire history. The Chamber has fostered new ideas and new organizations and has been practical in its search for answers to current problems and farsighted in its plans for the future.

Building Greenville's Economy

Major projects of the Chamber in the early 1900s included bringing the American Cigar Factory to Greenville to diversify the city's cotton-centered economy and encouraging the development of the Municipal League, which worked for beautification and sanitation. The Chamber helped local merchants avoid bankruptcy and business failure during the depression of 1907 and recruited outside businesses and industries to the area by publishing an illustrated guide to the city in 1911.

In 1929, the Chamber turned its attention to aviation, successfully bringing passenger and airmail service to the city. Members also began lobbying for a federal building and a new city hall, and they celebrated the

completion of Shriners Hospital. Post-World War II plans included working for a veteran's hospital, expanding Greenville General Hospital, and establishing a naval reserve armory.

In the 1950s, the Chamber celebrated the opening of Memorial Auditorium, saw Main Street become the Upstate's retail center, and cooperated with the

Greenville-Spartanburg Airport in 1962.

During the 60s, 70s, 80s and 90s objectives were set to help diversify the economy as the textile industry was changing through automation and off-shoring. GE's location in the mid-1960s and Michelin's arrival in the early 1970s brought additional manufacturing job

and Visitors Bureau both began with Chamber leadership in the 1980s and have continued to function on their own.

The business landscape changed again in 1992 when BMW Manufacturing announced its first North American facility next door in Spartanburg County. That first announcement promised 600

◄▼ The Greenville Chamber was awarded 4-Star Accreditation by the U.S. Chamber in 2015. Left to right: David Lominack/Chamber Board Chair-Elect and Accreditation Committee Chair, Pamela Gregory/ Manager, Southeast Region at the U.S. Chamber of Commerce, Julie Godshall Brown/Chamber Board Chair, and Ben Haskew/Chamber President/CEO.

county and state in establishing Greenville Technical College. Combined efforts of volunteers and staff brought Bob Jones University to Greenville in 1947, and the Chamber's deepest continuing interest was the opening of

opportunities. About a decade later, Michelin would locate its North American Headquarters in Greenville.

The Greenville Central Area Partnership and the Convention

jobs. Today BMW employs 8,000 with major suppliers accounting for many more jobs. In 2003 Clemson University began construction of its International Center for Automotive Research with part-

▲ The Greenville Chamber began its Presidential Series in 2015, inviting candidates to speak to and meet with local constituents. April Stagg and Elizabeth Edwards meet former Florida Governor Jeb Bush.

The Annual Greenville Chamber Night at Fluor Field with The Greenville Drive's traditional Tug-of-War between Leadership Greenville classes.

Grand Design

▼ The Greenville Chamber helps promote new businesses and celebrate milestones with ribbon cuttings and other business celebrations. Maserati Lotus Greenvile ribbon cutting ceremony.

ners BMW, Michelin, and others to provide research facilities and train the next generation of graduate-level automotive engineers.

Other developments in the 1990s included the Peace Center for the Performing Arts and the

Bon Secours Wellness Arena, as well as the establishment of the South Carolina Governor's School for the Arts and Humanities in downtown Greenville.

The 21st century has seen the Chamber as a major supporter of the establishment of the

Clemson University International Center for Automotive Research in Greenville. As the new millennium continues, focuses of the Chamber moving forward will be the support of entrepreneurialism, high-tech businesses, and a strengthening workforce.

A POWERFUL VOICE FOR GREENVILLE TODAY

The Greenville Chamber today is at the center of helping entrepreneurs start and grow high-impact companies ranging from software to life sciences to advanced manufacturing. Service to existing business and industry is also at the forefront of the Chamber's mission.

To accomplish its mission, the Chamber's leadership has initiated a five-year plan designed to continue enhancing Greenville's economy through the implementation of five strategic objectives:

• Growing new company headquarters

◀ Annual Meeting–The Greenville Chamber's Annual Meeting draws an attendance of 1200+ interested in the progress of the business community and to celebrate the accomplishments of many annual award recipients.

includes thirteen chambers of commerce dedicated to advancing a public policy agenda aimed at protecting and enhancing the business climate. This program is highly regarded by legislators, business leaders, and other business groups in the state.

With more than 2,300 business investors, the Chamber is the largest organization of its type in Upstate South Carolina. The staff totals twenty-six with specialists in economic development, diversity and inclusion, governmental affairs, leadership development, communications and education/workforce. According to Chamber President and CEO Ben Haskew, the organization also gains strength from its volunteer leadership. "Greenville has been fortunate for all of its history to have engaged leaders from the private sector involved in making a difference for this community," Haskew noted. "While our staff is small, active Chamber investors now number in the hundreds, all working together to make this community a special place to live and work."

- Increasing the number of and the performance of minority-owned businesses
- Continuing an environment that is both pro-business and pro-community
- Leading new transformational projects

- Selling Greenville to the Millennial generation.

While the Chamber primarily serves the greater Greenville area, many of its programs impact the region. The Upstate Chamber Coalition, managed by the Greenville Chamber,

▼ The Greenville Chamber presents an annual Business Fair for Investors to promote their businesses.

GREENVILLE'S

Where Christ Makes the Difference

In the foothills of the Appalachians, on the slopes of Glassy Mountain, lies the community of Tigerville, South Carolina, home to the 400-acre campus of North Greenville University. NGU provides exceptional opportunities for higher education in a biblically sound, Christ-centered environment. The University strives to prepare students to become better, contributing members of society by educating the whole person through the integration of academic discipline, a Christian lifestyle, and an enriched cultural experience.

Founded in 1892 as a non-government academy by private individuals, NGU evolved over the years to its position today as a co-educational liberal arts institution affiliated with the South Carolina Baptist Convention. The University is accredited by the Commission on Colleges of the Southern Association of Colleges and Schools, and awards Bachelor, Master, and Doctoral degrees. In addition to the main campus in Tigerville, NGU operates the Fairview Campus in Greer, South Carolina and the Tim Brashier Center in Greenville, South Carolina. Graduate programs are offered at these two sites.

NGU is consistently highly ranked in US News & World Report's list of "Best Colleges." The University also received top honors as the most efficient school among Regional Colleges in the South in an exclusive U.S. News analysis that compared spending and educational quality.

The fundamental purpose for which NGU was founded has remained constant over the institution's nearly 125 years of service: to provide a quality educational experience in the context of genuine Christian commitment. It fulfills its mission by presenting distinctive, innovative programs that attract and meet the needs of students. NGU also achieves high academic standards through the employment of qualified professionals and by furnishing appropriate educational support services to its enrollment of more than 2,600 students.

A VISION OF SERVICE

With exceptional leadership, NGU has grown from an all-time low enrollment of 329 in 1991 to today's 2,600 undergraduate, graduate, and doctoral students. Incoming freshmen host a "Make A Difference (MAD) Saturday" each fall to assist area non-profit organizations with various service projects. Students lend a helping hand to the elderly with their landscaping and housework, assist at nursing and children's homes, and provide free car washes. The University's Baptist Student Union sends out Impact Teams every week during the semester to assist local churches with D-Now and other children-and youth-related events. In addition, the school sends out over 500 students annually on missions to places all across our globe during the summer and the school's fall and spring breaks.

A rarity among many institutions of higher learning in the United States, NGU requires each and every member of its faculty and staff, from entry-level hourly employees to Vice Presidents, to be professing believers in Jesus Christ. Additionally, each employee is expected to maintain a lifestyle consistent with Christian moral standards. "North Greenville University offers something unique to its students. We strive to integrate Christian principles into quality higher education," said Dr. Randall Pannell, NGU interim president.

"We want our graduates to have had the best opportunities for spiritual growth and academic training and to be ready for a lifetime of Christian service."

▲ Over 87 percent of Pre-Med/ Biology graduates applying to medical schools have been accepted.

▼ Todd Prayer Chapel.

Grand Design

Day & Zimmermann

A Strong and Steadfast History in Greenville

▲ Rick Domyslawski, Executive Vice President, responsible for Day & Zimmermann's Engineering Services.

▶▼ Day & Zimmermann is the #1 ranked O&M contractor in the U.S. Power Industry.

▼ A values-driven company, safety is our number one corporate value.

Day & Zimmermann has been an integral part of the Greenville community for more than 20 years and services a growing portfolio of Fortune 500 companies and leaders in the power, process and industrial markets. Greenville is home to more than 400 employees who support the company's engineering, construction, and maintenance business.

"We made a strategic decision to locate in Greenville because it offers a diverse economy, skilled workforce, and a superior quality of life," said Rick Domyslawski, Executive Vice President of Engineering Services. "This is a great location for us to service our many customers in the Upstate and throughout the Southeast."

The company history and customer base extend well beyond the city's borders. Day & Zimmermann is a family-owned company founded more than a century ago. Its first work was to develop "Betterment Reports" that helped modernize American factories. Day & Zimmermann is still in the business of betterment. We specialize in construction & engineering, staffing and defense–helping leading corporations and governments make the world a better place.

Over the last century, we helped construct the Panama Canal, put men on the moon, and brought the Olympics to American households. Today, we're maintaining the nation's power infrastructure, protecting American freedoms, and driving technological advancements around the world. Behind every project is our promise of relentless reliability–we do what we say, so our customers can do their best work, better.

Day & Zimmermann employs 23,000 people at 150 locations worldwide and continues to deliver innovation and efficiency to its customers around the globe. The Greenville office is one of three Regional Design Centers that provide engineering services to clients in the chemical, advanced manufacturing, petroleum refining, and food & beverage markets. Greenville is also home to the company's open shop maintenance and construction group,

the largest craft labor employer in the Southeastern U.S.

"Day & Zimmermann is the top-ranked O&M contractor in the power industry and we are working with all of the major utility companies in the Southeast," said Guy Starr, President, DZ Atlantic. "Our location in Greenville is attractive to customers who benefit from our close proximity, and it is attractive to employees who appreciate the warm climate and quality of life that Greenville offers."

The nature of Day & Zimmermann's work requires access to skilled craft labor. The company's large industry footprint in Greenville and surrounding communities, and its zero injury safety program, enhances its ability to attract and retain exceptional talent. However, the company recognizes the impact the retiring Baby Boomer generation has on the industries it

serves and is working diligently to provide solutions to ensure a prosperous future for its customers and the communities where it operates.

The U.S. Department of Labor reports that the Baby Boomer generation will reach age 65 at the rate of about 8,000 people per day through the year 2029. This group is moving out of the workforce at the same time the U.S. construction industry is facing a critical shortage of skilled labor. In South Carolina, an estimated 1.7 million jobs for welders, I&C technicians, electricians, pipe fitters, and valve technicians will need to be filled in the next two to three years.

Day & Zimmermann is tackling the problem head-on by partnering with technical schools in South Carolina and throughout the country to develop training programs to prepare workers for careers in the engineering, construction, and maintenance industry. Day & Zimmermann is determined to get the word out to the community about the kinds of jobs that are available.

"Skilled craftspeople are in high demand throughout the country and often can command a six-figure salary," said Mr. Starr. "There is plenty of opportunity for rapid advancement as the Boomers retire. Trade and vocational programs typically take less time to earn a certification, which gets the person into a paying job faster. This is a very attractive option for a lot of people."

Through a number of recruitment, training, and job placement initiatives, Day & Zimmermann is helping workers learn trade skills so they can enter the workforce both in South Carolina and across the country. The company has partnered with

trade schools developing curricula, providing instructors, and recruiting students for job openings. Some of the local trade schools the company works with include Florence-Darlington Technical College, North Georgia Technical College, and Tri-County Technical College.

"Vocational programs can facilitate long-term career advancement," says Mr. Starr. "We have a number of people within our own organization who have come up through the trades to hold leadership and executive management positions. If you're dedicated to being a life-long learner, there are plenty of opportunities for growth. It will take a full industry-wide effort to solve this worker issue. We are committed to doing our part to find new talent so that our customers have the services they need to grow their businesses."

GROWING WITH GREENVILLE

Greenville consistently ranks among the fastest growing cities in the nation and the fastest growing city in the state. For two

decades, Day & Zimmermann has been committed to growing with Greenville and has become a dependable business partner in the community.

As the company looks towards its future, it hopes to expand into new markets while continuing to serve its existing customers in the power and industrial sectors. Its location in Greenville will continue to give it a key competitive edge. Combined with its efforts to build a more robust skilled workforce, Day & Zimmermann is well positioned for success.

"Since our founding in 1901, our mission has been to make Day & Zimmermann the preferred provider in the industries its serves," said Michael P. McMahon, President of the company's Engineering, Construction & Maintenance business unit. "Our customers associate Day & Zimmermann with safe delivery and excellent execution. Our Greenville location is part of our long-term growth strategy and an ideal location for our future business plans."

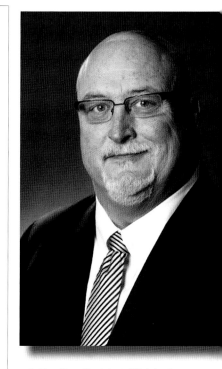

▲ Guy Starr, President, DZ Atlantic, responsible for Day & Zimmermann's Open Shop Construction Services.

▼ The Greenville office is one of three Regional Design Centers serving customers nationwide.

Grand Design

—Photo by Paul Ringger

G R E E N V I L L E ' S

Duke Energy—South Carolina

An Industry Leader in Providing Efficient Energy Solutions

As the largest electric power company in the United States, Duke Energy is at the forefront of new beginnings. We're investing in more efficient power plants, renewable energy, smart grid technologies, and innovative energy efficiency programs and services.

But while Duke Energy is a company that knows where it is going, we're also one that never forgets the people and the events that got us where we are today.

For many decades, Duke Energy has managed its South Carolina operations from its regional headquarters in Greenville. Of the more than 720,000 retail customers in South Carolina, Greenville County is our largest customer base, and we have been instrumental in recruiting, retaining and serving some of the largest manufacturers in the Upstate. More than 4,000 employees and 3,000 retirees live in and support communities in the Upstate and across South Carolina.

Duke Energy's history began with the Catawba Power Company in the early 1900s. Three visionaries, Dr. W. Gill Wylie, James Buchanan Duke and William States Lee, founded the company to spur economic revival of the Carolina countryside. They felt the South's heavy dependence on agriculture was prohibiting growth of other industries. By developing an integrated electric system of hydro-powered generating stations, they envisioned linking customers by transmission lines and creating new opportunities for economic growth.

They took the first big step toward this goal in 1904 when the first power plant, Catawba Hydro Station in South Carolina, began providing electricity to Victoria Cotton Mills in Rock Hill. Over the next several years, the company's hydroelectric fleet continued to grow to serve not only commercial textile mills, but also the region's growing appetite for the conveniences that electricity could provide.

The company's leaders also felt strongly about giving back to the communities they served. Their strong philanthropic commitment advanced the region's quality of life by funding health care and education in the Carolinas. It's a tradition that lives on today through the Duke Energy Foundation.

By the mid-1950s, Duke Power was looking ahead to nuclear power as a clean, safe and economical alternative for meeting growing electric energy needs. The first nuclear project, the Keowee-Toxaway Project, was launched in 1965. The project added the company's first nuclear plant and a pumped-storage hydro plant. The Oconee Nuclear Station was completed in seven years at a cost of less than half the industry average. Today, six of the company's eleven operating nuclear units are located in South Carolina.

Today, energy is about more than keeping the lights on. The twenty-first century electric company is a technology company disguised as a utility – identifying, integrating and scaling up new technologies that make electricity cleaner, more reliable and affordable. Duke Energy is poised as an industry leader in sustainable innovation, providing solutions that help its customers and communities thrive and grow.

▲ Duke Energy traces its beginnings to 1904 when the company's first power plant, Catawba Hydro Station, began providing electricity to Victoria Cotton Mills in Rock Hill, S.C.

◀▼ Our crews are some of the best and safest in the business. They work hard to make sure that your service stays on – 24/7. Most customers don't give it a second thought, and we wouldn't have it any other way.

▼ Oconee Nuclear Station is located on Lake Keowee in Oconee County, S.C., eight miles north of Seneca, S.C. Unit 1 began commercial operation in 1973, followed by units 2 and 3 in 1974.

Grand Design

199

Serving the Upstate for More Than a Century

The City of Greenville had been chartered for only 43 years when City Hospital, forerunner of today's Greenville Health System, opened in 1912. Originally an 84-bed facility with a training school for nurses, the hospital grew to keep pace with the city that was fast becoming known as the "Textile Center of the World." Name changes and expansions over the years reflected the

▲ GHS Children's Hospital offers more pediatric subspecialties than are found at most major U.S. medical centers.

▼ In addition to housing a four-year medical school, GHS has 15 fellowship and residency programs.

expanded scope of services the hospital was providing to Upstate South Carolina.

By the 1960s, the small hospital that had opened a half-century earlier had grown to become Greenville Hospital System, and in 1982 Greenville Memorial Hospital became the state's largest acute care facility. Greenville

Hospital System officially became Greenville Health System (GHS) in 2013.

GHS locations—hospitals, physician practices, urgent care centers and specialized facilities—are conveniently positioned throughout the Upstate. With eight campuses, there is a GHS site to meet the needs of everyone:

- Greenville Memorial Medical Campus
- Patewood Medical Campus
- Greer Medical Campus
- Simpsonville Medical Campus
- North Greenville Medical Campus
- Laurens County Medical Campus
- Oconee Medical Campus
- Baptist Easley Hospital (of which GHS is 50% owner)

GHS is the state's largest not-for-profit healthcare system and an advocate for healthy living initiatives, such as LiveWell Greenville, the GHS Swamp Rabbit Trail and Greenville B-cycle, the city's new bike share program. GHS also serves as a health resource for the community and a leader in transforming the delivery of healthcare for the benefit of the people and communities served.

"Greenville Health System is dedicated to being part of the social fabric of this great community," said Michael Riordan, GHS' president and CEO.

"This means not just striving to deliver the right care, at the right time, in the right place and at the right cost, but also ensuring that the communities we serve benefit financially, socially and educationally."

GHS' commitment to medical education has also advanced over the years, most notably with the recent opening of the University of South Carolina School of Medicine Greenville on Greenville Memorial Medical Campus. This medical school is focused on transforming healthcare delivery by training physicians to connect with communities, patients, colleagues and technology in a new, more progressive way.

Today's Greenville Health System is more than just buildings. It is a multi-faceted group of physicians, nurses, teachers, researchers and other highly skilled, highly specialized medical professionals committed to providing the best possible healthcare for a healthy lifestyle. From preventive medicine and routine procedures to ongoing treatment and complex surgeries, GHS is equipped with the expertise and facilities to help patients achieve total health.

Transforming Care for People & Communities

As a public not-for-profit academic health center, GHS is committed to medical excellence through clinical care, education and research. That commitment requires unparalleled, compassionate treatment in a multitude of medical disciplines:

HEART & VASCULAR INSTITUTE

The mission of GHS' Heart & Vascular Institute is to provide the highest quality, most efficient cardiovascular care for our patients. Through collaboration and a commitment to excellence, we care for patients in the Upstate and throughout the region.

CANCER INSTITUTE

The GHS Cancer Institute brings our community the most highly skilled physicians and healthcare team members with the latest in diagnostics, treatment, rehabilitation and research options available. This institute is accredited by the American College of Surgeons Commission on Cancer and is affiliated with the National Cancer Institute. It is also accredited by the Commission on Cancer and is the only academic comprehensive cancer care program in South Carolina.

The National Cancer Institute (NCI) has proclaimed GHS Cancer Institute among the nation's best in research. GHS is the only community-based site originating in South Carolina to receive a multi-million dollar award from NCI to conduct clinical trials and research studies aimed at improving patient outcomes and reducing health disparities.

ORTHOPAEDICS/NEUROSURGERY

Whether a patient is undergoing orthopaedic surgery, orthopaedic trauma surgery, hand surgery, orthopaedic oncology, rehabilitating from a sports injury or has neck or back pain— GHS orthopaedic and neurosurgical specialists provide the professional services needed.

PRIMARY CARE

It's important to have a medical home, and GHS has pediatric, family medicine, internal medicine and OB/GYN practices conveniently located across the Upstate. These physicians can follow a patient's health status over time and spot potential problems before they become life-threatening.

PEDIATRIC CARE

GHS Children's Hospital has board-certified physicians who care for over 360,000 infants, children and adolescents annually. From primary to specialty care, they are dedicated to providing outstanding medical care for every child and to serving not only the patients' well-being, but also the well-being of their families.

REHABILITATION

Roger C. Peace Rehabilitation Hospital is part of Greenville Health System. The aim of Roger C. Peace is to promote improved function and health of individuals with physical and/or cognitive impairments.

A VISION FOR THE FUTURE

The 15,000 employees of GHS continue to transform healthcare for the benefit of the people and communities we serve. While the present GHS is a far cry from the 84-bed building that opened in Greenville more than a century ago, the original mission and vision of those founders will remain the same – to heal compassionately, teach innovatively and improve constantly.

"GHS' vision is to transform health care to benefit the people and communities we serve," said Jim Morton, chairman of the GHS Board of Trustees. "With help from our many ter-

rific community partners, GHS provides educational opportunities such as Safe Kids™ Upstate and physician panels and wellness opportunities like the Minority Health Summit."

▲ GHS Clinical University is a unique partnership with Clemson University, Furman University and the University of South Carolina.

▼ GHS women's health services will expand to Patewood Memorial Hospital in 2016 with breast health and OB/GYN procedures.

Love to the Rescue

▲ J.T. Glisson (pictured with philanthropist W.W. Burgess) was 5 months old when he became the first patient at Greenville Shriners Hospital. Glisson reportedly continued treatment to correct his Club Feet until age 9, spending three to six months each year at the hospital and away from his home in Florida.

▼ Club Foot, which occurs in approximately 1 out of every 1,000 live births, has been treated by the skilled physicians at Greenville Shriners Hospital since the hospital first opened more than 80 years ago. Today, the hospital's Board-certified orthopaedic surgeons treat more than 80 conditions.

The course of countless lives was changed on September 1, 1927 when, due to a generous donation from Greenville businessman W.W. Burgiss along with the financial support of the Duke Foundation and Hejaz Temple, Shriners Hospitals for Children®—Greenville opened its doors. The $350,000 medical facility's mission, then called Shriners Hospital for Crippled Children, was to provide expert orthopaedic care. It would be the fourteenth in an eventual network of twenty-two medical facilities first opened by Shriners International in 1922.

What continues to make Burgiss's philanthropic gift noteworthy is that the Greenville facility remains the only hospital in the Shriners system built through majority funding of a third party.

Today, Greenville Shriners Hospital is the only free-standing children's hospital in the state of South Carolina, and continues to provide exceptional orthopaedic specialty care to children, regardless of the family's ability to pay.

UNCOMPROMISING COMMITMENT TO EXCELLENCE

By the late 1980s, it became apparent that the facility had outgrown its original home and the hospital was moved to a new location on West Faris Road. Throughout its history, the state-of-the-art Greenville Shriners Hospital has remained dedicated to its three-fold mission of treatment, education and research.

World-class pediatric specialty orthopaedic care and services are offered to children up to age eighteen if, in the opinion of the physicians, there is a reasonable possibility the child can benefit from the specialized services available. Acceptance is based solely on a child's medical needs.

The 50-bed pediatric orthopaedic facility includes two operating rooms, fifteen outpatient exam rooms, an in-house prosthetics and orthotics department, as well as a motion analysis laboratory. A team of dedicated physicians, nurses, therapists, specialists and support staff deliver the highest quality of care to children with a host of orthopaedic and neuro-musculoskeletal disorders and diseases.

A comprehensive spine program utilizes numerous options to treat all stages of scoliosis. The hospital features one of the largest Risser casting programs in the country—a non-surgical option to treat the condition.

"We focus on the way we deliver healthcare," notes Randy Romberger, the hospital's administrator. "That does not only mean having the most cutting-edge equipment and some of the best surgeons, which we do. It also means focusing on the day-to-day patient experience to make clinic visits more efficient and guaranteeing our outcomes are the very best they can be,

from both a clinical and customer satisfaction perspective."

The hospital's inpatient and outpatient units are colorful, kid-friendly and designed to put

Through its history, technology at Shriners Hospitals for Children – Greenville has been state-of-the-art. Greenville Shriners Hospital was the first in the region to offer an EOS Imaging Center, which delivers a radiation dose up to nine times less than a conventional radiography X-ray and up to 20 times less than a computer tomography (CT) scan.

patients and families at ease. Facilities include a KidZone, complete with video games, pool and air hockey tables, and a handicap-accessible playground.

"Greenville Shriners Hospital creates an environment where the kids are free to be kids," states George Thompson, the hospital's 2015 Board of Governors Chairman. "Here they are in a setting with other children with like challenges and in an atmosphere that is not only healing, but also colorful and comforting. This helps create a truly enjoyable environment."

Like all the Shriners Hospitals for Children, the Greenville facility enjoys close affiliations with several medical teaching facilities that provide a variety of educational opportunities, as well as sharing world-class doctors who are part of a total medical team dedicated to providing the highest quality of care.

Cerebral palsy, foot deformity and bone/joint malalignment are the three leading diagnosis of the more than 14,000 children who have been evaluated in the hospital's Motion Analysis Laboratory since it opened in 1994. Quantitative data provided by the analysis provides clinical insight necessary for determining the best treatment planning for patients.

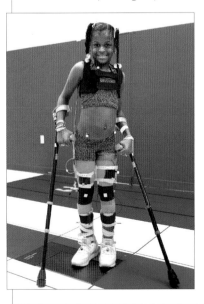

A Trusted Member of the Community

Greenville Shriners Hospital is known for offering exceptional care not only to patients in South Carolina, but to those in Virginia, North Carolina, Georgia, Alabama, and Tennessee as well. In keeping with its commitment to making that care more easily accessible, a satellite facility to serve patients in the Lowcountry and surrounding areas opened for regular service in Bluffton, South Carolina in Spring 2015.

The Bluffton facility offers services locally including post-operative visits, wound checks, new patient consultations, and follow-up appointments. Services such as surgeries, access to movement analysis laboratory diagnoses, and the benefits of the low-dose radiation EOS Imaging System remain at the main campus in Greenville. Shriners who live in the Beaufort area offer transportation to the Upstate facility at no expense to the family.

"Our goal is to take our services outside of our four walls where our patients are and where our expertise is most needed," points out J. Michael Wattenbarger, MD, the hospital's chief of staff. "We offer a multi-disciplinary approach to delivering the highest quality of care to our patients, and we want to continue to pursue ways to make it more convenient for patients to access our holistic services."

Greenville Shriners Hospital is proud of its history of service to patients in South Carolina and beyond. The legacy of W.W. Burgiss, the Duke Foundation and the 1920s visionaries of the Hejaz Temple lives on in Shriners Hospitals for Children—Greenville.

▼ Shriners Hospitals for Children-Greenville provides a fun and comfortable atmosphere for patients and visitors. The current building, erected in 1989 is home to an in-house Prosthetics and Orthotics Department, Motion Analysis Laboratory as well as Physical, Occupational and Recreational Therapy Departments.

Grand Design

Bon Secours St. Francis Health System

A Tradition of Quality and Compassion

Founded in 1932 by the Franciscan Sisters of the Poor, St. Francis transferred sponsorship in 2000 to Bon Secours Health System. The words Bon Secours mean 'good help,' but they have always been more than a name for our health ministry. These words are an ever-present reminder of our heritage and our call to serve. Here in the Upstate, Bon Secours St. Francis

provided a unique blend of quality healthcare and community service, offering an unmatched level of excellence and a caring, compassionate staff. Bon Secours St. Francis Health System continues to be recognized on regional and national levels for maintaining the highest standard of patient care and patient safety.

▼ ST. FRANCIS downtown is the flagship hospital of the health system and home of the Osteopathic Fracture Center, a national model. Consistently recognized for outstanding quality, it provides inpatient acute care, outpatient surgery, rehabilitation services, 24/7 emergency services and urgent care.

A QUALITY NETWORK

The Bon Secours Medical Group is comprised of more than 275 board-certified physicians in 70+ Upstate locations. This thriving network of healthcare professionals brings together practitioners, physicians and surgeons to offer a wide range of specialties, from primary care to highly specialized surgery.

The health system is comprised of two hospital locations—ST. FRANCIS downtown and eastside—plus a medical office building and the St. Francis Cancer Center on our Millennium campus.

ST. FRANCIS downtown, an all-private room facility near downtown Greenville, offers a complete range of comprehensive medical, surgical, diagnostic and around-the-clock emergency services. Among the top ten percent in the nation, our cardiac program maintains a door-to-balloon time that is well below the national average. A national model, our patient-centered Osteoporotic Fracture Center sets a new standard for the care of older patients with hip or femur fractures to help them

safely achieve the best possible outcomes.

ST. FRANCIS eastside serves this expansive area of Greenville with 24/7 emergency care and outpatient/inpatient surgical and diagnostic services. Designated as a Baby Friendly facility, it provides comprehensive obstetrics, with an award-wining, level II neonatal care unit and one of the Upstate's most successful lactation programs. The Pearlie Harris Center for Breast Health provides a comprehensive approach to breast health, with advanced diagnostics and one-to-one patient care. The St. Francis Joint Camp performs the most knee and hip surgeries in the state. WorkWell Occupational Health offers a single integrated source for work-related injury prevention and employee wellness proven to enhance productivity, reduce employer healthcare costs and bring a strong return on investment.

ST. FRANCIS millennium offers a holistic approach to healing with a wide range of advanced services including cardiac and oncology rehab, sports medicine and diabetes care. St. Francis

▼ ST. FRANCIS eastside is the site of the Pearlie Harris Center for Breast Health, St. Francis Joint Camp and WorkWell Occupational Health. A Baby Friendly facility, it features an innovative family centered neonatal care unit, an outstanding lactation program and natural birth options. The hospital provides round-the-clock emergency services, plus outpatient/inpatient surgical and diagnostic services.

Cancer Center is the Southeast's newest advanced cancer center combining state-of-the-art technology with compassionate care and emotional support for patients and their families. Extensive outpatient cancer treatment—infusion therapy, clinical trial research, palliative care and nurse navigation—are located conveniently under one roof.

BEYOND HOSPITAL WALLS

St. Francis HomeCare offers skilled nursing, physical therapy, occupational therapy, speech-language pathology, social work services, home health aide services, nutritional counseling, spiritual care and in-home health monitoring. Our service area extends throughout Greenville, Anderson, Spartanburg and Pickens counties. Open Arms Hospice, a ministry of Bon Secours St. Francis Health System, provides palliative or comfort care to those with life-limiting illness. Open Arms Hospice is the operating hospice for Greenville County's first and only hospice facility, the McCall Hospice House of Greenville.

And, in the tradition of the Sisters of Bon Secours, St. Francis brings health and wholeness to the communities it serves. Community Wellness Outreach brings the same level of quality healthcare services to neighboring uninsured and underinsured populations, such as Triune Mercy Center and the San Sebastian Misión. Our Mobile Dental Unit provides screenings and oral health services to individuals and families. The Pearlie Harris Mobile Mammography coach provides the same level of state-of-the-art diagnostic services to women in four counties, regardless of their ability to pay.

▲ The St. Francis Cancer Center on the Millennium campus combines leading-edge technology with compassionate care for patients and their families. A distinctive array of patient-centric outpatient cancer treatment services are centralized in one location.

◄▲ Services provided at ST. FRANCIS millennium focus on the whole patient. In addition to cardiac and oncology rehab, sports medicine and diabetes care, its in-house HealThy Self gym is staffed by medical professionals who share a passion for empowering patients to take charge of their health.

▼ Open Arms Hospice, a ministry of Bon Secours St. Francis Health System, operates the McCall Hospice House of Greenville, a 30-bed facility providing compassionate medical care in comfortable surroundings for patients in the final stages of life.

Blue Ridge Electric Cooperative, Inc.

Celebrating 75 Years of Service

When Blue Ridge Electric Cooperative was organized on August 14, 1940, only about two percent of South Carolina farms had central station power. The idea of electrifying rural America was itself a relatively young initiative, having been born just a few years earlier in an effort to bring power to homes and farms that had never enjoyed that service. Blue Ridge began

operations with 1,680 members inherited from the four-year-old South Carolina Rural Electrification Authority.

PUTTING MEMBERS FIRST

In its 75 years of supplying electricity to its Upstate members, Blue Ridge has earned an enviable reputation for its unwavering focus on providing quality, dependable service. Every aspect of the cooperative's operation is member-driven, as opposed to profit-driven. Substantial resources are devoted to maintaining the electrical-distribution system in optimal condition. In addition, employees are dedicated to delivering reliable service in ev-

ery phase of the operation. Cutting-edge technology is applied throughout the cooperative enterprise, but the human touch at Blue Ridge ensures that the member receives the highest priority. Quality service is at the heart of a cooperative organization. Blue Ridge endeavors to operate to the fullest extent possible in accordance with that philosophy.

Membership in an electric cooperative brings with it some very special advantages, not the least of which are capital-credit refunds. Capital credits are the remaining margins after all expenses for a year have been paid. The cooperative uses the annual revenues that exceed

operating costs to build equity. These funds, along with borrowed capital, allow the cooperative to continue to expand electric service to growing areas, as well as to employ new technologies for the improvement of power quality. At a later time, as the financial position of the cooperative permits, the assigned margins are then returned to the members who originally paid them as part of their electric bills.

In 2015, Blue Ridge refunded $1 million in patronage capital to those who were co-op members in 1986 and/or 1987. To date, the cooperative has paid back a total of $23.2 million.

▼ Blue Ridge Security Solutions is a wholly owned subsidiary of Blue Ridge Electric Cooperative. The company is now providing security services to more than 35,000 clients. Following the Blue Ridge tradition of unparalleled customer service, the company has set itself apart from other security providers and has made the Blue Ridge name one on which people can rely for peace of mind.

Geographically, the Blue Ridge service area encompasses more than 1,800 square miles. Terrain ranges from gently rolling farmland on the southern side of the system, to the state's most mountainous and wooded areas to the north.

Today, Blue Ridge serves more than 64,000 households and commercial/industrial establishments. Stretched across five Upstate counties, membership includes about 9,700 accounts in Anderson County; 4,700 in Greenville County; 32 in Spartanburg County;

and the remainder divided equally between Oconee and Pickens counties. The cooperative also maintains about 7,000 miles of power lines within in its service area.

Blue Ridge ranks as the fourth-largest of South Carolina's 20 cooperatives that together now serve over 750,000 members. That makes the co-ops larger than any other utility in the state in terms of the total number of accounts served. Each of these cooperatives has its own unique features, but all are member-owned and take pride in delivering the best possible service to their members.

In 1995, the cooperative established a subsidiary company, Blue Ridge Security Solutions. This regional operation has experienced rapid growth and is now ranked among the top 100 of America's 3,000 security providers. With a current workforce of 80 employees, Blue Ridge Security markets its full array of products and services to residential, commercial, and industrial customers. The preponderance of these accounts fall into the C&I category. Other major product lines include emergency standby generators and automatic gates.

An Even Stronger Voice in the Future

In 1998, Blue Ridge Electric joined with other cooperatives across the nation to become a Touchstone Energy co-op. Touchstone Energy is a national alliance of local, member-owned electric cooperatives committed to providing high standards of service at affordable rates to all customers, large and small. As independent, individual cooperatives, Touchstone Energy co-ops serve their members with integrity, accountability, innovation, and commitment to their communities. Each and every day, more than 550 Touchstone Energy cooperatives in 39 states deliver energy and energy solutions to more than 16 million members.

"As a Touchstone Energy cooperative, we're proudly united with other electric cooperatives across the country who share our dedication to delivering quality, community-minded, personal, and responsive service," said Charles E Dalton, Blue Ridge Electric president and CEO. "The Touchstone Energy brand provides us with a visible means of demonstrating and communicating to our members the competitive edge we offer as a cooperative.

"Blue Ridge Electric Cooperative exists to provide safe and reliable service to each and every member located on our network of power lines. That commitment was born on that August night in 1940, and it has grown ever stronger with the passage of time."

▼ Blue Ridge Electric Cooperative is headquartered in Pickens, South Carolina with offices in Oconee, Anderson and Greenville. Providing face-to-face opportunities to meet with its members is one of the value-added services that sets the cooperative apart.

Fluor Corporation

Designing and Building the World's Most Challenging Projects

In the early 1930s, Georgia native Charles E. Daniel used a colossal vision and a paltry $25,000 loan to found Daniel Construction Company. His mission was to help build the "New South." His masterful plan was set in motion in 1934 when operations started in Anderson, South Carolina, playing an important role in America's World War II industrial output. The company completed

▼ Charles E. Daniel, founder of Daniel Construction Company, poses in his office where some of the world's most dynamic building ideas were conceived with his namesake Daniel Building (the Landmark Building), in downtown Greenville, being chief among them.

▼ AMECO debuted its new energy efficient building, at the corner of Anderson Road and South Washington Street, in October 2014. The tool and equipment subsidiary of Fluor Corporation has called this location home since 1969. Designed to promote collaboration, the office houses 100 employees and is currently seeking LEED® certification.

numerous defense projects, including setting a world record for constructing an aluminum plant. In 1942, operations moved to Greenville, South Carolina, following the opening of an office in Birmingham, Alabama.

By the mid-1950s, tremendous growth made the company a southern construction leader. After completing industrial, commercial, and power projects across South Carolina, the company expanded, opening offices in Jacksonville, Florida; Richmond, Virginia; New York City; Atlanta, Georgia; and Greensboro, North Carolina.

Daniel's success was marked by quality construction and exceeding client expectations. "Mr. Daniel worked harder than

we did," stated Mary Neese Rubino, who worked 50-plus years with the company. "He set the pace, and we tried to keep up."

Soon, Daniel offices opened across the United States, followed by a European expansion starting in Belgium. Even with its global impact, Daniel never forgot the city that helped forge his future. In 1964, Daniel Construction broke ground in Greenville, South Carolina, on its 25-story skyscraper – later hailed as the most modern building south of Washington, D.C.

"It is my hope that Daniel Construction Company's expression of faith in a great future for Greenville in erecting the state's tallest office structure will cause others to join in building a 'new' city for the Carolinas," Daniel said.

After Daniel's passing in 1964, the company's new management transitioned Daniel Construction into a design and engineering leader. By 1971, the renamed Daniel International Corporation,

had 23,000 employees on four continents. In 1973, growth continued into Mexico, South America, France, Austria, and the Netherlands. Just three years later, Daniel offices stood in Ireland and Saudi Arabia.

A New Name, A New Vision

In 1977, Fluor Corporation purchased Daniel International. Founded at the turn of the 20th century by Swiss immigrant John Simon Fluor, Sr., the company evolved into one of the world's largest publicly traded engineering, procurement, construction, maintenance, and project management companies. Numerous governments and a long list of satisfied global clients came to rely on Fluor to deliver capital projects safely, on schedule, within budget, and with the quality they expected.

The entities merged in 1986 in what industry analysts hailed as a perfect alignment of management philosophies. As Fluor Daniel, the company grew even stronger by continuing in the power, process, government, industrial, and hydrocarbon sectors. The result was a more robust bidding position. A South Carolina gold mine contract was awarded based on the strength of the Greenville location and the expertise of Fluor's mining group, while a San Francisco biotech project was won on Daniel's experience and Fluor's robust local presence. Fluor absorbed the Daniel name in 2000, but Charles Daniel's fingerprint remains on places as nearby as the Greenville campus to far away climes such as Poland and Australia. Standing between those distant lands is a legacy of

expertly crafted design, start-up, procurement, construction, engineering, and operations and maintenance projects.

Today, the company ranks 109 on the Fortune 500 list and boasts more than 40,000 employees in 81 countries. These professionals boost the company's standing as one of the world's top contractors. Fluor was ranked Number One in Fortune's annual survey of World's Most Admired Com-

nerships led by Fluor, the Fluor Foundation, and the Fluor Cares employee volunteer program. Fluor's primary focus areas are education, social services, community and economic development, and the environment. These areas leverage the company's capabilities as a global engineering and construction company and align with its business priorities. This alignment allows Fluor to have a greater positive impact in the communities in which it operates.

▲ A hallmark of the Fluor brand is its standing as an elite global company dedicated to executing large and complex procurement, construction management, and precommissioning services. Representative of that status is Baxalta's (previously Baxter BioScience) new biotechnology facility near Covington, Georgia. The Baxter Program Covington project is located approximately 45 miles southeast of Atlanta.

▲ Over the last 25 years, Fluor's Golf for Greenville® (GFG) tournament has raised more than $3.5 million—$475,000 of which was raised last year alone. Founded in 1989 by a group of employee volunteers, GFG uses the funds to support local charities.

panies in the "Engineering, Construction" industry category in 2015 for the third year in a row. The company was also listed as one of Ethisphere's 2015 World's Most Ethical Companies. Additionally, Fluor was ranked first on Fortune Magazine's 2015 Engineering, Construction industry list of America's largest corporations.

SERVING THE LOCAL COMMUNITY

"One of the key tenets of Fluor's culture is making the communities where we live and work better places for future generations," stated Fluor Chairman and CEO, David Seaton.

Fluor's approach to community investment includes an involvement strategy set by executive leadership and implemented via programs, initiatives, and part-

Employee volunteering can be a powerful act of service for improving the lives of those in need, strengthening and transforming communities, and supporting important social initiatives. In 2014, Fluor employees volunteered approximately 41,000 hours to community projects around the globe.

Fluor also equipped nearly 47,000 students with more than 3.3 million hours of science, technology, engineering and math (STEM) academic training and enrichment by partnering with schools and youth-serving organizations in a variety of curricular and STEM outreach activities. Whether it is STEM education, $75 million given by Fluor and its employees through its employee giving campaign, or helping provide more than one million meals through meal-service providers

like Meals on Wheels, the intent has always been to give back to the communities where the company has a presence.

As Fluor grows, company leaders are steadfast in the goal to propel economies, provide employment, and raise global living standards. Through it all, Fluor Corporation remains a place where talented people help build on the strength of experience, knowledge, and skill to achieve one amazing milestone after another.

▼ Daniel helped design Greenville's downtown skyline in constructing the eight facilities in this photo to include (from left to right) the Daniel Building (Landmark Building), Phase I—First Union, Calhoun Towers, Phase II – C&S, Greenville Memorial Auditorium, Greenville County Courthouse, Greenville Commons and the Daniel Building Annex. All but the auditorium remain standing.

Grand Design

Bob Jones University

Build Faith. Challenge Potential. Follow Christ.

It began in the early 1900s when a timid vegetable-selling Alabama farm boy decided to give his life to Christ and became a spirited, Bible-heralding evangelist of international renown. Through the course of his travels, Bob Jones Sr. grew burdened for young people who were losing their faith as they went off to college. Ever a solution-oriented man, Jones directed his burden into prayer.

Over a picnic lunch with his wife, Mary Gaston, he announced that he was going to found a school—specifically, a non denominational Bible college with "high cultural and academic standards." Though she blurted out "Robert, are you crazy?", she knew her husband well enough to realize that "with him, to think was to act."

And so with counsel and assistance from his friends, Bob Jones Sr.'s vision became a reality, and Bob Jones College opened its doors in Florida in 1927. During the years of the Great Depression, BJC moved to Cleveland, Tennessee. And after World War II ended, an influx of students taking advantage of the GI Bill forced the college's leaders to

▼ Through instruction in Bible, communication, science and the arts, BJU Core develops students' critical and creative thinking with a biblical worldview.

begin searching for additional space.

The city officials of Greenville, South Carolina shared Dr. Bob Sr.'s passion for the arts and cultural experience and urged him to select their city for the school's new location. In the course of providence, Bob Jones College became Bob Jones University and welcomed students to its present home on Wade Hampton Boulevard in 1947. Since that time, the BJU family has sought to build meaningful relationships and make positive contributions within the Greenville community.

BUILDING FAITH

Through three states, the addition of six academic schools,

and four generations of Joneses, the mission of Bob Jones University remains: "Within the cultural and academic soil of liberal arts higher education, Bob Jones

▲ "In the arts, as in our other undertakings, what God has struck aglow will flame beautifully when a love for Him and a concern for His glory blaze on the altar of our lives."
—Dwight Gustafson,
A Brighter Witness

University exists to grow Christlike character that is scripturally disciplined, others-serving, God-loving, Christ-proclaiming and focused above."

In 2014, Steve Pettit, also a well-loved evangelist with Southern roots, was named BJU's fifth president and expressed his heartbeat "to focus on chapel and discipleship." Pettit's preaching is both powerful and intensely practical. He writes e-study materials on each semester's chapel theme for students' personal use as well as a tool for discussions in student-led discipleship groups. And he, along with many other faculty and staff members, can frequently be found mentoring students professionally, engaging in casual conversation along the sidewalk, or sharing stories and encouraging one another

over lunch and a tall glass of sweet tea.

CHALLENGING POTENTIAL

Academic excellence is not only a BJU mantra, but it is also a capstone of the school's reputation. BJU offers 56 undergraduate and 17 graduate programs—from fine arts and

▲ BJU President Steve Pettit connects with students one-on-one and invests daily in their lives.

communication to business and education, including terminal degrees from the Seminary. Most courses are taken on campus, but an increasing number are available through BJUOnline, including dual credit opportunities for high school juniors and seniors around the globe.

In addition to the BJU Core and classes specific to the student's chosen degree program, BJU encourages students to customize their program of study by strategically electing classes that will strengthen their individual interests and abilities.

The University's graduates consistently outperform the national average on certifying exams in engineering, accounting, education and nursing. Eighty percent of BJU premed graduates applying for entrance into medical school are accepted. That rate is over thirty percent higher than the national average.

In 2014, Educate to Career recognized BJU as the fifteenth Best Value College in America, and GSA Business ranked BJU as the tenth largest college/university and the twenty-fifth largest employer in South Carolina's Upstate region. Vicki Peek, COO at Find Great People noted, "BJU grads make a great impact as employees in companies within the Greenville community. Their values, outstanding character, discipline, hard work, and knowledge within their field set them apart."

FOLLOWING CHRIST

Students come to BJU from all fifty states and forty-eight countries to be equipped—not just for a career, but for all of life. In chapel and in classes, through positive interactions and personal reflections, BJU students grow in both character and competency.

These students, along with faculty, staff members and local grads invest themselves every day in Greenville-area churches, retirement homes, public schools and prisons. The student-run Community Service Council coordinates volunteer efforts with the Generous Garden Project, The Blood Connection, the American Heart Association and Special Olympics. The University also facilitates networking opportunities for local business professionals, provides MinistrySafe and other seminary-sponsored training events, and hosts a variety of summer camps for fifth through twelfth graders.

BJU welcomes members of the Greenville community to enjoy the rich cultural opportunities available through the Museum & Gallery and the award-winning Concert, Opera & Drama Series.

▲ Each spring, BJU partners with the Greenville County Recreation District to sponsor Washington Center Day—an inspiring day on campus, complete with a torch-lighting parade, fun athletic challenges, and tons of smile-making opportunities for all involved.

Enriching Lives Through Art Awareness and Appreciation

Part of the enduring legacy of Bob Jones, Jr. is the world-renowned art collection that complements the schools of Fine Arts and Religion at Bob Jones University. A man of many talents during his lifetime - accomplished university administrator, preacher, scholar, and actor–Dr. Jones also had a passion for art. In 1948, Carl Hamilton, a friend and an art collector himself, suggested

to Dr. Jones that he channel his interest in the visual arts into collecting paintings for an art gallery.

Dr. Jones discussed the possibility of a University Art Gallery with the Executive Committee who embraced his vision, and the Museum & Gallery at Bob Jones University was created. An acquisition fund was established and Dr. Bob was empowered to begin collecting art.

On Thanksgiving Day in 1951, the Gallery's first 25 acquisitions went on display in a two-room setting adjoining the Bowen Collection of Antiquities. The collection quickly outgrew its original home and moved twice over the years to accommodate its many additions.

By 1991, what began as two dozen paintings in two rooms has evolved into a world famous collection of religious art that now numbers more than 400 works.

Those works represent one of the largest and most interesting collections of European Old Master paintings in America. Aesthetically exhibited with period furniture, sculpture, and tapestries, these works of art from the 14th through the 19th centuries beautifully trace the religious, artistic, and cultural history of Western Europe. Included are important works of many major artists such as Rubens, Botticelli, Tintoretto, Veronese, Cranach, Gerard David, Murillo, Ribera, van Dyck, Honthorst, and Doré.

The Greenville community and visitors have always been an important focus of the Museum & Gallery. As the art collection has grown, M&G has expanded its community outreaches through special monthly events and programs for art educators, students, and all who appreciate fine art. In addition, each year M&G loans paintings from its collections to international museums ranging from the Uffizi Gallery and the Metropolitan Museum of Art to the National Gallery in Washington, D.C. and The Hague.

MUSEUM & GALLERY AT HERITAGE GREEN

In 2008 a second location, the Museum & Gallery at Heritage Green, was added in downtown Greenville. M&G uses art as a springboard and bridge to link history, literature, science, and culture that allows the collection to have a universal appeal.

Through its collection of Old Master paintings, the Bob Jones University Museum & Gallery exists to promote the appreciation, understanding, and preservation of quality fine art that enriches the whole person—mind, heart, and soul.

The collection of European Old Master paintings at the Museum is one of the largest in America. Thousands of visitors tour the Museum each year, including school children who are introduced to fine art during visits to the gallery.

Heritage Green

Culture, Education, & Art in Downtown Greenville

THE GREENVILLE LITTLE THEATRE is the oldest performing arts institution in the Upstate and has been producing popular plays and Broadway musicals since 1926. It has resided in the 600-seat Charles E. Daniel Theatre on Heritage Green since 1967. Today, it is the largest locally producing theater in the Upstate, entertaining more than 50,000. From farce to drama to comedy to

musicals both classic and modern, their high quality professionally produced shows draw patrons from the Upstate and beyond.

HUGHES MAIN LIBRARY

Located at the heart of the Heritage Green campus, the Hughes Main Library is the hub of a vibrant Greenville County Library System. Opened in 2002, the library now attracts 338,000+ visitors each year who take advantage of the extensive collection of more than 650,000 print and audio-visual items, public technology center, and one of the state's foremost regional history and genealogical collections.

GREENVILLE COUNTY MUSEUM OF ART

Home to the world's largest public collection of watercolors by iconic American artist Andrew Wyeth, the Greenville County Museum of Art also has an impressive collection of works by contemporary artist Jasper Johns. The museum's permanent collection explores the breadth of American art through the Southern experience from the colonial era to the present, including an array of works by such 20th century masters as Georgia O'Keeffe, Romare Bearden, and Andy Warhol. Changing exhibitions and challenging and fun educational offerings make every visit to the GCMA a unique experience.

UPCOUNTRY HISTORY MUSEUM—FURMAN UNIVERSITY

The Upcountry History Museum–Furman University, a Smithsonian Affiliate, is the largest history museum in the Upstate.

The museum tells the story of the Upcountry through a year-round calendar of changing exhibits and programs that preserve and interpret historical subjects pertaining to the Upcountry of South Carolina while bringing quality museum offerings from around the world to encourage people to discover the world and the Upcountry's role in it. Through an innovative and diverse program plan, the Museum has increased local and out of town attendance by 70 percent in the past year.

CHILDREN'S MUSEUM OF THE UPSTATE

Since opening its doors in 2009, the mission of The Children's Museum of the Upstate has been to spark a lifelong passion for curiosity and learning through play. Once inside this state-of the-art 80,000 square-foot facility, pure magic happens. Visitors can land a virtual space shuttle, star in a TV broadcast or even drive a formula one race car. "I Can Be Anything!" is the motto at the nation's seventh largest children's museum where you can find hundreds of hands-on activities that stir the imagination. In 2014, TCMU became the first children's museum to be named a Smithsonian Affiliate.

▲ Greenville County Museum of Art

◄▲ Les Miserables at Greenville Little Theatre

▼ Children can learn through play at The Children's Museum of the Upstate, a Smithsonian Affiliate.

▼ Upcountry History Museum –Furman University

Grand Design

213

Delivering the Ultimate Customer Experience

▲ Founder Dick Hendley during his days as a star football player at Clemson University.

▶▼ Ryan Hendley, Chairman and CEO provides the leadership and vision that guides and directs the efforts of all companies in the pursuit of delivering the "ultimate customer experience.".

▼ Erwin Carter, President of Newbold Services has shaped a workforce of experienced professionals around a foundation of strength through diversity and focused all efforts on delivering the highest level of service possible.

College and professional athletes are often disappointed when the success they achieved in their respective sports is not followed by similar achievements in the business world when they retire from the field of competition. The journey of Dick Hendley after he chose to hang up his Pittsburgh Steelers football jersey is a notable exception.

A two-sport star lettering four years in football and three years in baseball at Clemson University between 1946 and 1951, Hendley was drafted by the NFL's Pittsburgh Steelers. After only one year with the Steelers, Hendley and his wife, Lucille, and their growing family would make Greenville their home. With a houseful of mouths to feed, Hendley looked around for job opportunities.

One day while accompanying Doc Blackmon, a long time friend who worked for the local Health Department, as he made his inspections Hendley noticed that the bathrooms in one of his stops was in dire need of cleaning. Indicating this to Blackmon, his friend replied, "Why don't you offer to clean them?"

That offhand remark set in motion a string of events that resulted in the founding of a cleaning and janitorial business that today has a nationwide presence offering positive outcomes and solutions to a wide range of satisfied clients.

A SOPHISTICATED COMPANY IN AN UNSOPHISTICATED BUSINESS

Hendley founded Restroom Sanitation, Inc. in Greenville in 1955. Originally operating out of his home and the trunk of his car, he focused on cleaning restrooms in gas stations, nightclubs, and small offices. By bringing the same fierce work ethic to his business venture that he displayed on the football field, Hendley quickly grew his business to the point where he was able to hire cleaning crews. He began courting industrial clients who needed round-the-clock janitorial services and was soon expanding his services to include new, sustainable processes that result in cleaner, safer workplace environments.

A true pioneer in industrial outsourcing, Hendley began providing janitorial services to manufacturing customers who needed round-the-clock cleaning. In just a few years, Hendley's business had become one of the largest of its kind in South Carolina. His vision helped manufacturers outsource indirect jobs, such as sweepers, haulers, packers, and cleaners, and allowed clients to focus on their core business—making products—not cleaning up.

In 1980 Hendley partnered with Joel Wells, another football standout at Clemson, to take the business to its next level. He also brought his son, Ryan, onboard to learn the business from the ground up. The company's name was changed in 1984 to IH Services to reflect its primary focus of providing clean working environments for industrial, commercial, distribution, schools, healthcare, and institutional clients. Ryan assumed the role

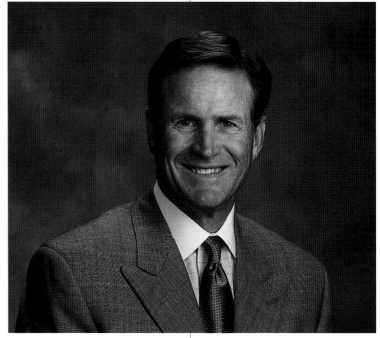

of President and CEO of IH Services in 1993.

Continued Growth and Expansion

The selection of David Ballinger in 1996 to head a new start-up company took the family business to an even higher level. Pinnacle Staffing offered clients an exclusive staffing service utilizing the most technologically advanced processes in the industry. Pinnacle provided recruitment, job assessments and skills testing, behavioral and personality testing, and competency modeling for all contracted personnel. So successful was Pinnacle's unique onsite approach that the company was selected to the Inc 500 list of "Fastest Growing Privately Held Companies in the U.S."

A subsequent move into facilities management and maintenance in 1997 under the leadership and vision of Taylor Bruce brought even more services to those already offered. Clients could now take advantage of the quality landscaping, forklift operations, overhead cleaning, painting, lighting mainte-nance, and baling and recycling that IH Services offered.

With a stellar management team at the helm of the business, IH Services continued its record of growth and expansion into the new Millennium. Gatekeeper Maintenance was brought under the company's umbrella to provide commercial real estate property managers with a one-stop service provider capable of handling the myriad issues that arise in the management and maintenance of commercial real estate, including strip malls and commercial office space. In 2007, Newbold Services under the leadership of Erwin Carter was added to the portfolio of companies as a janitorial and facilities management organization that offered customers a strategic supplier diversity solution. In 2012 Peak Workforce Solutions was formed as the newest member of the family of companies to provide a similar diversity solution to the staffing industry that Newbold Services provides to the janitorial and facilities management customer.

A Legacy for the Future

The entire staff of the companies under the IH Services umbrella and the Greenville community was saddened with the passing of Dick Hendley in 2014. The legacy of excellence he leaves, however, is indeed a testament to the vision and dedication of one man who embodied the true American success story. The small business that Hendley founded in 1955 now encompasses IH Services, Newbold Services, Gatekeeper Maintenance, Pinnacle Staffing, and Peak Workforce Solutions. Over six decades, its footprint has expanded beyond South Carolina to twenty-three states and provides employment for more than 4,200 people. The ultimate goal remains the same that Dick Hendley had for his original business – "delivering the ultimate customer experience."

▲▲ IH Services provides janitorial and facility maintenance programs for a wide range of industries all designed to deliver the "ultimate customer experience.".
▲ Pinnacle Staffing provides its customers with a customized on-site staffing solution that delivers a 21st century workforce that can compete in today's competitive global environment.

▼ The corporate office in Greenville provides customer support for over 300 client locations throughout the U.S.

The Greenville Zoo

Education – Conservation – Recreation

The Greenville Zoo serves the Upstate community by promoting an appreciation of nature and wildlife and providing a unique opportunity to participate in innovative programs for education and conservation. Upwards of 300,000 visitors a year explore the 14-acre hillside site enjoying animal exhibits set against a backdrop of plants and greenery that provide a naturalistic feel.

A division of the Greenville Parks and Recreation Department, the Greenville Zoo is small enough so that even the youngest visitors can visit every animal and exhibit over the course of a 90-minute tour through the facility. In addition, the zoo offers education programs for children and families focusing on its strong commitment to conservation, allowing families to discuss issues that affect not only themselves locally, but others around the globe.

▲ Red Pandas have been a featured animal in the Asian area for years and a breeding succes story for the Greenville Zoo.

in 1957. They selected a five-acre piece of land in Cleveland Park to bring that idea to life. The Jaycees donated $3,200 and adopted the creation of the zoo as their project.

The dream was realized when the Greenville Zoo opened to the public in 1960 with a collection of indigenous animals. New animal enclosures were constructed the following year. The collection grew to include exotic animals. In 1976, The Friends

▲ The African Overlook area opened in 2008 features the Greenville Zoo giraffe and lion exhibits.

▲ Saied is one of the zoo's male African lions, sharing the exhibit with his brother Chuma.
▶▲ The toco toucan brightens up the South American area.

"The Greenville Zoo is one of the Upstate's grand treasures and will continue to be so for generations," stated the Greenville Zoo Foundation Director, Amanda Osborne. "Like the development of Greenville, the Zoo's growth has been by design. Its development goes beyond just animals. It offers fun and educational programs for toddlers, conservation lectures for adults, and everything in between."

AN IDEA COMES TO LIFE

The Greenville Zoo began as an idea of the Greenville Jaycees

of the Greenville Zoo (now The Greenville Zoo Foundation) was established with a goal of supporting and expanding the work of the zoo.

The zoo's footprint expanded in 1982 from its original five to fourteen acres and a new Master Plan was proposed for the site. The zoo closed for construction in 1984 and reopened two years later with Phase I completed. A new Education Center, Reptile Building, Gift Shop and Concession, South American area, Primate area, and waterfowl lagoon were added.

Phase II opened in 1987 with the new Asia and Africa areas. Improvements and changes since that time have included several renovations of the elephant exhibit and the creation of the orangutan and leopard exhibits as well as the addition of the giraffe exhibit.

THE ZOO'S MISSION CONTINUES

With this strong foundation, the Greenville Zoo and the Greenville Zoo Foundation are moving forward on a new Master Plan. Developed in 2012 and approved by the Greenville City

Council and the Greenville Zoo Foundation Board of Directors, the new Master Plan will affect the entire 14-acre footprint of the zoo.

▲ The orangutan exhibit opened in 2003 and was the first new exhibit constructed since the 1985 renovation of the zoo.

as well as musical concerts, festivals, and other events and activities.

The animal areas will be expanded and more species will be featured, including endangered tigers, bears, gibbons, birds, leopards, and orangutans from Asia and Malaysia. In the African area, an expansion of the lion area will allow for the zoo to begin a breeding program. There will also be a large commitment to Madagascar and the unique animals that can only be found there.

The Blue Ridge Backyard will feature native animals and enhance the zoo's ability to educate

Behind the scenes, the zoo will be expanding its animal health clinic to keep up with the growing animal collection.

The relationship between the City of Greenville, the Greenville Zoo Foundation, local colleges and universities, businesses, and the community as a whole has been and will continue to be the driving force behind transforming the Greenville Zoo. The zoo will continue reaching out to the community to develop plans that will have a positive impact on children and families of the Upstate. Greenville is a thriving and prosperous community and the zoo has a direct link to that downtown experience.

▲ The Masai giraffes are a favorite of many zoo guests.
▼ The ocelots are part of the cooperative breeding program for these rare and endangered cats of South America.

When completed, the zoo will feature a large entry complex complete with gift shop and café designed to be accessible to park users in Cleveland Park as well as zoo guests. A large three-story South American rainforest exhibit tied to a full service restaurant and a special events center will greet guests as they enter.

In addition, a new education complex will be constructed with direct access to the parking lot for school groups. An adjacent amphitheater will also be available for large educational programs and demonstrations,

our guests on the many animals found right here in the Upstate region.

For our younger guests, the zoo will be developing a touch area that will allow them to get up close and personal with our Zoo Ambassador Animals, thus adding an educational element to their experience. There will also be an activity area for children near the entrance that will include a themed play area, a carousel, and a birthday pavilion.

"For the last fifty years, The Greenville Zoo has delighted and educated our community," noted Bill West, Chair-elect for the Greenville Zoo Foundation. "The transformation that will take place through the Master Plan will insure that the zoo remains an amazing destination for the next fifty years, as well as being a leader in species survival, conservation, and research."

◄▲ White-faced whistling ducks are a key feature in the zoo's lagoon exhibit.

GREENVILLE'S

Greenville Technical College

Advancing Skills, People, and the Economy

In 1960, South Carolina faced a critical need to build a skilled workforce in order to attract industry to the state. The South Carolina Technical College System was created, a game changing decision by the state legislature that paved the way for the future.

partnership between industry and education and a greater degree of integration between all educational providers than the state has seen before.

Manufacturing will draw strength from a new approach to the skills gap challenge, as other sectors in the Upstate continue to benefit from innovative collaborations. From four campuses across the community, Greenville Technical College works closely with employers in the health care, business, public service, and technologies sectors to see that they have a supply of skilled workers on the job and in the pipeline. Strong relationships with business, industry and community partners assist us in serving a diverse student body with varying needs and goals and allow us to build on the blueprint for success that leaders created decades ago.

Greenville Technical College (GTC) opened in 1962, creating a mechanism for advancing skills and people, but workforce development wasn't checked off the list with that launch. As the state made a successful shift from textiles to manufacturing attracting global names such as GE, Michelin and BMW, partnerships that meet the needs of employers continued to be an emphasis that saw the Upstate and South Carolina succeed and grow.

A focus on employer needs has only grown sharper over time. More than 50 years after the technical college system began, GTC's Center for Manufacturing Innovation (CMI) is a strong example of fulfilling our mission of driving personal and economic growth through learning. The CMI represents a new level of

◄ Health care employers rely on Greenville Technical College for graduates who've received a strong combination of classroom instruction and hands-on experience.

◄▼ The Center for Manufacturing Innovation will support the workforce needs of advanced manufacturing and encourage additional economic development.

▼ In technology programs, students learn skills that will allow them to earn a comfortable living by making things work.

–all photos FishEye Studios, Inc.

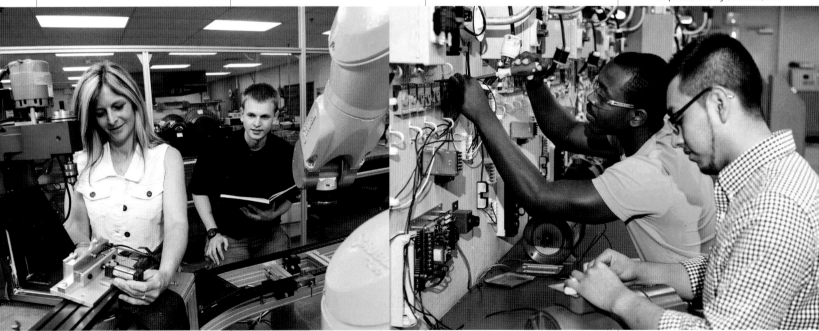

Grand Design

KEMET Electronics Corporation

Charged!

The name KEMET is an amalgamation of the words "chemical" and "metallurgy." This name represents a leading global supplier of electronic components offering customers the broadest selection of capacitor technologies in the industry, along with an expanding range of electromechanical devices, electromagnetic compatibility solutions and supercapacitors.

▲ KEMET is a leading global supplier of electronic components, offering the broadest selection of capacitor technologies in the industry. Electronic components store, filter and regulate electrical energy in anything that plugs in, turn on/ off or uses a battery. KEMET ships over 1,145 components per second.

▼ In late 1963, KEMET opened a 50,000 square foot plant in Simpsonville, SC. Today, this facility serves as its headquarters.

KEMET's vision is to continue to be the preferred supplier of electronic component solutions for customers demanding the highest standards of quality, delivery and service.

A CENTURY OF GROWTH AND EXPANSION

Just a year after the peace treaty that ended World War I was signed in Paris, KEMET Corporation was founded as a business of Union Carbide Corporation to manufacture component parts for vacuum tubes. The new company's first product was a high-temperature alloy for grid wires in vacuum tubes. In 1930, the product line was expanded to include barium-aluminum alloy getters, an essential element in vacuum tubes.

Shortly afterward, KEMET's development of automatic machinery allowed production of high-quality getters in the vast quantities needed to match the rapid expansion of vacuum tube usage. In fact, it is estimated that over 80 percent of the vacuum tubes used by the Allies during World War II contained KEMET getters.

The company continued to grow and prosper until the early 1950s when Bell Telephone Laboratories invented the transistor which would soon displace vacuum tubes in electronics.

Bell Laboratories had also invented the solid tantalum capacitor, which complemented the use of low-voltage transistors (semi-conductors) in electrical circuits. With its background and experience in the fields of high-temperature metals and alloys, KEMET changed its market focus in 1958 to the solid tantalum capacitor as the product to complement the getter product line and to provide the vehicle for the company's future growth.

That growth was rapid through the end of the 1950s and in 1963 KEMET opened a new 50,000 square foot plant in Simpsonville, South Carolina. The plant was designed from inception

as a capacitor production facility.

By the late 1960s, KEMET was clearly established as a major U.S. capacitor producer, with the leading market share in solid tantalum capacitors. In order to expand KEMET's product scope and enable its rapid growth, the decision was made to enter the multilayer ceramic capacitor business. The original plant in Cleveland, Ohio was phased out of service and all personnel and equipment were moved to South Carolina in 1971.

KEMET continued its rapid expansion, and by the early 1980s was adding plants in Mauldin, Greenwood and Fountain Inn, South Carolina; Columbus, Georgia; Shelby, North Carolina; and Matamoros, Mexico. In 1986, Union Carbide announced its decision to divest itself of businesses that no longer fit its strategic business plans. On April 1, 1987, the management group bought the company from Union Carbide Corporation and formed KEMET Electronics Corporation.

On December 21, 1990, a group of investors, including KEMET senior management and Citicorp Corporation, formed the present-day KEMET Corporation. This sale ended all ties with Union Carbide Corporation. KEMET stock, originally traded on the NASDAQ National Market System under the symbol KMET, is now traded on the New York Stock Exchange under the symbol KEM.

In 2003, the company expanded operations into Asia, opening its first plant in Suzhou, China. Beginning in 2007, KEMET expanded its tantalum capacitor offerings through the acquisition of the tantalum business unit of EPCOS AG. Further expansion continued in 2008 when KEMET entered into markets for film, aluminum electrolytic and paper capacitors with the acquisition of Evox Rifa Oyj and Arcotronics Italia S.p.A. In 2012, KEMET acquired two companies, Cornell Dubilier Foil, LLC (renamed KEMET Foil Manufacturing) and Niotan Incorporated (renamed KEMET Blue Powder Corporation) to allow for the vertical integration of certain manufacturing processes. Most recently, KEMET acquired a 34 percent economic interest in NEC TOKIN Corporation.

(continued on next page)

▲ An inside look at a KEMET organic polymer capacitor (KO-CAP). Some capacitors are smaller than a grain of salt. Capacitors are extremely useful in ultra-portable electronics like smartphones, tablets, smart watches and small medical devices.

▼ The flags in front of KEMET's headquarters represent over 9,800 employees and 30 countries in which KEMET has business operations.

Grand Design

▲ KEMET and its partners have helped establish a sustainable income from the mine for the people of Kisengo, empowering them to determine the future of their own community.

▼ Children of Kisengo line-up outside the newly built school. Over 1,800 children have had the opportunity to attend the school.

A GLOBAL CONSCIOUSNESS

Today, KEMET Electronics Corporation is a global company with its corporate headquarters in Simpsonville, South Carolina. Manufacturing facilities are located in Matamoros, Monterrey, and Ciudad Victoria Mexico; Suzhou and Anting-Shanghai, China; Pontecchio, Italy; Weymouth, United Kingdom; Évora, Portugal; Suomussalmi, Finland; Granna, Sweden; Skopje, Macedonia; Batam, Indonesia; Kyustendil, Bulgaria; Knoxville, Tennessee and Carson City, Nevada. KEMET also owns two specialty electronics companies—FELCO in Chicago, Illinois, and Dectron in Farjestaden, Sweden. Sales offices and distribution centers are located around the world.

Globally, KEMET's electronic components are used in the many millions of consumer and industrial electronic products manufactured each year. Smartphones, tablets, smart watches and small medical devices are just a few of the products that use KEMET's tantalum capacitors. These capacitors are made using tantalum powders produced from mined tantalum ore. The growing popularity of electronic products has generated an increase in demand for tantalum capacitors of various types and sizes.

Large natural deposits of tantalum ore can be found in the Democratic Republic of Congo (DRC). Sadly, this country has been the scene of constant fighting between rival factions for years. Many of these groups have been stealing and selling the country's natural resources, including tantalum, to fund their operations while terribly abusing human rights and terrorizing civilians. Companies in the tantalum industry are acutely aware of the human rights atrocities associated with conflict minerals (tin, tungsten, tantalum and gold), specifically those in the DRC and surrounding countries. The widespread use of cell phones has made tantalum a lightning rod for this issue.

As the world's largest user of tantalum, KEMET took an early leadership position in the electronics industry on the issue. Rather than avoid sourcing tan-

talum from the DRC altogether, KEMET saw an opportunity to develop a comprehensive and sustainable solution. Since 2010, KEMET has taken a leading role on the sourcing of conflict-free tantalum from the DRC, and has developed one of the electronics industry's first comprehensive, socially and economically sustainable sourcing model based on tantalum ore from the DRC; culminating in the only closed-pipe, vertically integrated conflict-free tantalum supply chain. The closed-pipe aspect of this supply chain is critical: this allows KEMET to be sure that no tantalum ore or processed products from unknown and possibly non conflict-free sources can enter the supply chain undetected. Companies looking to use tantalum capacitors for optimum performance of new designs can rely on a secure and stable long-term supply of verifiable conflict-free parts. The supply chain begins with tantalum ore sourced from the conflict-free Katanga Province of the DRC, through processing and smelting, and finishes with the delivery of conflict-free capacitors to KEMET customers: component distributors and electronic product manufacturers in all regions of the world.

To ensure that the sourcing of tantalum in the DRC remains conflict-free and socially sustainable, KEMET was instrumental in establishing the Kisengo Foundation. The goal of the foundation is to embrace lasting prosperity and security for all the involved parties, as well as demonstrate that solutions combining social sustainability and economic interests are not mutually exclusive. As a result, the KEMET initiative, Partnership for Social and Economic Sustainability, was formed. The Partnership along with the Kisengo Foundation is responsible for defining the needs of the mining village and community in Kisengo, the individual projects, and how the money is

spent. It is projected that the Partnership's social programs will be self-sustaining in the long run using proceeds from the mine output.

KEMET's financial commitment to the residents of the mining village of Kisengo supported the development of a new hospital and school, fresh water wells, solar powered street lights, and improvements to infrastructure. The hospital and school were little more than a series of thatched roof huts. Now, the hospital and school provide a much-appreciated resource for the mineworkers and the people of Kisengo. The hospital is well equipped and medical professionals from the USA and worldwide are helping to train local workers to run the hospital independently in the longer term. Since the hospital opened, over 13,000 cases have been treated. Additionally, over 1,800 children have had the opportunity to attend school.

KEMET and its partners established a sustainable income from the mine for the people of Kisengo, empowering them to determine the future of their own community. For KEMET and its customers, a closed-pipe, vertically integrated tantalum supply chain ensures a reliable supply of verifiable conflict-free parts to the global electronics industry, positively impacting the lives of the people of the village of Kisengo and the industry in general, both now and into the future.

"For more than 50 years, KEMET has had a long and productive history with Greenville," stated Per-Olof Loof, the Chief Executive Officer of KEMET Electronics Corpora-

tion. "KEMET continues to grow as a leader in research and development in the industry. I am proud that KEMET has helped secure the region's reputation as one of the fastest growing business destinations and best places to live. The quality of life, talented workforce and engagement with the community are just a few of the reasons KEMET is fortunate to be headquartered in Greenville. We are honored to be part of the Upstate, and help put the city on the map for nearly 10,000 of our employees worldwide. Because of our dedicated employees and support from the community, we have grown to become a leading global supplier of electronic components. Greenville has always been at the forefront of innovation, and together, KEMET is committed to continuing the legacy of expanding possibilities here and abroad for the generations to come."

▲ Per-Olof Loof, CEO at KEMET, visits with children of Kisengo in the Democratic Republic of Congo. Through the Kisengo Foundation, KEMET has enriched the lives of residents in this mining community with a new school, medical clinic, fresh water wells, solar street lights, and infrastructure improvements.

Mitsubishi Polyester Film, Inc.

World Class in Polyester Films

It is rare in today's business landscape across the U.S., to find a company manufacturing the same product in the same location for more than a half-century. But that is exactly what Mitsubishi Polyester Film, Inc. has been doing at its plant in Greer, a close neighbor to the city of Greenville, South Carolina. It was in 1963 that Celanese Corporation announced plans to transfer ICI's film plant from its location in Dumfries, Scotland into a Celanese plant in the Carolinas. Site selection was the project team's first task and, after reviewing several communities, the Greenville area was chosen because of the availability of well-trained employees, a strong technical education system, transportation infrastructure, proximity to other Celanese plants and the overall quality of life in the area.

Hiring at the new plant began in 1964 and about 100 employees were on site to start the 95,000 square-foot plant with two production lines. The first roll of polyester film was produced on November 5, 1964.

Today the plant employs more than 600 in a one million square-foot facility on 193 acres with a total of ten production lines manufacturing films and polymers. The company's 24-hour polyester film and polymer manufacturing processes provide a broad range of value-added performance options for its HOSTAPHAN® products through its polymer variations, inline coatings and co-extrusion capabilities. These same processes utilize on-line monitoring of process parameters and product characteristics to provide high quality products for its customers. Mitsubishi Polyester Film, Inc. is committed to its Quality Vision to provide products that meet or exceed its customer's expectations and is ISO 9001 certified.

"Constantly innovating has been and will continue to be the key to the success of our business", stated Chief Executive Officer Dennis Trice. "By keeping abreast of the changing market trends and then introducing innovative products for new emerging applications, we have been able to adjust and prosper in an ever changing global market."

Trice's comments were echoed by Mitsubishi Polyester Film's President and Chief Operating Officer Bill Radlein along with his appreciation to the city and the state the company calls home. "With our technology and the skill of our people," Radlein noted, "we always have opportunities to differentiate and bring value to our customers. And the support we receive from the Greer community and the state of South Carolina provides us with the advantages to compete in a global environment."

KNOWLEDGE AND EXPERTISE IN A GLOBAL MARKET

Mitsubishi Polyester Film, Inc. operates as a North American affiliate of Mitsubishi Plastics, Inc., part of the Mitsubishi Chemical Holding Corporation. The company offers a wide array of polyester films for existing markets such as industrial labels and liners, flexible packaging, and for many of today's emerging markets in energy and electronics.

Recognized as a global leader and one of the largest suppliers of polyester PET (polyethylene terephthalate) film in the world, with locations in Japan, Germany, Indonesia, and China, Mitsubishi Polyester

▼ Mitsubishi Polyester Film is committed to producing a quality product that meets or exceeds our customer's expectations.

Film, Inc. is proud to be the partner of choice for customers who depend on them for a wide range of high-quality customized Diafoil® and HOSTAPHAN® brand PET films. The company's knowledge and expertise can provide the perfect solution for a product design, manufacturing, logistics, or process challenge.

A COMMITMENT TO SAFETY, HEALTH AND THE ENVIRONMENT

The management team at Mitsubishi Polyester Film, Inc. believes that creating and maintaining a safe and healthy workplace is everyone's responsibility, and these values define the behaviors they use when dealing with their customers, employees, and the community.

Mitsubishi Polyester Film, Inc. is committed to World Class Environmental, Health and Safety Management Processes and is ISO 14001 and OHSAS 18001 Certified. The site has won many awards associated with safety, health and the environment. Some of the most recent include the Advance SC Manufacturing Competitiveness Grant for improvements in energy efficiency; the Tag and Label Manufactures Institute's (TLMI's) Environmental Leadership Award (2012); the Society of the Plastics Industry (SPI) Special Bronze Recognition Safety Statistics Award (2012–2014); the L.I.F.E. Label Initiative for the Environment Certification (2009-present); and the Renewable Waste Resources (ReWa) 2014 Pollution Prevention (P2) Award and Compliance Excellence Award for sixteen years

of pretreatment compliance and environmental stewardship.

The company goes an extra step in creating a healthy environment for its employees by providing on-site health and wellness programs. It is one of the first employers in the country to provide a free on-site medical clinic, exercise facility, health assessments and health coach.

A COMMITMENT TO THE COMMUNITY

You cannot operate as a company in a small community for over fifty years without having a significant effect on the community and its growth. The Mitsubishi plant was one of the first high-tech industries to locate in the Greenville area following the downturn of the textile industry helping the community not only to survive, but to grow and prosper.

Over the years the company has formed a strong partnership with the local community and has provided leadership, sponsorships and donations.

▲ Mitsubishi Polyester Film Americas' Headquarters located in Greer South Carolina is home to 10 production lines as well as its Sales, R&D and Operations Support Functions.

A Family's Imprint on the Upstate

Just two years after choosing a career in real estate, Greenville native C. Dan Joyner was ready to open his own real estate business in his hometown. Joyner launched his venture in 1964 and over the next half-century, would see it evolve into the leading real estate company in the Upstate. Joyner's original staff of three has grown to nearly 350 real estate professionals serving in ten offices across the Upstate.

▲ President Danny Joyner (left) and Executive Vice President David Crigler lead the Upstate's largest real estate company.

▶▼ Company founder, the late and beloved C. Dan Joyner.

Greenville was the logical choice for Joyner's business venture. The Joyner name has long been recognized in the area as a beloved member of the community in which the family played an integral role in numerous key community development projects.

"You can't talk about Upstate real estate without talking about C. Dan Joyner, REALTORS," states Danny Joyner, the late founder's son and president of the company. "We've probably sold hundreds of thousands of homes and helped launch successful careers for hundreds of real estate professionals. We're committed to this community and ensuring that people see it in a way that blends its South-ern charm with the economic opportunities available here."

A New Name for a Trusted Friend

The company converted from Prudential to Berkshire Hathaway HomeServices in 2014, and now carries the world's most respected brand name in addition to its strong local brand. "Our unrivaled brand power and leadership position in the Upstate sets us apart from any other real estate agency," noted David Crigler, the founder's son-in-law who serves as executive vice-president. "We achieved this market leadership position through our commitment to professionalism, our passion for quality, and our service delivered with a friendly smile. We're proud to be selling more homes than any other company in the Upstate."

Joyner and Crigler are also proud that the business they lead has been ranked among the best in its field in the Upstate and the top company in the Southern Region of Berkshire Hathaway HomeServices.

Carrying on a Tradition

C. Dan Joyner is remembered today as a giving person, and his generous spirit lives on through the company's involvement with the United Way each year. Also, in C. Dan's honor, the company participates in the annual Heart Walk for the American Heart Association. The company sponsors several community programs and events, including Artisphere, Furman Sports, South Carolina Children's Theater, Peace Center, and Summer on Augusta, to name a few. "We believe in giving to our community," Danny Joyner relates, "and encourage all our agents and associates to be involved in charitable organizations important to them."

Finding Solutions for the Toughest Challenges

From the late 19th century, when Thomas Alva Edison introduced the first successful incandescent electric lamp to the world and founded the Edison General Electric Company, GE has evolved into one of the world's most recognized names. Relying on dedicated people and cutting edge technology, over the years the company has expanded into finding solutions in areas that affect people's lives, including energy, health, aviation, and transportation.

GE Power & Water's history in Greenville dates back more than four decades with the opening of a 340,000 square foot gas turbine manufacturing plant, employing just 250 employees. GE now works in all areas of the energy industry: natural gas, oil, coal, and nuclear energy, as well as renewable resources such as wind and solar, biogas and alternative fuels.

The original site has grown into more than 1.5 million square feet of factory and offices, housing wind turbine and gas turbine engineering, services, and gas turbine manufacturing for customers worldwide. GE now has more than 3,000 employees in Greenville and, in the past five years, has invested more than $500 million to bolster critical manufacturing and engineering activities housed on the GE Power & Water campus. The company has established valuable relationships with local community schools, universities and technical programs to develop new technologies and create a system to support those who are passionate about growing with the industry.

A FAMILIAR NAME CONTINUES TO GROW

GE's relationship with Greenville and the Upstate took another giant leap forward in 2014 with the company's announcement to build the company's first advanced manufacturing facility and invest $400 million in the Greenville site over the next ten years. The new Advanced Manufacturing Works serves as an incubator for innovative advanced manufacturing process development and rapid prototyping for the Power & Water businesses, including wind turbines, heavy duty gas turbines, distributed power gas engines, nuclear power services, and water processing.

Dignitaries, including South Carolina Governor Nikki Haley and Senators Lindsey Graham and Tim Scott, hailed GE Power & Water's planned expansion. "The Greenville community has a long standing relationship with GE, and it welcomes the new GE Power & Water Advanced Manufacturing Works facility," Governor Haley said.

Senator Scott added, "Today's announcement builds on a well-established relationship between Greenville and General Electric. The Upstate continues to be at the epicenter of South Carolina's manufacturing renaissance, as our state is home to a well-trained workforce that is eager to produce world-class products."

"GE's continued development in the state demonstrates that South Carolina is a great place for business," Senator Scott noted, "and we will continue to lead in the development of innovative solutions that solve today's toughest challenges."

◀ GE's HA high-efficiency, air-cooled gas turbines are the industry leader among H-class offerings. A single 9HA.01 gas turbine in combined cycle can generate 600 MW, or enough to power 600,000 homes.

◀▼ GE Power & Water has built world-class heavy duty gas turbines at its facility in Greenville since 1968 and has earned a reputation for the highest quality and an unwavering commitment to customer fulfillment.

▼ The Greenville site is home to the world's largest and most powerful variable speed, variable load, non-grid connected gas turbine test facility. Capable of replicating a real-world grid environment at full capacity, the facility tests 50 and 60 Hz gas turbines well beyond normal power plant conditions seen in the field.

Grand Design

GBS Building Supply

By Builders, For Builders

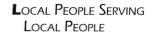

It is often said that if you want something done right, you might just have to do it yourself. Adhering to that adage, a group of ten homebuilders from South Carolina's Upstate decided in 1972 to establish their own building supply company. They reasoned that the very people who purchase building supplies would be best qualified to run a supply business. Under the leadership of R. Buford Landers,

the ten homebuilders launched Greenville Builders Supply intending the company to serve as the supply source for their own home construction needs as well as meeting the needs of area professional builders.

The founders' vision proved to be twenty-twenty. Word soon spread about GBS and the business expanded to the point where today they are meeting the needs of professional builders throughout South and North Carolina and parts of Georgia. The start-up with just ten employees has evolved into an employee-owned company with a staff of more than 100 due to strong leadership, superior customer service, and a supportive board of directors made up

▼ Bob Barreto CEO

▼ One of many 'Turn-key' kitchen solutions from GBS

of pillars of the homebuilding community.

Building on their solid foundation, the company's management continued expanding and in 2011 added enhanced products, services, and solutions to better serve their customers. Focusing, as ever, on its building-based clientele, GBS rebranded itself with additional expertise in installed sales, green products, remodeling/renovation design services, and commercial applications.

"It's our people that set us apart," stated Nick Campbell, Vice President of Sales. "GBS is a large company that acts like a small company. We have a ton of heart and determination."

LOCAL PEOPLE SERVING LOCAL PEOPLE

GBS now ranks among the largest building supply companies in South Carolina. The GBS management team is justifiably proud that much of the company's growth over the years was recorded despite the economic downturn after the Millennium. They point to their local roots as a major contributor to the company's success.

"We have been an important part of the local economy for over forty years," explained Bob Barreto, the company's CEO. "Many of our employee-owners were born, raised, and continue to live here. Everything we do is with our local economies and our customers uppermost in our minds. As the premier supplier in our service areas, we can adjust our businesses and our products to the needs and preferences of our customers. GBS is truly customer focused. We understand that their success is ours as well. When we were asked by our customers in 2011 to fill a void in our markets, we responded by launching our Commercial Division and our Cabinet Divisions. We hired the best people we could find, outfitted the best facilities available, and partnered with our customers despite the economy at the time. Our customers asked, we delivered, and we all benefited. That is the partnership that is at the heart of our culture at GBS."

BUILDING LOCAL COMMUNITIES

Professional builders look with confidence to GBS to supply all their home construction needs, including windows, doors, siding,

Community Service was followed in 2013 with a "Best Performing Large Company" listing in the SC Biz News 'Roaring Twenties'. In 2014, GBS was ranked on the Inc. 5000 list of "Fastest Growing Private Companies."

involvement," Barreto added. "It's been part of our DNA since 1972 and remains so today. We support many local organizations ranging from Boy Scouts and church groups to the local Children's Museum, Greenville Fire Department, and various charities. We support and encourage our employees to be involved in their communities

roofing, lumber and plywood, insulation, millwork, columns, moulding, cabinets, locks, decking, and much more. They also know that GBS offers unparalleled services ranging from kitchen and floor system design to a millwork center and lumber yard.

The GBS combination of quality products and personal service has been recognized with numerous awards from both the business and the building communities. Their garnering in 2012 of the Better Business Bureau's "Business of Integrity Award" for Outstanding Customer Service and Outstanding

The unwavering focus of GBS in providing the finest building supplies and services carries over to their desire to build and strengthen the communities in which they live.

"Beyond the impact our business has had on the economy of the local community, we also have a forty-year culture of community service and

as well. From our Board to our newest employee, this is the finest group of people with whom I have ever had the privilege to work."

Narramore Associates, Inc.

Four Decades of Excellence in Architectural Design

David Narramore founded Narramore Associates, Inc. in 1973 with two primary objectives uppermost in his mind: to provide quality architectural design and planning services while establishing long-term relationships with his clients. He has succeeded in accomplishing both.

A 1969 graduate of the Clemson University College of Architecture, Narramore's firm has become a leader in commercial/retail design. His first commissions included custom homes, residential additions, multi-family projects, small to moderate commercial projects, and shopping centers. Over the course of more than forty-two years of successfully completing a wide range of projects, each with unique challenges, for satisfied clients, Narramore and his staff of professionals have designed over twenty million square feet of commercial retail space and have completed projects in twenty-eight states.

The firm's success in achieving the founder's goals is demonstrated by the fact that, in addition to steady controlled growth, eighty percent of its business has been with repeat clients. There is probably no greater testament to a firm's proficiency, especially in the field of architectural design where a client puts his ultimate trust in the person responsible for the design of his business, than to be defined by that remarkable amount of work from previous clients. Although licensed to practice architecture in twenty-eight states, Narramore Associates currently has active projects in sixteen states ranging from Florida to Indiana, Nebraska, Texas, and Colorado.

Today, e-mail and the Internet are an integral part of business, but in 1985 it was new, unchartered territory. Narramore broke new ground in 1985 when the firm realized the potential of computers in architecture and was also one of the first in the area to convert totally to electronic media.

Once the exclusive domain of hand-drawn artists, modern computer technology has now made 3D models and renderings a primary graphic presentation method of Narramore Associates. In addition to 3D graphic renderings, color rendered 2D elevations have become a very effective method to study a project's potential design impact, both in regard to color as well as lighting.

A MULTI-TALENTED TEAM FOR A MULTITUDE OF PROJECTS

Each of the firm's design professionals takes great pride in their adherence to the founder's goal of providing personalized service to each client. That business tenet applies to each and every client across the business spectrum on all projects the firm undertakes:

INDUSTRIAL/HEALTHCARE

Completed industrial projects have generally involved very large amounts of enclosed space with specialized uses and requirements that had to be sat-

▶▼ Walters Hunting Lodge, Waterloo, S.C.

▼ Shealy Hunting Lodge, Lake Greenwood, S.C.

isfied both for discerning clients as well as governing authorities.

COMMERCIAL RETAIL

Since its inception, Narramore Associates has specialized in designing quality retail space for clients ranging from shopping centers, specialty centers, big box retailers, local shops, grocery and food stores, theaters, drug stores, banks, and building supply stores. From Aldi stores in Emporia, Kansas; Harrisburg, North Carolina; and Milton, Georgia to Bi-Lo stores at Bee's Ferry and James Island in Charleston, South Carolina, clients turned to Narramore Associates with confidence for design excellence. The Garner's Ferry Marketplace in Columbia, South Carolina, and Riverside Office Park in Greenville, South Carolina also carry the Narramore signature.

RESIDENTIAL

Residential projects have varied from completely custom designed homes to additions and renovations to existing homes. Every residential project presents a different set of variables that must be satisfied. The Narramore design team has always enjoyed the challenge of residential projects in addition to being able to work closely with owners during the design and construction process.

RESTAURANTS

Over the years, the firm has completed a variety of restaurant projects, both custom-designed as well as for fast-food chains. Narramore professionals have designed some of Greenville's most recognized culinary landmarks, such as Sushi Marasaki, Azia, On the Roxx, Indigo Joe's, and Fried Green Tomatoes.

ADAPTIVE REUSE

The "adaptive-reuse" of an existing building for a purpose other than its original intent has been, and remains, one of the firm's primary services to clients. In most cases, this requires extensive field investigation as well as documentation of both the building structure itself and all of its support systems. Greenville's Old Parker Hardware —Paws and Claws, Mall Center, and 215 W. Stone are classic examples of Narramore's success in this field.

"Greenville has changed substantially over the past forty plus years as it continues to grow and advance," David Narramore notes. "Narramore Associates, Inc. is proud to have been a part of its history and growth as well as its future."

▲ Freeland-Kauffman Engineers, Greenville, S.C.

◄▼ Azia Restaurant Bar, Greenville, S.C.

▼ Azia Restaurant Bar, Greenville, S.C.

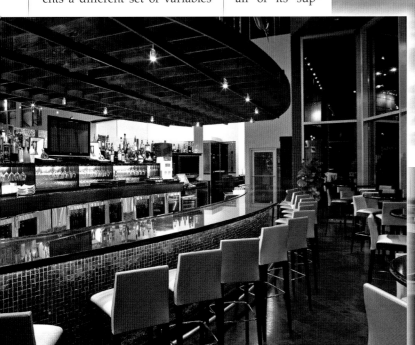

A Better Way Forward for More Than a Century

The year was 1975. Steven Spielberg's film *Jaws* was holding us spellbound in movie theaters. Saigon was about to fall to the Communists. The Watergate principals were being sentenced. And Michelin's very first radial passenger tire was coming off the line at the company's plant in Greenville, South Carolina. Part of the tire industry in the United States since 1907 when it purchased

▲ In 20112, Michelin announced an expansion of its Earthmover tire capacity in Anderson and Lexington, S.C.

▼ Michelin employees volunteer as part of the company's Michelin Challenge Education program in local schools and communities.

the International Rubber Company in Milltown, New Jersey, Michelin had grown to be a major player in the manufacture of tires and tubes with a reputation for durability and quality still prevalent today in the industry.

Michelin would continue to grow and expand through the 1930s and by the middle of the century, the company would introduce radial passenger tires in Europe and in the United States. By the mid-1960s. Michelin's worldwide growth proved phenomenal with the opening of twelve new plants and the announcement that a plant would be built in Nova Scotia, Canada in 1971.

▼ One of Michelin's largest Research & Development centers, Michelin Americas Research Corporation (MARC), is housed in Greenville.

Two major events in 1966 drew Michelin into the largest passen-

ger tire market in the world. Until that year, Michelin had been importing only small quantities of radial passenger tires to service consumers with European cars originally fitted with Michelin radial tires. Ford decided in 1966 that the 1968 Lincoln Continental Mark III would have radial tires as original equipment and Michelin was selected to be

the supplier. This was a major boost for both the acceptance of the radial tire and establishing Michelin in North America.

The second major event that made Michelin a part of the U.S. tire market occurred when SEARS went shopping for a radial tire. In an effort to get ahead of its competition and realizing the impending radialization of the tire industry, SEARS sought out a supplier and ultimately selected Michelin on the company's reputation for high quality and technical expertise in building radial tires. By the end of 1969 expansion necessitated another move to a larger headquarters.

MICHELIN'S IMPRINT IN SOUTH CAROLINA

Michelin had led a revolution in the transportation industry with the introduction of the radial tire. As the global demand for radial tires accelerated, Michelin responded with an expansion plan that opened 23 new plants, all producing radial tires. Michelin made the decision in the early 1970's to produce only radial tires and eliminate production of the old-style bias ply tires.

Two plants had been opened in Nova Scotia in 1971 and the company announced that construction would soon begin for two plants in western South Carolina. Michelin's US2 plant in Anderson would build semi-finished products to supply the

other plant, US1 in Greenville, that would produce tires. The plants opened in 1975, and just three years after the very first radial passenger tire came off the line at US1 in Greenville, a third plant, US3 in Spartanburg, came on line. That plant would produce radial truck tires for the rapidly growing radial market in the trucking industry.

Expansion in the 1970s in the U.S. was completed with the opening of US4 in Dothan, Alabama. In addition to the three plants already in operation in South Carolina, Michelin opened a research and development center in the Palmetto State.

▲ Michelin operates 10 major manufacturing sites in South Carolina.

The company's management team had always believed in developing products exclusively for a North American market where huge geographical distances demanded different tires from those in the established European markets.

The 1980s brought the challenges of consolidation and recession to the tire industry. Fully recovered from the effects of World War II, Japanese and European countries were competing toe-to-toe with American companies in a global economy. Michelin invested heavily in the expansion of its North American operations. An additional plant in Lexington, South Carolina, and one in Nova Scotia, Canada, were opened in the early 1980s. To consolidate headquarters operations and manufacturing, Michelin made the decision to relocate its North American headquarters from New York, where it had been since 1950, to Greenville, South Carolina. The doors opened at its present loca-

tion in Greenville in September 1988.

Michelin in North America now operates 20 plants in 16 locations that employ some 22,000 people in North America. With annual sales of more than \$10 billion, the company has a substantial economic footprint across North America.

The effect of Michelin's presence is felt in numerous ways beyond sales. Total capital investment is more than \$6 billion in the state of South Carolina.

In addition to the more than 22,000 people the company employs in North America, another 35,000 jobs are created outside Michelin in support businesses.Upwards of 8,900 of Michelin's U.S. labor force live, work, shop, and play in South Carolina with plants in Greenville, Spartanburg, Lexington, Sandy Springs, Starr, and Duncan.

Michelin is proud to be a major player in the state's dynamic economy and looks forward to a future of continued service to each of the communities where the Michelin sign is part of the business landscape.

▲ The Michelin Tweel was developed by a team of engineers in Greenville and named one of **TIME Magazine's** "Most Amazing Inventions of 2005".

▼ Greenville is home to Michelin's North American Headquarters.

Centennial American Properties, LLC

Building Relationships, Not Structures

One need not look far to see the imprint of Centennial American Properties on the Greenville skyline. The company's headquarters at 935 South Main Street are within a stone's throw from downtown condominiums and the stadium that is home to the city's baseball team. The Lofts at Mills Mill, with styling reflecting the cotton and textile era that once identified Greenville, offers

▼ An historic old mill from Greenville's textile heydays has been stylishly converted to 104 residential condominiums at the Lofts at Mills Mill.

the ultimate "true loft" living experience as a gated community with pool, gym, conference room, and other amenities. The Field House at West End and office buildings at Falls and Broad Street are also part of Centennial's resume.

Originally established by David W. Glenn in 1976, Centennial American Properties has successfully developed more than seven million square feet of commercial space in many of the Southeast region's most prominent and competitive markets. Throughout the company's 35-year history, the professionals of Centennial American Properties have developed, leased and managed a variety of projects, including neighborhood and community shopping centers, free-standing retail stores, specialty centers, and professional office buildings.

A COMMITMENT TO QUALITY

The success of Centennial American Properties is the result of an unwavering commitment to deliver on promises. The firm's clients and customers depend upon Centennial for the quality infused into each and every development and the firm's ability to deliver projects on time and within budget. The commitment to quality continues long after a grand opening, and this dedication is one of the reasons Centennial's clients and customers turn to them time and again for their real estate and investment requirements.

Centennial has also built a strong reputation as a real estate management firm, providing the necessary management resources to oversee the critical day-to-day operations of leasing, maintenance, and tenant services. Centennial's development expertise has uniquely positioned the firm to offer clients market research and site identification services throughout the Southeast. Retailers such as Target, Lowes, Wal-

greens, Home Depot, Harris Teeter, Publix, BI-LO, and Staples have secured excellent locations in 15 states from Washington to Virginia through the efforts of Centennial's licensed brokers.

A COMMITMENT TO COMMUNITY

In addition to its physical imprint on the region, Centennial American Properties has had a considerable impact on the Greenville area through the Glenn family's philanthropic activities that have benefitted numerous civic and charitable organizations. The family is on the "Distinguished Benefactor" list of contributors to the Greenville Health System, and was pleased to establish a scholarship at the University of South Carolina in honor of Marcus Lattimore, the school's record-setting running back. David Glenn was named as the 2015 Green Day Honoree by the Greenville Drive. A recipient of the Greenville Real Estate Award honoring companies whose commercial real estate activities have significantly enhanced the local community, Centennial American Properties is well-positioned to continue successful operations throughout the Southeast for many years to come.

►▼ The GHS/Suntrust Plaza features 170,000 square-feet of prime office space.

▼ Business offices and retail shops fill the 58,000 square feet of space in The Fieldhouse.

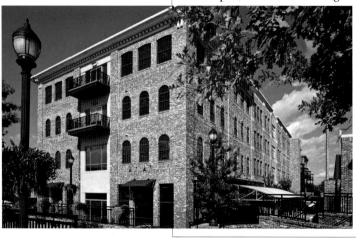

—Photo by Paul Ringger

Grand Design

Creating Innovative Technologies and Solutions

It was a natural extension of Surendra Jain's family background in textiles for him to expand that expertise into the manufacturing of textile adhesives and coatings. The native of Amritsar, India combined his knowledge and experience with a degree in chemistry from the University of Bombay and further study at the Philadelphia College of Textiles to enable him to open Jain Chem, Ltd. in 1977.

Originally specializing in the marketing of adhesives and coatings to the textiles, packaging, disposable nonwovens, and fiberglass industries, Jain later expanded his venture to include the manufacture of chemicals with a focus on developing environmentally friendly "green" products through the use of natural and recycled raw materials.

Manoj Jain, the founder's son, became the second generation of the family to enter the business. Born and raised in the Greenville area, Manoj worked with his father while in middle and high school, engaging in plant activities and learning the basics of the chemical business. Upon graduating from the University of South Carolina with a BA in Humanities and Social studies, Manoj worked in the insurance industry and later as a financial advisor.

In 2005 Manoj joined his father full time as Vice President of the company. Six years later, he oversaw the acquisition of Ulterion International, a company that primarily focused on "green chemistries" for the tex-

tile and paper industries. Manoj has remained an integral part of the Jain Chem family and now serves as President and CEO, actively managing the financial aspects of Jain Chem Ltd. and all its subsidiaries.

Today, Jain Chem, Ltd. specializes in designing customized and unique chemical solutions for its customers across the chemical industry and for related downstream businesses. The company's research and development and technical strength helps it to better understand its customers' needs while delivering performance and adding value to their products and processes. Jain Chem's product innovation strategy is focused on developing environmentally friendly, green and sustainable products. Its business philosophy is based on providing a competitive edge with Jain Chem's products and services that help differentiate its customers from the competition in the global marketplace.

Jain Chem has over three decades of experience in the production of chemical products. The company's highly qualified staff is completely customer focused and service-oriented, fully capable of designing solutions for the problems and challenges its customers face. Jain Chem's primary goal is to satisfy its customers' requirements with the highest regard for safety in our operations and our environment. The company adheres to the highest quality standards and its manufacturing facility, CPJ Technologies located in Taylors, South Carolina, is ISO 9001:2008 certified. Being in close proximity to

Greenville, Jain Chem is ideally located to supply not only its customers' domestic locations, but can deliver globally as well. Jain Chem's recent acquisition of Ulterion International has given the company a strong global presence and offers its customers a more diverse portfolio of products and services.

Jain Chem's business model is focused on building partnerships with its customers to provide them the highest level of support in their areas of interest. The company's management team understands that Jain Chem will grow and prosper only if its customers grow and prosper. They are, therefore, totally committed to supplying products and services that meet rigid quality standards while providing a safe and rewarding work environment for the company's associates.

SERVING **D**IVERSE **M**ARKETS WITH **C**UTTING-EDGE **P**RODUCTS

Jain Chem, Ltd. serves a wide range of industries and applications, including textiles, auto-

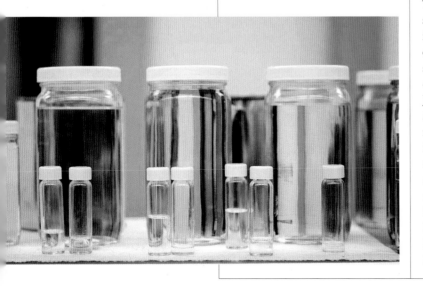

motive, paper and packaging, fiberglass, and others. The products the company provides to its customers is an indication of its imprint in those markets:

- Textiles, polymers, scours and surfacants, specialty coatings
- Binder chemistries for non-wovens
- Lubricant chemistries
- Fiberglass treatments
- Denim specialty chemicals
- PET-based polyols
- Dyeing auxiliaries

- Resins and catalysts
- Mold and mildew resistants
- Flame retardants
- Floor polish
- Adhesives
- Coatings for the paper and packaging industry

Jain Chem's broad technology know-how enables the company to leverage its manufacturing capabilities to perform a variety of chemical reactions and syntheses. Through close association with its partners, Jain Chem develops custom or exclusive products to meet their specific needs. In addition, Jain Chem has several proprietary chemistries available to meet customers' requirements.

SUPPORTING CUSTOMERS LOCALLY AND WORLDWIDE

With chemists who have decades of experience in their field comprising more than thirty percent of its technical staff, Jain Chem stands ready to provide its customers with complete support for its technical development needs. That support extends from the laboratory bench to pilot scale, to commercial scale-up, to providing technical support at the customer's facility. The goal is to provide innovative and sustainable solutions to ensure each customer's competitiveness in the global marketplace. Jain Chem's Technical Sales and Support team members are always available to help improve or optimize a customer's process, provide

cost saving ideas or provide a customized solution approach. The company's analytical lab is fully capable of troubleshooting a customer's chemical problems with state-of-the-art analytical instruments such as FTIR, GC, and other tools. Jain Chem's strength in wet chemical methods is complemented by its instrumental access, which also aids the company's product development projects.

With its cutting-edge technology, global capabilities, and

laser-like focus on customer satisfaction, Jain Chem, Ltd. is poised to remain a leader in its field and a strong contributor to the diversified economic base of Greenville.

Ogletree, Deakins, Nash, Smoak & Stewart, P.C.

Employers and Lawyers Working Together

▲ One of the founders and named partners of the firm, J. Frank Ogletree's portrait hangs in the corporate offices.

▼ The Ogletree Building is a prominent fixture on the Greenville skyline.

Businesses today are faced with myriad federal and state laws and regulations that govern the workplace. In order to comply with these laws and to provide a positive workplace, employers must dedicate tremendous resources to labor and employment law issues. The law firm of Ogletree, Deakins, Nash, Smoak & Stewart, P.C. is comprised of 700 lawyers in

more than 40 offices around the United States and abroad who work daily with employers in connection with their workplace needs. From traditional labor issues to employment litigation, to workplace safety, to employee benefits and other areas, Ogletree Deakins has experienced professionals in all areas of labor and employment law who provide efficient, client-focused service to each and every client. The firm's labor and employment law practices are complemented by thriving practices in immigration, construction, and environmental law, and commercial litigation.

A PROUD TRADITION OF SERVICE

Ogletree Deakins was founded in 1977 by eight partners and eight associates, several of whom had practiced law together since 1966. The first offices opened by the firm were in Atlanta, Georgia, and Greenville, South Carolina. The firm's Greenville office today is located, aptly enough, in the Ogletree Building on North Main Street.

Ogletree Deakins' leaders today understand what the founders realized when they opened the practice more than three decades ago: clients have choices among labor and employment counsel. They proudly point to the reasons why so many satisfied clients have chosen Ogletree Deakins:

• Ogletree Deakins represents employers of all sizes and across many industries, from small businesses to Fortune 500 companies.
• The firm offers distinguished labor and employment counsel that has been recognized as "Law Firm of the Year" in both the "Litigation-Labor & Employment and the Employment Law-Management" categories by U.S. News -Best Lawyers in their "Best Law Firms" rankings.
• More than 150 of the firm's attorneys are listed in the 2014 edition of Best Lawyers in America.
• Ogletree Deakins provides coverage through 40 offices in 27 states, the District of Columbia, the U.S. Virgin Islands, Europe, and Mexico.
• Through representative agreements with major corporations based on alternative fee arrangements structured for individual situations, the firm offers rates and rate structures that meet the needs of each client.
• Ogletree Deakins attorneys offer value added client service through multiple seminar programs, briefings and webinars for their clients. Client assessment surveys are conducted to assess and improve the performance of the firm's attorneys. Clients are updated

with newsletters and e-alerts on new developments to keep them abreast of the latest developments in their respective fields.

Ogletree Deakins is also constantly striving for improvement in the firm's internal processes through such initiatives as Legal Lean Sigma training for key firm leaders and administrative staff, and development of best practices for efficiently and effectively handling employment litigation and discovery.

A COMMITMENT TO DIVERSITY

Ogletree Deakins is proud to have a tradition of professional development, diversity, and inclusion. In its more than 40 offices, lawyers of diverse gender, age, race, ethnicity, national origin, gender identity, marital status, sexual orientation, and physical abilities have significant positions of responsibility. These positions include a seat on the Compensation Committee and more than a dozen managing shareholders of our offices.

The firm's partners believe that professional development, diversity, and inclusion are integral to the outstanding performance and exceptional client service for which Ogletree Deakins is known. It is this commitment to having a highly talented, vibrant workforce that reflects the growing diversity of our communities and our clients.

We believe that such a workforce is able to contribute unique perspectives and creative approaches. This, in turn, generates the highest quality of legal service and serves the needs of our clients and the communities where we live and work.

"Our firm has its roots in a bold decision that the sixteen original Ogletree Deakins lawyers made 35 years ago," states Kim F. Ebert, Ogletree Deakins' Managing Shareholder. "That was to leave a law firm dictatorship and establish a new model to service clients. The principles adopted in those early days of the firm remain core values of our firm today: premier client service; teamwork and collaboration; treating each other with respect; hard work; and open governance. These core values permeate the firm's culture and are the bedrock upon which we build our diversity and inclusion initiatives."

PEER RECOGNITION

Ogletree Deakins was named for the fourth year in a row "Law Firm of the Year" in the Labor Law-Management category in the 2015 edition of the U.S. News-Best Lawyers "Best Law Firms" list. In addition, the firm maintained its national "First Tier" practice area rankings in six categories.

"We are honored to be named a U.S. News—Best Lawyers 'Law Firm of the Year' for the fourth consecutive year," Kim Ebert noted when the rankings were announced. "Our continued selection for this honor underscores the firm's steadfast commitment to providing our clients with outstanding service and value." In 1984, two young engineers founded an electrical consulting group in Greenville with a primary focus on superior client service, delivered with quality and integrity. The founders, who had begun their careers in Greenville, selected the city because of its reputation as a center of engineering excellence.

▲ The Dedication and Ribbon-Cutting for the Ogletree Building was an exciting day for the firm's founders and employees.

▼ Pictured are many of Ogletree, Deakins, Nash, Smoak & Stewart, P.C.'s founding shareholders, some of whom had practiced together as early as 1966.

Bradshaw, Gordon & Clinkscales, LLC

Accounting Services for the Upstate for More Than Three Decades

The roots of the accounting firm that would become Bradshaw, Gordon & Clinkscales (BGC) go back to 1980 when Greenville native Del Bradshaw sought to fulfill a dream of owning his own business by opening an accounting office in his own hometown. Bradshaw launched his business with no clients, but saw his firm quickly evolve into something far beyond anything he had ever dreamt.

—Photo by FishEye Studios
▼ Del Bradshaw works diligently to provide excellent service to his clients.

—Photo by FishEye Studios

▼ The firm has been at home in downtown Greenville since 1984.

Bradshaw was joined over the next four years by Mike Gordon and Roger Clinkscales who shared the founder's vision and passion for making the lives of their clients easier by improving the bottom lines of their businesses. Originally they focused on providing accounting services to individuals and small to mid-sized businesses.

As their reputation for excellence grew, the firm expanded its size and its range of services. They were joined over the years by Andy Foth, Susie Repko (now retired as partner), Dell Baker, Roger Duncan, Peter Tiffany, Mandy Satterfield, Sandy Watkins, Laura Foster and Ellison Smith, all of whom shared the same dedication to excellence as the firm's founders.

Additional managers and staff allowed for further expansion. Today, the professionals at BGC help individuals, small to mid-size companies and large corporations with their decisions relating to accounting and taxation issues. While serving small to mid-size companies continues to be the bedrock of the firm's business, their clients today include large companies with more than $50 million in revenue.

While the company has experienced phenomenal growth over its three decades of existence, its goal has remained the same: to provide the highest quality auditing, accounting, tax, management consulting, litigation and business valuation services to each and every client.

"We are totally committed to promoting client prosperity, community involvement, internal harmony, staff fulfillment and quality service while continuing to expand our client base," explains Peter Tiffany. "That means we're more than just number crunchers offering commodity services. Our clients choose us and stay with us because they know that we stand beside them to offer solutions and help solve problems regardless of size. And we are constantly striving to improve what we do."

A Trusted Partner

Accounting services, like clothing, are not a one-size-fits-all package. The accounting professionals at BGC understand that each client is different and faces unique challenges requiring highly personalized tax and accounting services. Their strength is their ability to form strong partnerships with their clients to assist them in navigating the often confusing waters of bookkeeping, income taxes, payroll, auditing, management consulting, litigation, and business valuation.

Another strength is the depth of experience of their team members, 19 of whom are certified public accountants. That experience allows them to meet the needs of larger, more complex businesses while maintaining the personal contact that clients expect. They provide that elusive combination of small firm

—Photo by FishEye Studios

"feel" with larger firm resources and capabilities.

Bradshaw, Gordon & Clinkscales professionals provide a wide range of highly personalized services for individuals and businesses in several distinct service areas:

- Audits of financial statements for various industries

- Compilation and review of financial statements

- Advice on financial statements and accounting issues

- Employee benefit plan audit services

- Internal control studies

- Implementation of new accounting standards

- Forecasts and projections

- Preparation of corporate, partnership, LLC, individual, estate, gift and trust tax returns

- Federal and State income tax examination and appeals representation

- Sales and use tax analysis and examinations

- Exempt organization applications and returns

- Planning and projections

- Monthly bank reconciliations

- General ledger bookkeeping and analysis

- Quarterly and year-end payroll returns, W-2s and 1099s

- Sales and use tax return preparation and compliance

- Reporting for household employee wages

- Business license preparation

- Accounting software consulting, implementation and training

- Business valuations for management use, divorce, estate and gift or transactional purposes

- Litigation support services and expert testimony

- Forensic accounting

BUILDING ON GREATNESS

Bradshaw, Gordon & Clinkscales is proud to be among the largest accounting firms in Greenville, but they are prouder still to be an integral part of the social fabric of the Upstate of South Carolina. The firm's partners and employees demonstrate

their commitment to community service in numerous ways, from supporting civic and charitable organizations ranging from Hands on Greenville, the Meyers Center, and Habitat for Humanity to the Boy Scouts, Rotary Club, Meals on Wheels, and others.

"Even though Mike Gordon is retired and Roger Clinkscales recently passed away, we are proud of the legacy they started and to have pooled together a very talented and dedicat-

▼ Peter Tiffany chats with a client in his Greenville office.

—Photo by FishEye Studios

ed group of people who have helped our firm and our clients grow along with Greenville," Peter Tiffany notes. "We are very excited to see what the next 30 years brings to Greenville and to our firm."

▼ The firm's partners pictured (left to right) are Peter Tiffany, Mandy Satterfield, Ellison Smith, Laura Foster, Del Bradshaw, Sandy Watkins, Andy Foth and Dell Baker..

—Photo by Carol Stewart

Grand Design

Automation Engineering Co.

Three Decades of Automation Precision

Automation Engineering Company (AEC) was founded in Gaffney, South Carolina in 1981 by an engineer with a focus on automation, controls and integration. The organization moved to Greer in 1989 and relocated to its current Greenville location in 2002. When a company has to supply tires, steel pipes, fiber, carbon or other products to their customers,

Automation Engineering receives the call. "We enjoy the challenge of helping a company

design and build the equipment that takes raw materials through a manufacturing process to produce a final product, " says John Malsch, Partner and Vice President of Sales.

"If a customer can develop a product, we will develop the electrical controls, the mechanical processes and the equipment to make more."

"Greenville has been a substantial hub for business growth in South Carolina", says Donna Rauch, CEO. And Automation Engineering is an integral part of that growth."

Automation Engineering, a leading provider of industrial automation equipment for manufacturers worldwide, has been engineering design-build solutions since 1981. "We are unique in that we have strong capabilities to design it, build it here on site in Greenville and install wherever the customers are," Malsch says.

"We have equipment working all over the world, including China, India, Poland, France, Canada and Brazil, among others. We realized the other day, the only continent that doesn't have AEC equipment is Australia!"

John Fisher, Director of Business Development, adds, "AEC designs, manufactures and installs complete industrial automated equipment—each system tailor-made to the customer's specific requirements. It's important to us to have exceptional support after the installation, too. We expect to have a long-term relationship with our customers. As they grow, so do we."

AEC is also in tune with the growth of manufacturing here in the state of South Carolina, as well. "We are excited about what's been happening all around us," says Donna Rauch, CEO. "We've met with the South Carolina Department of Commerce and those folks do an outstanding job connecting business to business. Our projections for 2016 and beyond will focus on being a more integral part of what's around us, from growing our current local relationships to being in on the ground floor when new companies decide to make South Carolina their home."

Jennifer Mann, Director of Marketing, has been tasked with increasing AEC's footprint in South Carolina, "AEC has a lot to offer our customers, our community and our employees," says Mann. "We received the 2014 Award for Best Places to Work in South Carolina as well as the Michelin Vendor Performance Award. We have a great partnership with Clemson

University and hire engineering students through their Co-Op Program. Building on an established footprint won't be hard."

Brooke Bowman, Global Channel Partner Director, is working to develop partnerships that allow AEC to provide more effective delivery of a quality product. "We find that when we have relationships that produce a turn-key solution to our customers, it's a 'win-win' all the way around. We are not re-inventing the wheel with our suppliers, and many of our supplier relationships are really synergistic with the customers we serve. We are always looking for new partnerships with the same quality and delivery philosophy."

"We've spent the last couple of years adding fabrication and build-work centers in the plant," says Matt Kelley, Plant Manager. "We invested in new equipment and systems and are continually looking for state-of-art technology. I am proud of the skilled craftsmen we have on our staff. It's impressive to see raw materials come in and then trucks shipped out with tons of equipment that will make fiber, tires, plastics and other products. Further, to see the equipment come to life at the customer's site is something else."

Over the next three decades AEC evolved into one of the foremost automation and integration companies in the Upstate of South Carolina serving many larger production companies, including Michelin, Bosch, Timken, Alcoa (Howmet Castings), GE Nuclear Energy, and others. Its position in the marketplace today is that of a leading provider of industrial automation equipment for manufacturing companies throughout the United States and in Canada, Japan, China, India, Romania, France,

England, and Central and South America, many of them Fortune 500 companies.

AEC provides mechanical and electrical engineering design for factory automation systems, especially high-end industrial automated handling systems. AEC engineers produce custom fabricated machinery and control panels and complete electrical and mechanical installation and startup. Each system is tailor-made to the client's specific requirements.

Not only does AEC provide great custom material handling equipment, the company's engineers and staff offer exceptional service and support that are unmatched in the industry.

AEC team members seek to reduce equipment maintenance cost, optimize energy efficiency, improve operator safety and minimize operational noise in the machinery the company designs, installs and supports.

BEHIND EVERY MACHINE . . .

While AEC's reputation is built on the design and construction of custom material handling equipment, the company's leadership understands that the foundation of AEC's thirty year old success story is its people: talented, passionate, driven individuals with an eye for precision and a commitment to the highest standards of engineering for finishing room material handling equipment.

The AEC team today is composed of more than fifty professionals operating from a single story, 55,000 square foot facility. The building is air conditioned throughout, which is unusual for a traditional manufacturing plant. Mechanical design, control system engineering, fabrication and assembly take place

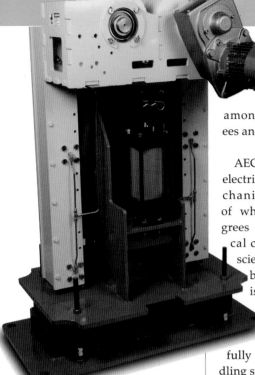

on-site, allowing maximum collaboration among the company's employees and with its customers.

AEC professionals include electrical, chemical, and mechanical engineers, several of whom hold advanced degrees in engineering, physical chemistry, and computer science. They are supported by highly skilled machinists, welders and fabricators who have produced some of the most intelligent, low impact, fully integrated material handling systems.

The "can-do" attitude, flexibility and adaptability of AEC employees allows the company to design and build the most intelligent, fully-integrated material handling systems, taking precision automation equipment solutions to new levels.

AEC hand selects a team for each project from start to finish, bringing a wide array of skills and expertise to each customer's unique challenges. By housing all project disciplines on one campus, AEC is able to deliver optimal integrated solutions on time, on budget and to specifications.

Beyond the economic benefits of AEC's low impact handling system design improvement process and the reliability of its solid machine design concepts, what sets AEC apart from the competition is the company's collaborative approach with its customers to deliver an effective custom-built solution.

AEC team members understand that from the front door to the shipping dock, each industrial facility is different. Whether working from new site plans or within an existing plant with physical restraints, AEC finds a way to reduce congested zones, reconfigure underutilized areas and improve material flow.

AEC's highly skilled professionals can perform a production flow analysis to examine both product and processing requirements, delivering maximum performance for each individual client.

GIVING BACK TO THE COMMUNITY

In fulfilling its mission to serve as a good corporate citizen in the community it calls home, AEC supports numerous local charities, including Greer Community Ministry's Meals on Wheels program. The company also offers a cooperative (co-op) learning program primarily with Clemson University that provides students with hands-on work experience in the fields of design and manufacturing engineering. Through the company's university partnerships, what is taught in the classroom

is applied to practical work experience.

AEC participates twice a year (spring and fall) at the Clemson University co-op fair during which some twenty potential co-op students are interviewed. These students spend a total of three semesters at AEC where they work in manufacturing, design and engineering to hone their practical work skills. They have the opportunity to learn the design processes and acquire valuable "shop time"

working with industrial components, which includes the fabrication, machining, and assembling of AEC machinery. Students are then tasked to complete their own engineering calculations, subassemblies, and design reviews. By the end of the training, students are functioning as project engineers. Once students graduate, they may be candidates to join Team AEC full time. Most of AEC's mechanical engineers are hired from this pool of co-ops once they have finished their education at Clemson.

AEC's thirty years of serving a wide range of customers has led to a series of impressive accolades, including the "Salute to Manufacturing's Silver Crescent Award" that recognizes outstanding manufacturers in South Carolina based upon economic impact, commitment to workforce, and involvement and contributions to their communities.

"AEC will continue to provide the best engineered equipment for handling the Upstate's manufacturing needs for the next 34 years and beyond," said Donna Rauch.

Grand Design

Crowne Plaza Greenville

Greenville's Prestigious Address for Business and Leisure Travel

With a population of more than 850,000 people, the Greenville-Anderson-Mauldin Metropolitan Statistical Area (MSA) is the largest in South Carolina. And Greenville, located halfway between Atlanta, Georgia and Charlotte, North Carolina, is the largest and fastest growing city in that MSA. It is imperative, therefore, for a city such as Greenville, the largest in the 10-county "Upstate" region of northwestern South Carolina, to have a hospitality facility commensurate with its impressive credentials.

The Crowne Plaza Greenville meets that need.

WHERE SOUTHERN HOSPITALITY MEETS MODERN FUNCTIONALITY

The Crowne Plaza Greenville is conveniently located directly off the city's I-385 inner loop eight miles from the Greenville-Spartanburg airport. The hotel is also just minutes from Greenville's vibrant uptown entertainment and dining district, the Bon Secours Wellness Arena, and TD Convention Center. Just up the street is the Haywood Shopping Mall. Anchored by Belk's, Dillard, Macy's, JC Penney, and Sears, and featuring 150 specialty shops including Apple, Banana Republic, J. Crew, and others, The Mall is a favorite shopping destination of the Upstate.

In 2012, Rialto Capital Management, LLC, a major real estate developer, purchased the hotel and engaged Valor Hospitality Partners, a professional hospitality management firm to manage and operate the Crowne Plaza Greenville. In 2013 the hotel went through a $5 million dollar total renovation that included all 202 guest rooms, the lobby and public spaces. The investment was recognized by members of the Greenville Chamber of Commerce, local dignitaries, and esteemed guests at the Crowne Plaza Greenville's ribbon cutting on January 9, 2014.

The Crowne Plaza Greenville's new look, feel and design provide an atmosphere of sophistication, style, comfort, taste and distinction. The stylish new rooms, great lobby, lounge and bar, fitness facilities and the warm caring attention from the staff provide the new gold standard for today's travelers.

Each of the 202 deluxe king and double bedded rooms and two executive suites features the Crowne Plaza's Sleep Advantage seven layer beds and TempleSpa amenities. There is also complimentary wireless high-speed internet access in all guest rooms and public spaces and a variety of cable channels to enjoy on the high-definition flat screen TV's in all guest rooms. The 24-hour business center, with remote printing capabilities, is very convenient for business travelers. Guests will also enjoy the hotel's 24 hour fitness center for a vigorous work out and can unwind in the indoor heated saline swimming pool.

Complimentary airport transfer service is offered from six a.m. until eleven p.m. daily. Local shuttle service is also available within a five-mile radius of the hotel on a first come first serve basis. The Crowne Plaza Greenville offers ample free parking for cars and motor coaches.

Nationally renowned Ruth's Chris Steakhouse provides all food and beverage service throughout the hotel, including room service, banquets, and in the hotel's new lobby bar and all day dining room that features six large flat screen TVs. Guests also have the option to visit the Ruth's Chris Steakhouse's main dining room located in the hotel to enjoy their famous mouthwatering, custom-aged beef broiled to perfection.

▲ The Crowne Plaza Greenville offers a relaxing cosmopolitan atmosphere for both business and leisure travelers.

▶▼ Open 24/7, the fitness center provides a mix of aerobic and weight training machines.
▼ The heated indoor saline pool is a year 'round source of fun for children and families.

THE CROWNE PLAZA GREENVILLE WILL PUT THE WOW FACTOR INTO YOUR NEXT BIG EVENT

In addition to its laurels as the city's top choice for leisure travelers, the Crowne Plaza Greenville has established its reputation as the area's preferred host for business meetings, banquets, and social events. The hotel's extensive renovations included 7,200 square feet of first-class meeting and banquet space, including a 4,200 square foot Metropolitan Ballroom that accommodates up to 500 people.

team understands that helping you successfully orchestrate all of the little details leads to a truly unforgettable event," said Greg Greenawalt, the Crowne Plaza's General Manager.

Ever attentive to the needs of meeting and event planners, the hotel's meeting specialists offer a unique Two-Hour Response Guarantee. Each call for a quote on meeting/event space is guaranteed to receive a response within two hours and a proposal by the next business day. Event planners can enroll in the IHG Meeting Planner Busniness Re-

• Furman University; Bob Jones University; Wofford College; and Clemson University
• Greenville Zoo
• Liberty Bridge and Falls Park
• Fluor Field at the West End— home of the Greenville Drive Baseball team
• Swamp Rabbit Trail—17.5 miles of beautiful walking and biking trails

The perfect place to stay when visiting these attractions or attending a special event is Crowne Plaza Greenville.

▲ The lobby bar and all-day dining room serves breakfast, lunch and dinner as well as a selection of your favorite beverages and appetizers seven days a week.

▲ With over 7,000 square-feet of meeting and banquet space, the hotel can accommodate events with 10 to 500 guests.

▲ The hotel's professional event-planning team will help put the "Wow-factor" in your meetings and conferences.

The Crowne Plaza Greenville features meeting space that includes ten meeting rooms and two new executive boardrooms with executive style seating. Banquet food and beverage service is provided by the experienced chef and attentive staff of Ruth's Chris Steakhouse.

The hotel has the ability to dedicate up to 100MB of internet bandwidth to its meeting space for seamless Wi-Fi connectivity.

"Event and meeting planning is more than just blocking space and guest rooms at a hotel. It's about the details that inspire a memorable experience for your guests. At the Crowne Plaza Greenville, our professional

wards loyalty program and receive three points for every dollar spent on qualified meetings at The Crowne Plaza Greenville.

The City of Greenville offers a plethora of historical, cultural, educational, and scenic attractions:

• BMW Zentrum featuring exhibits of classic BMW cars and motorcycles.
• The BMW Performance Driving School
• Roper Mountain Science Center
• TD Convention Center
• Bon Secours Wellness Arena
• The Peace Center—Greenville's cultural and performing arts center

▼ The hotel offers 202 newly-remodeled king and double-bed guest rooms with free Wi-Fi and HD cable television systems.

DeVita and Associates, Inc.

Excellence in Engineering

DeVita & Associates provides professional Mechanical, Electrical, Plumbing, Structural, and Precast engineering services to meet the specific needs of client for projects large or small. The DeVita team offers a commitment to innovation and a proven ability to engineer great ideas, backed by professionalism and the energy that sustains long term relationships.

▲ River Pier Landing, Chattanooga, Tennessee.

►▼ Research Park Innovation Center, Clemson University.

▼ Anthropologie, various locations.

Over the years, clients have discovered the important qualities that have become the hallmark of the professional services provided by the DeVita team.

First is the firm's intense focus on client satisfaction by hiring, training and retaining excellent people, often from excellent local educational institutions such as The Citadel, Clemson University, the University of South Carolina, and Greenville Technical College. Second is a keen awareness that excellent service requires operational excellence. In particular, DeVita focuses on project management and seeks to develop client-interfacing skills in all its staff members.

A RECORD OF SUCCESS

DeVita & Associates is understandably proud of its impressive portfolio of projects completed successfully for a wide range of satisfied clients.

DeVita has contributed to the area's rich automotive heritage, providing engineering services to a variety of automotive suppliers such as Plastic Omnium, Inergy Automotive, Pirelli, Draexlmaier, and many others, as well as to large full-service area automotive dealerships such as Fletcher BMW and Jim Hudson Toyota.

In the education sector, DeVita has provided services for scores of Greenville County School projects including precast design and detailing services for approximately 400,000 square feet of solid panels, insulated brick panels, tees, beams, columns and flat slabs for a five-phase project at Eastside High School.

Community projects include mechanical, plumbing, and electrical design services for fire stations throughout the state which include company living quarters, training and support areas, and emergency operations centers. System designs include energy recovery, solar water heating, and high efficiency lighting.

DeVita & Associates has also provided design services for some of the area's most prominent sites:

- Commercial Office – Administrative Office at Patewood for Ogletree Deakins Law Firm
- Engineering Center – GE Innovation Center
- Retail & Restaurant – Methodical Coffee, Mark's on Main, and City Range

- Mixed use – Camperdown Redevelopment (Greenville News site)
- Light industrial/Distribution - Marley Lilly Office and Production Space

These and numerous other projects, including work on the Peace Center, various area libraries, the 18,000 square foot St. George Greek Orthodox Church and the renovation of the 19th century Newberry Opera House, have cemented DeVita's reputation as one of the Upstate's premier engineering and design specialists.

The DeVita management team takes very seriously their responsibility to serve as good corporate citizens, repeatedly obtaining "Best Places to Work in South Carolina" status from the South Carolina Chamber of Commerce. In addition, DeVita & Associates has participated in the design of numerous local pro-bono projects over the years, including the Ronald McDonald House, Tiger Band Plaza at Clemson University, Pendleton Place Children's Shelter, and the Boy Scout Pavilion at White Pines. DeVita has also been a consistent supporter of the United Way and the Greenville and South Carolina Chambers of Commerce.

TRANSITION FOR FUTURE GROWTH

With an eye toward the future, the firm became an employee-owned company in 2008. In 2012, the firm completed a transition to a new management team including President Darren Springer, Vice-President Derrick Hiott, and Chief Technology Officer Trey Moran. Though he is no longer involved with day-to-day operations, Frank DeVita remains involved as Chairman of the Board.

Having celebrated its 30th anniversary in 2014, DeVita and Associates faces the future with confidence, investing heavily in Building Information Modeling (BIM) technology and seeking dynamic growth in its national and regional services, while always retaining its deep roots within the Greenville community.

▲ Caine Halter YMCA, Greenville, South Carolina.

▼ IBSH Research Center, Chester County, South Carolina.

DP3 Architects, Ltd.

PEOPLE PLACES PURPOSE

The talented professionals of DP3 Architects are proud to call Greenville, South Carolina their home. A perfect blend of historic Southern charm and cutting-edge innovation, the city has amassed an impressive list of accolades and media mentions for its numerous amenities and high quality of life. Having started the firm in a residential basement, it was not surprising that people

▲ The hub of Greenville's entrepreneur community, the NEXT Innovation Center, is one of DP3 Architects' most identifiable projects in the area.

▶▼ Supporting missions for programs like Camp Spearhead and Camp Courage, to hosting corporate events and weddings, Pleasant Ridge Camp and Retreat Center provides a welcoming environment in a natural and sustainable setting.

▼ Mac's Speed Shop located in the West end of Greenville, is an example of DP3 Architects' restaurant expertise.

so passionate about architectural design would seek out an inspiring environment in which to nurture their creative genius and address the dreams of their clients. In 2000, DP3 Architects renovated the 1890's Greenville Gas and Electric Light Company building, listed on the National Register of Historic Places, transforming it into an open studio office space. The space in the heart of downtown Greenville promotes collaboration and reinforces the team approach that DP3 Architects takes on each of

its projects, energizing the firm's team members to design innovative and functional spaces.

A focus on people has been a cornerstone of DP3 Architects' values since the firm's founding in 1984. Each member of the DP3 team understands that their ultimate business is people— the talented ones on their team, the visionary ones who retain them, and most importantly, the ones who will work and play daily in the spaces they create.

A penchant for creative and sustainable design motivates DP3 Architects to create places that invite, inspire, and invigorate users. Their passion is understanding the greater underlying purpose in the buildings they craft, and working relentlessly to fulfill it.

The firm is identified by the numerous high-profile projects it has successfully completed for a wide range of clients in the region including, Greenville's NEXT Innovation Center, Grill

Marks, Pleasant Ridge Camp and Retreat Center, new student centers at both Winthrop and Anderson universities, and numerous public safety, community, and recreation facilities around the Upstate.

The firm's influence is also evident in the impact DP3 Architects' team members have had serving community and professional organizations including the City of Greenville Architectural Review Board, United Way, Greenville Chamber of Commerce, Rotary International, U.S. Green Building Council, the Clemson University Architectural Foundation, and the American Institute of Architects. The firm's professionals have also given back to their community by providing pro bono architectural services for the renovation of Historic Sirrine Stadium, Cleveland Park's Rudolf Anderson Memorial, and the Clemson University Spirit Point at Tiger Band Plaza.

—Photo by Paul Ringger

Grand Design

More than houses.

In early 1985, a small group of concerned citizens in Greenville gathered at First Presbyterian Church to launch an initiative aimed at creating affordable housing for families who could not otherwise afford a safe, decent place to live. Among the group was Joe Barron, who, while helping Boy Scouts deliver firewood to those in need, had been touched by the plight of an elderly woman

Habitat Greenville's Homeownership Impact Study:
- 68% of homeowners earned a college or technical degree
- 70% of homeowners' children had improved grades
- 77% feel their family's overall health has improved
- 90% say they are more financially independent
- 87% know how to set long-term financial goals

▼ Habitat Greenville builds 10-12 homes each year, each constructed to Energy Star and NAHB ICC-700 building standards.

huddled in her 30-degree living room. She had been praying all night for heat, and saw Joe and the Scouts as the answer to her prayers.

"Newspapers were stuffed into cracked windows and there was cardboard on the walls," Joe recalls. "We built her a fire, but I knew it would never heat that shack."

Housing for the poor became a matter of conscience for Joe. He was instrumental in the creation of Habitat for Humanity of Greenville County. Founded on September 20, 1985, the new organization soon gained the support of the community. Joe and his wife, Becky, remained driving forces in the organization where Joe served as founding Board President.

Over the next ten years, the walls were raised on 50 homes for low-income families in Greenville. Since 1995, Habitat volunteers and donors have built 280 additional homes, and the building continues.

The dream of Habitat for Humanity's national founder, Millard Fuller, is championed by former President Jimmy Carter. "Habitat has opened up unprecedented opportunities for me to cross the chasm that separates those of us who are free, safe, well fed and housed, financially secure and influential enough to shape our own destiny from our neighbors who enjoy few, if any, of these advantages."

PRIDE IN OWNERSHIP, PRIDE IN GREENVILLE

"By building affordable, energy-efficient homes, Habitat Greenville works to eliminate poverty housing and the social and economic blight it fosters. The ministry's mission statement sums up its goal: putting God's love into action by bringing people together to build homes, communities and hope. Its fundamental belief is that affordable homeownership is foundational for creating family stability, ensuring academic success for children and eliminating generational poverty.

According to a 2001 Harvard University study, children raised in homes owned by their families score nine percent higher in reading, seven percent higher in math, and are 116% more likely to pursue post high-school education.

Habitat Greenville is the only agency providing zero-interest home loans in Greenville County. Its affordable mortgages and volunteer-based home construction enable families with low income to attain homeownership.

The Habitat model provides an opportunity for people to help themselves. The program has been carefully designed to ensure successful outcomes for the homes' recipients.

As they pay their mortgage, each family develops equity in their home. This helps to change their financial trajectory, breaks the generational cycle of poverty, and creates more responsible neighbors and involved citizens. In turn, families are more secure

and neighborhoods and communities are strengthened and improved.

ENGAGING THE COMMUNITY

What began as a grassroots effort has now become one of the largest non-profit organizations in Greenville. Habitat supporters—donors and volunteers—continue to be the backbone of the organization. Each year, more than 2,100 volunteers contribute approximately 22,000 hours to build Habitat homes, and hundreds of companies, organizations, churches and individuals in Greenville County lent their support.

In 2015, Habitat Greenville celebrates its 30th anniversary, and the construction of its 330th home. This milestone represents much more than houses. It symbolizes 330 families whose lives have been transformed through affordable housing.

Amy, who became a homeowner in 1994, shared, "Our home allowed my children to grow up in a close-knit community where neighbors looked out for each other and took pride in their property. One of my children is now a teacher and another is a respiratory therapist. I was able to complete my RN program and begin a career in nursing. I thank God for Habitat. Without this wonderful organization, I don't know where we would be."

Monroe Free, President and CEO of Habitat Greenville, said, "Through the efforts of thousands of volunteers and donors, Habitat Greenville has helped hundreds of families like Amy's become successful homeowners over the past 30 years. We honor these families for their commitment to improve their lives and the lives of their children

through affordable homeownership."

In 2015, Habitat for Humanity of Greenville County received the Nonprofit Excellence Award, given annually by SCANPO (the South Carolina Association of Nonprofit Organizations). The award recognizes Habitat for exemplary governance and management, and excellence in implementation of SCANPO's Guiding Principles and Best Practices.

In addition, Habitat was honored with the 2015 Max Heller Neighborhood Improvement Award, given by the Greenville Chamber of Commerce. The award was presented for use of a derelict property to create the Abigail Springs subdivision—an attractive, stable neighborhood providing affordable homes for 24 families.

"Everything we do at Habitat is centered on our homeowner families," said Monroe Free. "Our Board, staff and volunteers

▲ Greenville CEOs participate in the wall-raising for Habitat Greenville's 2014 CEO Build. Each year since the project was initiated in 2013, approximately 20 CEOs have funded, and with their employees, built a Habitat home.
Photo: The Greenville News

continuously work to the highest standards for their benefit, and we are honored to be recognized for that effort."

▼ Homes are built by volunteers, under the supervision of Habitat's construction staff and members of its Quality Assurance Team (QAT) who are trained in construction methods and safety.

Rolling Green Village

Embracing a Future Filled With Choice

Nestled in the Blue Ridge Mountains in South Carolina's pastoral Upstate region, Rolling Green Village is a premier retirement community offering a continuum of care through dedicated staff who are committed to serving the residents. Rolling Green has attracted retirees from around the country who have discovered the commitment of those dedicated staff members to providing services that create exceptional living at a great value. Operating as a not-for-profit, stand alone community run by local businessmen and women, Rolling Green Village consistently receives five-star ratings for its licensed areas due to its commitment to excellence and emphasis on resident centered care.

▼ Rolling Green Village is a continuing care retirement community that has been a part of Greenville for almost 30 years.

▶▼ RGV's patio homes provide a luxurious space in which residents can enjoy life any way they wish.
▼ There are three different lakes on RGV property, stocked with bass for the residents to fish.

Residents at the Village enjoy retirement living at its best. While the community's beautiful and serene setting evokes images of an artist's idyllic landscape, life at Rolling Green is anything but sleepy. In fact, the daily activities available to residents are so varied and numerous that the challenge is finding the time to take advantage of them all.

The Village is situated on 175 serene acres with the area's natural beauty setting the tone for the peaceful neighborhood. The site includes three fishing lakes surrounded by forest and a system of walking trails.

The community consists of 291 independent patio homes, 133 independent apartment homes, 72 assisted living units including an Alzheimer's unit, and 42 healthcare beds. Rolling Green Village offers service and amenities that support senior adults so that they can stay active and healthy and living independent lives much longer.

PUTTING DREAMS INTO ACTION

A great deal of praying and planning went into the creation of Rolling Green Village. The dream began in 1973 when John Bandy, the pastor of the Judson Mill Memorial Baptist Church in Greenville, was searching for a quality retirement community in which his parents could embrace an active, healthy lifestyle during their golden years. Reverend Bandy's search led him to conclude that there was nothing in the Greenville area that met his needs. He approached the Greenville Baptist Association with his conviction that the Association itself should establish a retirement community. In the fall of 1974, the Greenville Baptist Association formed a Task Study Committee for Housing of the Aging.

Troy Goodwin, pastor of Roper Mountain Baptist Church, had heard Reverend Bandy present his proposal to the Baptist Association. Reverend Goodwin shared Reverend Bandy's dream of such a retirement community with his own congregation at a worship service, emphasizing the need for acreage necessary to build the community.

Hoke and Mildred Smith were inspired by Reverend Goodwin's passionate plea and offered to donate a portion of their own farmland for the project as

a way to give something back for the blessings they felt they had received. The generous offer of the dairy farmer and his wife was gratefully accepted by the task force. The proposed retirement community would be built on Smith's land.

Rolling Green Village, under the leadership of Reverend Bandy, broke ground on June 30, 1985 with a target opening date in late 1986.

In April of that year, however, a fire destroyed much of the construction. The fervor of the dedicated individuals for rebuilding and completing the project was not dampened. Work resumed, and the healthcare facility opened in October 1986 even before the first residents moved into their residences the following month. Sadly, Hoke Smith had passed away before his dream had become reality. The philanthropy of his family is remembered today, however, with the naming of the healthcare facility after Mildred L. Smith.

COMMUNITY LIFE

Life at Rolling Green Village today is enriched by a Residents Association that strengthens the community through committees focusing on:

- Art
- Health Services
- Association Presidents
- History
- Buildings and Grounds
- Library
- Caring
- Publicity
- Crafts
- Recreation
- Financial Advisory
- Safety
- Food
- Woodshop

A rich community life for Village residents was a goal of the founders from the outset. An Activities Director was appointed even before the first residents moved in and continues to coordinate the Village's wide range of cultural and recreational activities today. Residents can participate in activities ranging from aerobics, Tai Chi, and Scrabble to bingo, chorale activities, and outings and trips

The services and amenities the Village offers its residents are also many:

- Restaurant-style dining with healthy, delicious options
- Tailored housekeeping services
- Complimentary local transportation
- Full-time maintenance staff
- Lawn and grounds care

- Well-supplied library with Wi-Fi
- Hair salon (for men and women)
- Multimedia club room
- Wellness and Fitness Center
- Access to Village Center activities and amenities

▲ RGV's saltwater heated pool is a great resource for residents, who use it for aquatic classes and independent swimming.

A community newsletter, *The Village Voice*, has been published regularly since 1986 and keeps residents updated on local events. In addition, an in-house television channel carries much of the same information as well as the day's menus and announcements of general interest.

Among the many rewards of the active and worry-free lifestyle of the residents of the Rolling Green community is participating in activities that serve the greater Greenville community. The Village actively supports a number of local civic and charitable organizations, including Meals on Wheels, Upstate Alzheimer's Association, Miracle Hill Ministries, Loaves and Fishes, and the St. Francis Foundation.

◀▼ RGV focuses on 8 areas of wellness, and provides a fully equipped exercise room for residents to work on their physical wellness.
▼ Situated on 175 acres of beautiful land, Rolling Green Village is a luxurious and relaxing place where your choices are our priority.

Peace Center for the Performing Arts

In the mid-1980s a group of visionaries in Greenville began making bold plans to revitalize their inner city and build a world-class performing arts facility amidst deserted sidewalks and boarded up storefronts on Greenville's South Main Street. Community leaders envisioned a place where people of all socio-economic groups could enjoy performances ranging from classical music to Broadway musicals to popular music and dance.

The visionaries quickly realized that dreams require inspired, committed people as well as substantial resources to become reality. The idea soon captivated the entire community that responded with donations from leading families and individuals, including an initial $10 million pledge by members of the Peace family whose multi-media company owned The Greenville News along with other local publishing and broadcasting companies. With donations from leading families and individuals, corporations, and even school children, the campaign to build the Peace Center for the Performing Arts eventually raised the $42 million needed to bring the idea to life.

The leaders of the initiative formed a unique public-private partnership and selected a six-acre site on the corner of Main and Broad Streets occupied by four deteriorating nineteenth

▼▼ Sitting on six acres in downtown Greenville, the Peace Center is the premier non-profit performing arts venue in South Carolina.
—Photo by Brenda Ernst

GREENVILLE'S

century buildings. Work began on transforming the site into a cultural institution and architectural gem that would attract the world's finest performing artists, provide arts education and outreach, and support local arts organizations. Care was taken to retain the original character of the historic buildings and incorporate it into the design of the new construction.

In November 1990, through tremendous leadership and determination, the vision became a reality and the Peace Center for the Performing Arts opened its doors, forever changing the landscape of Greenville.

In 2010, twenty years after the original groundbreaking, the Peace Center raised the bar again with plans for a $23 million renovation. The renovation included expanding the concert hall lobby; adding Genevieve's, a magnificent new patron lounge; and reconceiving exterior spaces including the TD Stage amphitheatre and Graham Plaza. In addition, extensive renovations to the Huguenot Mill included relocating the Peace Center administrative offices; adding the Ramsaur Studio, a new education facility; and building a unique meeting and event space, the Huguenot Loft.

In the past several years, the Peace Center campus has evolved along with its South Main Street neighborhood. In 2012, The Gullick Building was purchased in order to round out the Peace Center's street presence. The newly developed Graham Plaza, with its plantscapes, water features, and granite walkways and stairways, provides a sense of arrival.

THE DREAM TODAY

In November 2015, the Peace Center for the Performing Arts marked its 25th anniversary. It has much to celebrate. Operating as a not-for-profit organization, the Peace Center has evolved into the largest arts organization in South Carolina and is unique in Greenville due to its flexibility and the variety of venue options it provides. The original design and renovations of the Peace Center reflect a focus on meeting community needs to entertain, educate and inspire. The three main performance venues provide ranges in seating capacity and state-of-the art technology to meet the most demanding requirements of artists and performance companies at the local, national, and global levels.

The Peace Concert Hall has seating for 2,100; the Gunter Theatre holds 400; and the TD Stage can accommodate outdoor seating for 1,250. Additional spaces are ideal for meetings, parties and workshops, including the Ramsaur Studio, the Huguenot Loft, the Wyche Pavilion and the theatre lounge Genevieve's.

Performances are the heart and soul of the Peace Center. A critical goal has been to offer diverse programming to serve all communities and all ages. The Peace Center presents the best tours that Broadway has to offer, world-class classical music concerts and dance companies, along with popular musicians, comedians and speakers.

In addition, a number of local performing arts orga-

nizations have found performing homes at the Peace Center. These companies include the Greenville Symphony Orchestra, South Carolina Children's Theatre, Carolina Ballet Theatre and International Ballet. Other non-profit organizations that utilize the Peace Center are South Carolina Governor's School for the Arts and Humanities, Carolina Youth Symphony, Greenville County Youth Symphony, Greenville Chorale and Greenville Light Opera Works. These organizations work to engage the entire community in new and ex-

▼ The uniquely modern Genevieve's lounge is adjacent to the Concert Hall and has been taking care of hungry theatergoers for over two years.
—Photo by Brenda Ernst

▲ Megan Riegel, President/CEO
—Photo by Josh Norris

▼ With room for 1250 music-lovers at max capacity, the outdoor TD Stage is the best spot to see live Summer shows.
—Photo by Brenda Ernst

citing ways through an array of inspiring programs and performances.

A 44-member board currently serves the organization and day-to-day operations are handled by a professional management team. With its mixture of the old and the new, its variety of performance and event spaces, the Peace Center continues to create a home for cultural activity and energy for Greenville's downtown and economic development.

A Commitment to Greenville

The Peace Center's impact on Greenville's downtown revitalization has been well documented. Streets that were marred by abandoned and crumbling buildings are now filled with retail shops, hotels, award-winning restaurants and art galleries and most importantly, people. The Peace Center has brought in patrons numbering in the millions, creating a "buzz" that helps support Greenville as a destination—for vacations, new businesses and the recruitment of personnel. The Peace Center is the foundation for the economic engine of the region.

In 2003, the Peace Center received the Elizabeth O'Neill Verner Award, which recognizes outstanding achievement and contributions to the arts in South Carolina. The Peace Center has also received several education grants from The Broadway League and is part of the Kennedy Center's Partnership in Education program. In 2013, Peace Center President/CEO Megan Riegel was awarded the Order of the Palmetto, the highest civilian honor in the state of South Carolina, recognizing a person's lifetime achievements and contributions to the state.

More than a place for performances, the Peace Center enriches the Greenville community and the entire region, engaging students, teachers, parents and others through the education initiatives of the Peace Outreach Program. Every year, this nationally recognized program brings the arts to life for nearly 55,000 attendees. In addition, master classes, lectures, workshops, and specially developed performances give kids a whole new way to learn and help teachers grow in their profession.

Through the Peace Voices program, students learn to express their views and feelings through the art of poetry. Working with Peace Center Poet-in-Residence, Glenis Redmond, these students are learning from the best. In 2014, Redmond was invited by The President's Committee on the Arts and Humanities and

▲ Camp Broadway attendees perform their final show before the Summer's end.
—Photo by Staci Koonce

▲ The outdoor Wyche Pavilion is a great space for weddings or other large outdoor gatherings.
—Photo by John Macaluso

the Scholastic Art & Writing Awards to mentor the 2014 National Student Poets.

"As we celebrate a successful 25 years, we look ahead to meeting the needs and goals of the next 25 years," Megan Riegel noted. "Through our pursuit of artistic excellence and high standards, the Peace Center remains committed to providing Greenville and the region with an exceptional quality of service, facilities, and programming which are sure to be enjoyed by future generations."

▼ With over 2000 seats, the Peace Concert Hall has hosted some of the best acts in entertainment.
—Photo by Clint Davis

Grand Design

—Photo by Paul Ringger

Plate 108

A Cooking & Entertainment Venue

Where can you go to have fun learning cooking techniques, consult with a dietitian about a nutritional challenge, or book a catered lunch meeting? Plate 108 in downtown Greer is the place. Opened in 2012, Plate 108 a cooking and entertainment venue combining the culinary arts with the nutrition expertise of registered dietitians. Its contemporary setting provides a place where participants can transfer what they learn into creating their own healthy, delicious meals in the kitchen.

▲ Learning proper knife skills at Kids Culinary Camp.
—photo by Christa Mazak

Plate 108 classes are educational and entertaining, and they are wide ranging—from specialized nutrition education to local chef demonstrations. Kids culinary classes and summer camps, corporate team building events, bridal parties, and birthday parties are just some of the events on the Plate 108 calendar. And, every class concludes with a delicious taste of food prepared by participants.

With an expansion in 2013, Krumms on the Plate, a catering and events service was established. It provides chef-created foods for everything from weekday lunch meetings to lavish receptions, parties, and weddings. Customized menus are prepared and delivered in stunning presentations to make every event spe-

▲ Team building—pasta style with ZF Chassis Engineers.
—photo by Doug Smith

cial. Krumms on the Plate caters off-site and also has space to host meetings and special events.

Wendy Watkins, a practicing dietitian, is the visionary behind Plate 108. She has helped others make sensible and sustainable lifestyle changes. Whether the desire for change comes from a sense of urgency regarding a health condition or a recently sparked interest, she helps individuals with weight management, diabetic management, food sensitivities, eating disorders, and many other nutrition challenges.

"I love working with individual clients," Wendy stated, "so Plate 108 and Krumms were natural outgrowths. We are always looking for new ways to bring people together to enjoy learning and sharing food and good times."

◀ Guest Chef Teryi Youngblood of Passereile Bistro leads a cooking class featuring Moroccan delights.
—photo by Christa Mazak

EnviroSouth

Sustainable Solutions for Bringing Brownfield Sites Back to Life

In March 2001, Thomas Donn and Brendan Brodie decided to launch their own business specializing in environmental consulting. Both men were geologists and worked for another company when they recognized the need for a firm dedicated solely to providing practical solutions to environmental problems. Their goal was to launch and grow a firm that was able to clearly explain

▲ Soil cores collected for examination and chemical analyses.

complex technical and regulatory issues in a manner that was easily understandable to a wide range of clients. They also wanted to achieve a high level of personal communication with their clients so that their mantra of "on budget, on time, and no surprises" would be the standard for every project they accepted.

▲ EnviroSouth's groundwater remediation efforts protect the region's streams from becoming impacted by chemical contaminants from industrial and commercial sources.

▶ Shuttered factory that has been brought back to productive use through EnviroSouth's guidance in navigating through South Carolina's Brownfield restoration program.

The name of their new venture, EnviroSouth, reflected not only their business focus, but also their primary area of service.

The founders selected Greenville as the home of their new business as they were attracted to the vibrant, growing economy of the upstate of South Carolina. Their early experiences with meeting new and prospective clients was very encouraging. Donn and Brodie found that many of Greenville's business leaders were very receptive to listening to new ideas and affording the partners an opportunity to show them how EnviroSouth could put planned works into action.

Just six months after Donn and Brodie launched their business, the nation was reeling from the tragedy of 9/11. The American workplace became paralyzed with fear. Many older, established firms closed their doors or sharply curtailed their activities. With no clear direction of the economy at the time, it was

difficult for a new business venture to gain momentum, but Donn and Brodie doubled down on their marketing efforts and made certain that every client's experience with EnviroSouth was second-to-none.

Despite the cautious business climate of the day, EnviroSouth saw its base of repeat clients continue to grow. The firm's reputation of always providing honest and high-quality service helped them weather the ensuing business recession and is evident to this day as satisfied clients with environmental needs continue to call EnviroSouth.

One of the firm's earliest success stories involved EnviroSouth professionals creating a successful outcome to what had been a difficult and complex environmental problem for a Fortune 100 international chemical manufacturer. EnviroSouth provided environmental solutions and regulatory coordination to clean up significant groundwater contamination that allowed the sale of a former paint factory in Greenville to proceed. That facility now provides jobs to approximately 100 employees.

Earle Furman, an early client and the founder of Greenville's largest commercial real estate firm, weighed in on the role EnviroSouth played in that project. "I consider EnviroSouth a problem solver as opposed to a problem creator," Furman noted, "and have recommended the company to numerous commercial and industrial purchasers."

EnviroSouth's reputation continues to grow. Brisk business and continued growth in recent years led to the opening of an office in Spartanburg, South Carolina in addition to their original location on Augusta Road in Greenville.

SPECIALISTS IN THEIR FIELD

EnviroSouth now provides a complete range of environmental consulting services, including:

- Soil and groundwater assessment and remediation
- Building evaluations
- Soil vapor and indoor air testing
- Real estate environmental site assessment
- Brownfields property restoration

Unlike many other companies in this field that also provide geotechnical engineering, construction testing, and/or civil engineering services, EnviroSouth professionals remain focused strictly on environmental matters. They be-

lieve that this allows them to maintain a position of expertise, especially in the complex field of groundwater remediation.

The EnviroSouth team focuses on explaining in a clear and concise manner the chemistry and geology that are at the heart of their services. They understand that the main problem most clients had with hiring a technical consultant was that they didn't receive a clear explanation of the services in an easy to understand manner. Whether the scope of work involves environmental due diligence when clients are purchasing real estate or complex groundwater remediation, clients need to know exactly what they are paying for.

"Our biggest impact on the region has been assisting property owners with re-developing properties with environmental challenges," states Thomas Donn. "By assisting land purchasers and developers with addressing environmental concerns at Brownfield sites, we have played a key role in putting idle properties back to productive use. The role we play in these types of transactions is twofold. First, we help clients navigate the regulatory steps to protect themselves from becoming responsible for existing contamination on the properties they purchase. Second, we provide cost-effective and efficient

technical solutions for remediating, or cleaning up, contaminated soil and groundwater. We have successfully completed environmental remediation projects for numerous commercial and industrial properties that were impacted by petroleum or chemical products. These projects are located in the Carolinas and Georgia and include manufacturing facilities, petroleum terminals, dry cleaning plants, and gas stations among others. We are also working closely with Clemson University's Environmental Engineering professors

to develop new and innovative groundwater remediation methods."

Another positive impact EnviroSouth has had on the area is its heavy involvement in activities that benefit the local community. The company participates in "Hands On Greenville" community service day, sponsors local food banks, donates professional services to charities, and speaks about geology and environmental awareness topics to school groups and scout troops.

◄◄ EnviroSouth employees and local residents supporting a community gardening project through Hands On Greenville activities.

▲ Underground petroleum storage tank removal. EnviroSouth has assisted numerous clients with assessment and remediation of petroleum contaminants at sites throughout the region.

◄◄ Soil and groundwater assessment being performed at a former textile equipment manufacturing plant.

Context Design Group

Process Focused Design Since 2002

Dave Lewis was destined to become an architect. The Nebraska native's family had long-standing ties to the construction industry. A frequent visitor to work sites as a child, he became fascinated with planning and building. He watched projects grow from blueprints on the dining room table into thriving entities. While still in high-school, he designed a house that he'd like to live in.

The design so appealed to his family that his father built it. The house won a residential design competition and from that moment there was never a doubt about the young man's calling.

At the University of Nebraska, he won other awards while earning his degree in architecture. After completing an internship with a leading architectural

▼ Timken Plant Expansion, Walhalla, South Carolina.

firm in New York, the newly accredited *David W. Lewis, AIA*, immigrated to Greenville, South Carolina, a city busy transforming itself.

Formerly known as the "Textile Center of the World", Greenville was diversifying its economy and reshaping its urban landscape. In addition to having become the North American headquarters of major corporations such as Michelin and Hubbell Lighting, it had attracted numerous firms that are now household names, including Caterpillar, General Electric and Lockheed Martin as well as automotive giant, BMW.

While serving as Architectural Department Manager for Simons Engineering, Inc., BMW chose Lewis to serve as lead architect in charge of initial architectural programming and overall site master planning for their manufacturing plant in Spartanburg. In addition, he served as Architect of Record for the BMW Zentrum Visitor's Center and Museum.

The young architect continued to sharpen his focus on planning and design of automotive assembly plants and went on to serve as lead architect for programming, planning and conceptual design efforts on three other automotive plants locating in the Southeastern United States and

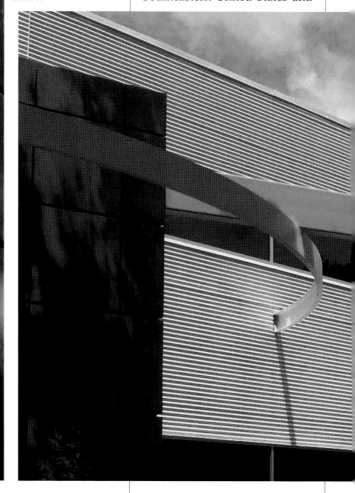

GREENVILLE'S

one in Germany. With his expertise and experience in industrial manufacturing and a specialty in the automotive market sector, he decided in 2002 that it was time to establish his own design firm. Context Design Group was born.

PROVIDING SOLUTIONS

Context Design Group has built an impressive reputation for providing clients with totally integrated design and planning services to align their facility and business objectives. Context Design professionals understand that their clients' building environments must respond to their operational objectives as well. They call it "Process Focused Design." Context's responsive and flexible business methods allow their professionals to understand, analyze, and prioritize the "big picture" objectives of each client.

"Our focus is on understanding and solving customer-specific needs with our building solutions," Lewis states. "We have an advantage over our competition due to our long and unique history of working with numerous European and other international clients. They expect an understanding of their own individual details and expectations of quality as they relate to their particular building needs."

"Our primary market sectors are commercial and industrial/manufacturing with a special expertise in the automotive manufacturing arena. Our clients are primarily domestic and international corporations doing business along the Interstate 85 corridor in the Southeastern United States."

Context Design Group's five design professionals operate from their office in Greenville's

downtown historic district and find the city a perfect match for their talents. "Greenville is a hot spot for architectural and engineering talent with the history of CRSS, Fluor, Lockwood Greene, and others in this part of South Carolina," Lewis notes. "There is a deep talent base in this area."

(continued on page 266)

▲ Exterior of BMW Zentrum – Museum & Visitors Center
▼ Interior of BMW Zentrum – Museum & Visitors Center.

Context Design Group

A RAZOR-SHARP FOCUS ON DETAIL

Lewis and the talented design professionals at Context Design Group understand that no detail is insignificant as they develop targeted solutions to fit their clients' business objectives. Using proven programming techniques, analysis methodologies, and design processes, they help their clients visualize and understand how their facility should respond to the changing needs of their business and the context of the surrounding environment for which a project is to be developed.

That attention to every detail has been recognized and appreciated. "Context Design Group was instrumental in the realization of Starlinger-Sahm's new North American headquarters and showroom," stated Jimmy Cranford, President of American Starlinger-Sahm, Inc., a global manufacturer of wholesale recycling/textile machinery and parts. "The project team systematically developed a facility program based on our company's needs, worked diligently on a design that reflects our Austrian corporate language, and provided the knowledge and direction for negotiating a construction contract within our budget."

Fritz Dräxlmaier, CEO and Chairman of the Executive Board of Dräxlmaier Group echoed Cranford's comments. This supplier of electronic systems and interior components for upscale passenger cars and luxury sports cars employs upwards of 38,000 people worldwide and notches annual sales in excess of $257 million. When searching for an architectural design firm to create the master plan for their U.S. headquarters, they selected Context Design Group.

"Innovation, customer-orientation, and quality," explained Fritz Dräxlmaier. "David Lewis and his team at Context Design Group have done an outstanding job to reflect these hallmarks of our business in the architectural design and layout of our U.S. headquarters in Duncan, South Carolina. This is evidenced by many positive comments on the visual appeal of our building that we have received from our visitors over the years. For more than two decades, Context Design Group has been a strong and reliable partner of the Dräxlmaier Group in all architectural aspects, from the initial building design to contractor selection and construction oversight. We know that we can count on the expertise of David and his team for all of our building needs."

By providing solutions and unparalleled design quality, Context Design Group has been directly involved with the geographical shift of the automotive industry from its traditional roots to its numerous new locations in Southeastern states. The company has worked closely with automakers

noted for developing state-of-the-art facilities. Context Design Group has been on the ground floor advancing the systems and procedures that the most innovative U.S. manufacturing and assembly plants are now implementing.

The company is intimate with the needs of both JIT (just in time) and JIS (just in sequence) manufacturing as well as the Toyota Production System. When asked to design Hyundai's first North American assembly plant in Alabama, Context Design Group was instrumental in the evaluation and benchmarking of Hyundai's Korean plants against the best automotive assembly plants in North America. Altogether, the Group has placed its signature on facility design, planning, and engineering activities on nearly fifty Tier 1 and 2 JIS and JIT supplier projects. Supplier facilities designed by Context Design Group have played a major role in defining the "New Style" building vocabulary, which has become the standard for process flow and facility design. They have been integral to the transition of automobile manufacturing to the Southeastern United States.

A Focus on Community

"At Context Design Group, we are involved in our community and support its economic development efforts, which we see as critical to our success," states Dave Lewis. "Through our architectural design practice, we collaborate with our domestic and international clients to design buildings that streamline their business operations and disseminate their corporate image. Over the years, our work with dozens of companies along the I-85 corridor accounts for hundreds of millions of dollars in capital investment and the creation of thousands of jobs. Many of our clients and projects have played a key role in the significant growth and development of Greenville over the past thirty years.

"For over a decade, it has been my pleasure to have supported the German American Chamber of Commerce of the Southern United States (GACC South) on whose board I have served as a Director and as President of the South Carolina Chapter. Through both professional and community service, we have fostered strategic growth and European cultural influence in our local market by assisting companies and individuals in their transition. We also assist local universities by serving as design consultants for student projects and by mentoring students."

Context Design Group is in step with Greenville's march into an innovative future.

▼ The Dräxlmaier Automotive of America Plastic Injection Molding Bay was an expansion project for the business in 2011.
▼▼ Dräxlmaier's North American Headquarters & Manufacturing facility, located in Duncan, South Carolina.
◄▼ An arching, linear design is a striking feature of the interior lobby and reception area.

On Time. On Budget. On Your Side.

The Proclamation by the Columbia City Council marking May 10, 2014 as "Alliance Consulting Engineers Day" and the South Carolina House of Representatives Resolution to recognize Alliance Consulting Engineers, Inc. for its "significant contributions to statewide economic growth and development" was the highlight of the celebration of the engineering company's tenth

anniversary of service. The honors underscored the role Alliance Consulting Engineers, Inc. has played in local and regional economic development in the state

▲ Taylor Street Parking Garage, City of Columbia, S.C.

▼ Lexington Medical Center, Lexington County, S.C.

with its assistance in projects totaling $8 billion in industrial investment and 24,000 new jobs in South Carolina.

The proclamations went on to commend the company for its excellence in providing engineering services to the City of Columbia and to communities throughout the entire state and the Southeast, highlighting the $100 million in grants and low-interest loans it has helped its clients secure in order to finance key infrastructure and industrial projects. Alliance was also praised for its dedication to community service and especially its efforts to give back to the City of Columbia.

PURSUIT OF A DREAM

A native of Sri Lanka, Deepal S. Eliatamby founded Alliance Consulting Engineers, Inc. in 2004 on the concept of providing unsurpassed, in-depth personal involvement on today's complex engineering projects. The hands-on approach and meticulous attention to detail that he envisioned for every project that his company accepted would begin from conceptual planning and continue through to final design, permitting, and construction. Using traditional business practices and the latest technology, Eliatamby's mission for Alliance Consulting Engineers, Inc. was to demonstrate the company's commitment to every client through responsiveness, experience, and quality results.

Eliatamby's formula for success has proven to be right on target. The young man who arrived in the United States with two bags and a backpack now heads a company of 75 professionals with five offices in South and North Carolina. In addition to the company's corporate headquarters at the Midlands Regional Office in Columbia, Alliance Consulting Engineers, Inc. also maintains their Lowcountry Regional Office in Bluffton, South Carolina; the Upstate Regional Office in Greenville, South Carolina; the Charleston Regional Office in Charleston, South Carolina; and the Charlotte Regional Office in Charlotte, North Carolina.

During the last decade, Alliance Consulting Engineers has grown into one of the state's largest civil and environmental engineering firms. As the firm celebrates its tenth anniversary, company leaders look to the promise of growth on the horizon.

"We are thrilled and honored to reach the milestone of our tenth anniversary, especially considering the economic challenges our nation has experienced in the last decade," states Eliatamby. "We believe our success is a testament to the talented people we have on our team and our great clients who have let us use our skills to streamline their projects and save them time and money."

To date, Alliance has worked on more than 900 projects, spanning all 46 counties in South Carolina and many projects in North Carolina, Georgia and other Southeastern States. One area of concentration has been economic

development and working with companies that are building new facilities or expanding existing ones. High-profile companies Alliance has assisted include Continental Tire, Nephron Pharmaceuticals Corporation, Adidas, BMW, QVC, Home Depot, Monster.com, Amazon.com, Toray Industries and numerous others.

Alliance has also assisted cities and counties in the Southeast with infrastructure projects. These projects include more than 200 miles of water and wastewater lines, numerous water and wastewater treatment facilities, speculative industrial buildings, industrial site certifications and master plans, and roadway plans.

While the size of the operation has continued to grow over its decade in existence, the core values on which Eliatamby founded his business have remained constant. "Our three core values - responsiveness, quality control and added value – are what separate us from other engineering firms," he notes. "Alliance's responsiveness is supported by its state-of-the-art equipment, which also helps with work quality. We have a very strict policy on quality control, and we always try to bring something to the table. We want to add value to every project we touch."

A Tradition of Service

The professionals at Alliance Consulting Engineers, Inc. take great pride in providing a complete range of civil and environmental engineering services to a wide range of clients.

Master Planning and Design

Project personnel from Alliance Consulting Engineers, Inc. provide a complete range of services for the site design and planning of industrial sites. The company's design specialists understand the unique infrastructure demands associated with the development of industrial sites. From family-owned operations to facilities of over two million square feet for Fortune 500 companies, Alliance personnel have been involved with the development of numerous industrial sites throughout the Southeastern United States.

Construction Services

Once the planning, engineering design and permitting are completed, Alliance professionals can provide construction administration and observation services during the construction phase of the project. Construction administration and observation are critical to assure that the construction proceeds in accordance with the expectations of the client and in accordance with the permitted conditions of the particular project.

Solid Waste Management

Since its inception, Alliance Consulting Engineers, Inc. has assisted municipalities, counties and individuals with solid waste management services. The company's solid waste related services are multifaceted ranging from planning to post-closure care.

By staying current with ever-changing regulations established by both state and federal agencies, the engineering design and permitting proficiency of Alliance Consulting Engineers, Inc. personnel have resulted in the successful permitting of numerous

solid waste related facilities. Additionally, the company has assisted South Carolina counties with maintaining solid waste management plans to govern the solid waste facilities within the county as required by regulatory agencies.

▲ McDaniels Acura, Richland County, S.C.

▼ Malls & Shopping Centers.

Alliance Consulting Engineers, Inc.

▲ Sarah Collins Special Needs Program Car Wash in Greenville.

▲ Adopt a Highway – 12th Street Extension, Lexington County, S.C.

GRANTS

The grant professionals at Alliance Consulting Engineers, Inc. have extensive experience in accessing grant and funding programs ranging from Community Development Block Grants and Economic Development Administration Funds to State Revolving Fund Programs of the Environmental Protection Agency.

WITH AN EYE TO THE FUTURE

Deepal Eliatamby and his staff appreciate the support the company has received over the years from their clients and look forward to continuing the business relationships that have been the cornerstone of their success. That commitment is evidenced in the recent expansion of their corporate headquarters to better serve the many clients who have put their faith in the myriad services provided by Alliance Consulting Engineers, Inc.

In June 2014, the company began expansion of its corporate headquarters which have been located on Main Street since the company's founding. One of several large companies to call downtown home, the expansion increases the firm's corporate footprint to 17,000 square feet - nearly an entire floor in Capitol Center Tower, making it one of the top ten largest tenants in the 25-story building that is also the tallest building in the state.

The expansion ensures that Alliance Consulting Engineers, Inc. will have the physical space to support its growing staff, to better serve its clients, and to promote economic and business development in the area.

"Our commitment to the Midlands and South Carolina is further strengthened as we continue to grow to serve our clients and be the largest locally owned civil and environmental engineering company based in the region," Eliatamby noted. "As we look to the next ten years, we will continue to expand our footprint to better serve our clients."

PEER RECOGNITION

The company's record of excellence and integrity has earned it numerous industry awards and accolades, including:

• On May 5, 2014, Alliance Consulting Engineers, Inc. was ranked by Engineering News-Record magazine (ENR), as one of the top ten design firms in South Carolina and one of the top 75

▼ Adidas Distribution Facility, Spartanburg County.

▼ Wastewater Treatment Plant, Orangeburg County.

▲ The Mayor's Isabel Law Breast Cancer Breakfast.

design firms within the Southeastern United States including Florida, Georgia, North Carolina, and South Carolina.

• In November 2013, Alliance Consulting Engineers, Inc. was named one of the fastest growing companies in South Carolina by Capital Corporation, Integrated Media Publishing and others in the annual "25 Fastest-Growing Companies" listing. Now in its thirteenth year, the "25 Fastest-Growing Companies" competition recognizes the achievements of top-performing private and publicly-owned companies that have contributed to South Carolina's economy through exceptional increases in revenues and employment.

• Also in 2013, Alliance Consulting Engineers, Inc. was ranked in the annual Grant Thornton "South Carolina 100" as one of South Carolina's 100 largest privately held companies.

"We are very pleased to be ranked on the 'South Carolina 100'," Eliatamby stated on receiving the award. "Being named one of South Carolina's largest privately held companies is an honor, and we are very grateful to our clients for their ongoing support and for helping us earn this honor. As we complete our tenth year of client service, we look forward to even more growth in South Carolina and the Southeastern U.S."

In an ongoing effort to return something to the communities that have been so supportive of the company he founded, Eliatamby encourages his employees to volunteer their time outside the office. "Find something that you are passionate about, wheth-er it's economic development or working with charitable organizations – that makes each of us a better person, which makes for a better company and helps make our communities stronger," he encourages them.

His employees have done exactly that. They now provide support to more than a dozen civic and charitable organizations ranging from the United Way of the Midlands, the Service Dog Institute of Greenville, and Bluffton Lions Club to the USO, Isabel's Law Breast Cancer Breakfast, and Big Brothers and Big Sisters of the Midlands among others.

◄◄ *(photo in margin page opposite)*
John W. Matthews Industrial Park
Water Tank, Orangeburg Cty, S.C.

▼ Timken Sports Complex, Union County, S.C.

▼ Amazon.com Fulfillment Center, Lexington County, S.C.

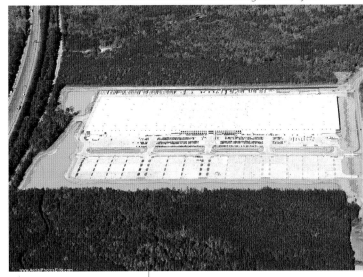

Grand Design

"There's financial planning and then there's wealth management," stated Rusty Cagle, President and Founder of ASE Wealth Advisors. "The difference is captured in the consolidated big-picture. Think of wealth management as one office working in collaboration rather than one person providing a range of services for a client. This includes personal financial planning and

▲ ASE Wealth Advisors' President and Founder, Rusty Cagle, M.S., MPAS℠, CFP®, CRPC®, CAP™

▶▶ Rusty Cagle has been interviewed by several major publications including multiple NPR interviews for the South Carolina Business Review.

▼ ASE Wealth Advisors provides objective, independent advice to clients.

investment management, tax reduction and estate planning strategies, and occasionally in-house legal resources."

Cagle, a native of the Upstate, brings nearly 25 years of experience advising individuals, professionals, and businesses in a wide range of financial strategies and solutions. A noted author, he co-authored the book *Plan of Action—Strategies to Help You Build and Preserve Wealth*. He has also been quoted in and written articles for national publications such as *Kiplinger's Personal Finance, SmartMoney.com, Yahoo!News, BusinessWeek,* and *Physician's Money Digest,* just to name a few. He can also be heard locally on the South Carolina Business Review through NPR radio.

His career in wealth management began at American Express Financial Advisors, Inc. where he was recognized with various awards including the "President's Advisory Award for Quality of Objective Advice." Today he is among a select group of national representatives that participate in an elite program focused on serving the affluent marketplace with strategic alliances.

Over the past decade, high income tax payers and retirement focused families have turned to the professionals at ASE Wealth Advisors for investment strategies designed to help them achieve their individual financial goals. Whether planning for a comfortable retirement, providing funds for a college education, the preservation of wealth, or the reduction of tax burdens, choosing the right wealth management team with whom to entrust a family legacy is crucial.

PUTTING CLIENTS FIRST

ASE Wealth Advisors serves as a comprehensive financial services firm committed to help-

ing its clients improve their long-term financial success. Using an in-depth consultative process, they learn the details of the client's financial picture so they can construct and implement a customized plan using a personal financial action checklist. The experienced team of professionals at ASE fully evaluates the client's situation to prepare personal solutions that integrate investment planning, tax reduction planning, retirement income and distribution planning, and family wealth planning.

After assisting clients in identifying their personal aspirations and most pressing concerns, the firm's skilled advisors are able to develop an appropriate strategy and tactfully direct its implementation. ASE Wealth

Advisors' trusted professionals utilize independence, transparency, and competence to provide each client with a comprehensive financial plan. They walk clients through the step-by-step process to make them more confident in their decisions and to ensure they understand the roadmap for success that has been created.

"Financial independence is not something that just happens in people's lives," Cagle explains. "We have to plan for it. At ASE Wealth Advisors, we specialize in strategies for sustaining family legacies and preserving wealth. Our focus is to create income that our clients can have confidence in, potentially improve their returns, and preserve their capital assets while mitigating taxes. We are committed to the highest standards of excellence, understanding each unique situation, and delivering exceptional value with helping our clients reach financial independence. We work in a fiduciary capacity that aligns our interests with those of our clients.

MAKING A DIFFERENCE

Cagle and his team of professionals remain passionate about making a meaningful difference

• The Corporate Strategic Planning and Asset Management Strategies model is designed for executives, privately held businesses, and large corporations.

In addition to their strong commitment to each and every client that entrusts them with their future, the ASE Wealth Ad-

with a number of non-profit organizations, outreach programs, and development of young leaders through the local educational system.

"I have always felt personally compelled to remain in Greenville," Cagle adds, "and to help make it a vibrant and emerging community that offers a unique

◀▼ ASE Wealth Advisors' office is conveniently located in Greenville.

▼ ASE Wealth Advisors' conference room provides a comfortable atmosphere for client meetings.

in the lives of their clients, providing them transition from success to significance. Assisting high performance individuals keep more of the wealth they have earned as a legacy for their families is paramount.

ASE Wealth Advisors has developed a proprietary system called "The Wealth Sustainability Model™" to deliver unprecedented, comprehensive services in three specific areas:

• Asset Management is available for clients who want advisory or fee-based investing while having a Certified Financial Planner ™ as a resource for investment and professional services.
• The Private Client Group option delivers comprehensive financial planning that focuses on tax reduction, asset preservation, estate planning, asset protection, and investment management.

visors team remains committed to their community. That commitment translates into giving back to Greenville in numerous ways, including involvement

environment that enhances the quality of life, education, and the arts, and makes this a great place to raise a family."

▼ ASE Wealth Advisors' team, left to right: Matt Van Name, CFP®, Kerin Galloway, Rusty Cagle, CFP®, Andy Hazle.

Play Ball!

More than three million fans over the years have filed through the turnstiles to watch their Greenville Drive compete as professional baseball's South Atlantic League affiliate of the Boston Red Sox, one of the best known and most popular brands in sports. The Drive team was founded in 1960 in Shelby, North Carolina before relocating to Columbia, South Carolina in 1983.

▲ Fluor Field welcomed over three million fans for Drive games over the first nine seasons in Downtown Greenville.

▼ Greenville is an extremely picturesque city, as evidenced by this beautiful sunset captured during a Drive game at Fluor Field.

There, the team was known as the Bombers to honor members of Lt. Colonel Jimmy Doolittle's Raiders who trained at Columbia Army Air Base for their raid on Tokyo in 1942. Following the 2004 season, the Bombers relocated to Greenville and began its long-term love affair with the South Carolina Upstate it now calls home.

As part of the relocation to the Upstate, the team changed its name to the Greenville Drive to reflect the determination and tenacity that is the hallmark of a great athlete, as well the character of the people who have made the South Carolina Upstate the success it is. The name was also a tip of the hat to the city's growing automotive cluster including Michelin, BMW, the Clemson International Center for Automotive Research, and a host of other companies that have catapulted Greenville into the top tier of U.S. cities known for an exceptionally high quality of life.

A New Home For a New Team

Following their initial season in Greenville, the Drive moved into their newly built home in the historic West End heart of downtown. A replica of Fenway Park in Boston, the privately funded stadium was named "Ballpark of the Year" by Baseballparks.com. People throughout the sports world were especially impressed by this honor as the stadium won that designation against such high profile baseball venues as Busch Stadium in St. Louis and other prominent new ballparks.

Soon afterwards, naming rights for the increasingly popular ballpark were claimed by the Fluor Corporation, a premier employer in the community and a global leader in the engineering and construction industry. Fluor Field has since become widely recognized for its charm, class, fan experience and comfort, including selection as the highest ranked ballpark in the South Atlantic League, and earning a top 100 positioning as one of the best stadium experiences in all college and professional sports.

That experience, which includes Greenville Drive Trolley rides from nearby parking at County Square, has become a popular Upstate destination. This popularity has translated into sustained success at the turnstile with record breaking attendance over each season of the Drive's tenure in downtown Greenville. The investment impact has been impressive as well, with the initial $20 million investment that went into the development of Fluor Field generating $125 million and climbing in new construction projects with West End tax revenues and property values soaring over 300 percent since 2005.

"We're proud of what Fluor Field has become in its first nine seasons: a beautiful stadium that's an important part of downtown Greenville and the Upstate community," said Drive owner and President Craig Brown in reference to the team's success. "We believe Fluor Field is one of the true gems at all levels of baseball, and to see it recognized with the best of the best is a tremendous accomplishment." The Greenville News underscored the ballpark's popularity and importance to the community, calling it "Greenville's Front Porch!"

CHAMPIONS ON AND OFF THE FIELD

The Greenville Drive management, staff, and players are justifiably proud of the numerous accolades the organization has garnered. On the diamond, the Greenville Drive has seen

more than 45 of the team's alumni reach the Major Leagues over its first nine seasons, including seven players on the 2013 Boston Red Sox World Series championship team.

As a community brand and business operation, the Drive won Baseball America's prestigious "Bob Freitas Award", recognizing the ball club as the top organization among 100 teams in its class for overall excellence in operations, franchise stability, and community engagement. And the Greenville Drive was also the first and only Minor League sports team to win the National Sports Forum "Overall Award in Excellence for Sports Marketing", beating out multiple MLB, NFL and NHL teams, all of whom operate with substantially more resources.

With that success on the field and in the front office the Drive have experienced similar achievements in the community. The Drive have posted an impressive batting average in helping cement Greenville's image as the shining star of the Upstate through a community partnership platform that is unequivocal in its support of the city: "To foster an atmosphere where family fun, customer service, community works, and baseball merge to create lasting memories."

Working closely with the leading corporations, associations and community based organizations that shape the quality of life in the Upstate, the Drive has formed strategic partnerships that positively impact a variety of critical initiatives. From education to entrepreneurism, from youth leadership to healthy living, and from regionalism to workforce development, the Drive has creatively and continuously leveraged the community engagement platform that is Fluor Field to positively impact these and other key quality of life drivers.

The Drive's commitment to good corporate citizenship continues with theme nights at Fluor Field that highlight everything from the area's First Responders and the Greenville Zoo to the city's birthday and legacy of great leaders and the region's patriotism and appreciation for its men and women in military service.

The Greenville Drive is proud of the role it has played in bringing quality family sports entertainment to Greenville, and in being part of the economic development engine that is making the Upstate a great place to live, work and raise a family.

–All photos courtesy of the Greenville Drive

▼ A capacity crowd during a Reedy River Rivalry game between Clemson and South Carolina. The game has produced five of the ten largest crowds in Fluor Field's history.

◄▲ Drive mascot Reedy Rip'It roams the crowd during a Drive game. With his friendly demeanor and impressive dance moves, Reedy continues to captivate fans of all ages.

▼ The Drive have made two South Atlantic League Championship Series appearances and seen over 45 players reach the major leagues.

—Photo by Paul Ringger

A New School. A New School of Thought.

There are merous reasons why national publications such as CNN Money listed Greenville as one of the "Top Ten Fastest Growing Cities in the U.S." and Forbes named the city to its list of "Best Cities for Young Professionals." Not the least of those reasons is the USC School of Medicine Greenville. One of the nation's newest medical schools, USC School of Medicine Greenville was

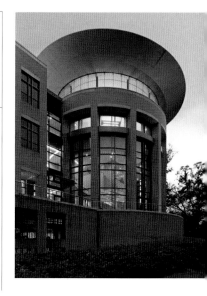

created in 2012 as a partnership between the University of South Carolina (USC) and Greenville Health System (GHS). Citing a common interest in health-care education, the partnership brought together the educational resources of the state's largest public university and Greenville Health System, the predominant healthcare resource providing healthcare services to the ten-county Upstate region and one of the largest healthcare systems in the country.

Instrumental in the founding of the school was Jerry R. Youkey, MD, the first Dean of the school, and Spence M. Taylor, MD, Senior Associate Dean for Academic Affairs and Diversity.. Their vision for the new facility was one of educating and advancing knowledge to transform healthcare for the benefit of the people in the diverse communities the school serves.

As a thriving metropolitan area with a diverse population and unique healthcare needs, Greenville was the logical choice to bring that vision to life. The area's climate, access to exercise facilities, and its active community complement the school's one-of-a-kind Lifestyle Medicine curriculum, which educates future physicians on the importance of exercise, nutrition and behavior in patient care.

The school truly reflects the uniqueness of the city that has played an instrumental role in the recruitment of some of the nation's best faculty. Our approximately 700 faculty members, many of whom are world-renowned in their fields of expertise, were excited to join

a new medical school which allowed them to continue living in or moving to Greenville.

In July 2012, the USC School of Medicine Greenville welcomed its charter class of 52 students – the Class of 2016. The school's maximum enrollment will be 400 students (100 in each of the classes – first, second, third and fourth year students).

The 90,000 square foot building, totally wireless and state-of-the-art, provides an exceptional learning environment to students from a variety of health professions in addition to medical students.

"Since opening its doors, the USC School of Medicine Greenville has had a tremendous impact on the city and its citizens," stated F. Ben Haskew, CCE, the President and CEO of the Greenville Chamber. "The faculty and students bring new intellectual capital to the area and have a direct economic impact through spending in the Upstate. We also believe the quality of life will be improved with many students

choosing to stay and practice in our community and region. Having this four-year medical school puts us in a different league."

The medical school is one of the first in the world to promote the importance of exercise and nutrition in wellness and disease prevention and treatment.

Established in 2012, USC School of Medicine Greenville is committed to creating modern physician leaders, ready to answer our community's unique health care needs.

USC School of Medicine Greenville is the first in the nation to require Emergency Medical Technician training to certification for first-year medical students.

Grand Design

Wilson Associates

Serving Greenville and the Upstate With Excellence

For most of us, the buying and selling of a home ranks near the top of the list of the most important decisions we will make during the course of our lives. It is imperative, therefore, to work with the most respected and trusted real estate professional to ensure that transaction will be a smooth, efficient experience.

A lifelong passion for helping people make the right decision in realizing their dream of home ownership led Sharon Wilson

▲ Sharon Wilson, President/BIC.

to launch Wilson Associates in Greenville in 2014. Sharon's roots in the area go deep. She is a seventh generation Greenvillian and a graduate of the University of South Carolina. As a veteran realtor with years of experience locally in the industry, she had built a reputation and an impressive track record that had

placed her among the leaders in the Greenville market as well as earning her top honors nationwide. Having done everything else in real estate except be part of a company with her own name over the door, Sharon felt the time was right to create a new synergy in real estate in Greenville and the Upstate. That synergy would be based on offering buyers and sellers the most innovative opportunities aimed at exceeding their expectations.

"Our skyline has changed, our community has changed, and the real estate industry has changed dramatically," Sharon relates. "I felt that it was time for a change in the way we do real estate in Greenville."

Sharon was joined by Nick Carlson, who shared her vision and her passion for connecting buyers and sellers of real estate. After graduating from Clemson University, Nick had settled in Greenville in 2005 and enjoyed watching the city grow and prosper. His professional growth paralleled that of the city

as Nick has been consistently named to his former brokerage's prestigious "President's Circle", an honor awarded to only the

▲ Nick Carlson, Vice President

top four percent of approximately 90,000 sales associates worldwide in the system.

"Everything then just came together to make it happen," Sharon relates. "We know real estate and we know Greenville's neighborhoods. We are dedicated to serving those neighborhoods and the entire Upstate."

THE HIGHEST STANDARDS

The Wilson Associates team now includes eleven real estate agents and three full-time staff members. Their headquarters is a downtown location in an historic brick building on East Broad Street which they restored themselves. Clients are welcomed into a relaxed setting of a fine home with the heart of pine floors, brick walls, and large exposed wood beams that identify the firm's offices.

The team takes great pride in the company's size - small enough to be agile and flexible while, at the same time, having the resources necessary to offer their clients the ultimate in cutting-edge service. Their "open office" concept includes exceptional marketing and branding as well as a large presence in social media.

"We employ in-depth fact finding, personal exploration, and meticulous attention to detail," Nick explains. "We strive to earn not only the trust of our clients, but their friendship and respect as well. Utilizing these skills and the personal dedication each of us brings to our work allows us to truly become trusted advisors to our clients."

Each member of the Wilson Associates team focuses on listening. They take time to thor-

oughly understand exactly what their clients are searching for in their dream home. Thorough analysis and assessment of market trends and data are essential in assisting their clients in making an informed decision. Seasoned professionals utilize effective tactics to negotiate favorable contract terms, and they manage the entire transaction in an organized fashion to ensure a stress-free experience from start to finish.

A VISION FOR THE UPSTATE

From new construction to the restoration of Greenville's historic heritage to the majesty of the mountains that surround the city, Wilson Associates is meeting the real estate needs of Greenville and the Upstate.

In addition, the company and its associates are pleased to be giving something back to their city and the region. A member of the Greenville Chamber of Commerce and the Better Business

Bureau, Wilson Associates can be counted on annually for their support of the American Heart Association, Lungs for Life, the American Cancer Society, and other civic and charitable organizations.

Sharon's personal involvement includes former service as a board member of Project Host, a culinary school created to address the root causes of hunger by equipping individuals with the skills and knowledge needed to gain and sustain employment in the food service industry. She was also a founding member of McCall Hospice House and is a member of the Junior League of Greenville.

"We are looking at a very bright future in Greenville," Sharon notes. "Our professional standards remain high and will always be rooted in exceeding the expectations of our clients."

Grand Design

Photo by Robert Clark

Robert Clark

Robert Clark has photographed South Carolina for over 30 years. A native of Charlotte, NC, Robert's photography has appeared in *National Geographic* books, *Newsweek, Smithsonian*, and photographic awards annuals such as *Print* and *Communication Arts*. Robert's specialties include architectural/interior photography, editorial, advertising and fine art photography. Robert has contributed the photography for six coffee-table books on South Carolina the latest of which, *Reflections of South Carolina—Volume Two*, was released in June 2014.

www.robertclarkphotography.com

803-348-2569

Stephanie Norwood

A Memphis-area native, Stephanie Norwood studied Graphic Design and Fine Art at Parsons The New School for Design in New York City.

She takes a photojournalistic approach to her lifestyle and fine art photography and specializes in portraits, figure, cultural events, and architecture. Stephanie developed her passion for photography during a 30-year career as an international model.

In addition to contributing heavily to two previous books in this series, *Knoxville: Green by Nature* and *Columbia, city of rivers, vistas, and dreams*, her work has been featured in *Cork It*, Memphis' *Downtowner* magazine, and *Memphis* magazine.

Studio Norwood Photography
www.StudioNorwood.com

info@StudioNorwood.com

901-217-2509

Tom Poland

Tom Poland first considered photography as a career but soon realized his talent lay in writing. More than that, legal pads and pens proved much more affordable than cameras, lens, and accessories. Many years later, digital cameras came to his rescue. He's often in the field researching unusual wildlife habitat, histories, and classic back-road venues, and he never leaves his camera behind. Now and then he admits he gets lucky.

tompoland.net

tompol@earnlink.net

Publisher's Note:

Yes, this intrepid photographer is the self-same individual who is the author of this book.

Paul Ringger

The abstract realism of Paul Ringger's photo-art has a large following on Facebook. This is no surprise to those whose work he has supported as a software engineer specializing in digital communication. Countless users of graphic and text systems have long been dependent on solutions such as those he delivered as leader of the world's first production team integrating text and graphics for print in the early 90s. His skills are equally leading edge today and are employed by some of the foremost technical companies on the planet.

His long-time study of the visual arts and the physics of their digital conveyance, has recently led to the creation of his impressive art portfolio.

facebook.com/paulringger

paul.ringger@gmail.com

Index

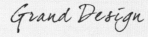

Copies of this book may be ordered at:
www.pubresgroup.com/greenville.html